ECONOMICS IN CANADIAN SOCIETY

Principles and Applications

To Dale, Kelli, Jeremy and Jessica
and
To Mariel, Ann-Marie and Christopher

ECONOMICS IN CANADIAN SOCIETY

Principles and Applications

Bruce A. Forster
Department of Economics
University of Guelph, Canada

Clement A. Tisdell
Department of Economics
University of Newcastle, Australia

John Wiley & Sons
Toronto   New York   Chichester   Brisbane   Singapore

Canadian Cataloguing in Publication Data

Forster, Bruce A. (Bruce Alexander), 1948-
  Economics in Canadian society

Bibliography: p.
Includes index.
ISBN 0-471-79778-2

1. Economics. 2. Canada - Economic conditions.
I. Tisdell, C. A. (Clement Allan). II. Title.

HB171.5.F67 1985   330   C85-099141-2

Design: Annette Tatchell & Associates
Illustrations: Annette Tatchell/David Windebank
Cover Design: Tibor Kovalik
Typesetting: Jay Tee Graphics Ltd.

Printed and bound in Canada by The Bryant Press
10 9 8 7 6 5 4 3 2

Contents

The ideas of economists and political philosophers, both when they are right and when they are wrong, are more powerful than is commonly understood. Indeed, the world is ruled by little else. Practical men, who believe themselves to be quite exempt from any intellectual influences, are usually the slaves of some defunct economist. Madmen in authority, who hear voices in the air, are distilling their frenzy from some academic scribbler of a few years back. I am sure that the power of vested interests is vastly exaggerated compared with the gradual encroachment of ideas.

John Maynard Keynes, *The General Theory of Employment, Interest, and Money* (London, Macmillan, 1936), p. 383

Preface

The starting point for this book was Professor Tisdell's *Economics in our Society*. In addition to discussing the fundamental principles that govern the operation of modern-day economies, the text contains a wealth of institutional, descriptive, and historical information concerning various features of the Canadian economic system. As a result, the book will appeal to economics and noneconomics students who desire more information about their economy and its behaviour. Whether we like it or not, we, as individuals, are important components of this economic system. We collectively affect economic outcomes; through government agencies or other groups, we attempt to control or manipulate outcomes; and in the end we are affected by the economic outcomes. A better understanding of these relationships is the desired result of reading this text. If, after reading this book, the reader is encouraged to pay closer attention to the economic section of the newspaper and of other media, then the book will have accomplished much.

The book does not attempt to be encyclopaedic, but rather it discusses selected issues in a survey manner while treating other topics in more detail. For those who desire more detailed discussions on certain topics, each chapter ends with a "Further Reading" section.

Acknowledgements

My first debt is to Professor Clem Tisdell for providing me with an opportunity to write the Canadian edition of his excellent textbook. I was able to benefit from discussions with Professor Tisdell while I was the Jayes-Qantas visiting lecturer at the University of Newcastle, Australia, during June and July of 1983. His perceptive comments were quite valuable in preparing the final draft.

Next, my thanks go to James Rogerson of John Wiley & Sons Canada Limited for his guiding hand and encouragement since the start of the project, and to Ms. Barbara Consky, also of John Wiley & Sons Canada Limited for her helpful suggestions in preparing the final manuscript.

During the writing of the first final draft, I benefited from the insightful comments of my colleagues Bram Cadsby, Brian Ferguson, John J. Madden, and David Prescott who kindly read selected chapters. The comments of the following reviewers also provided valuable input for the preparation of the final draft: Gary Berman & Michael Hatton, Humber College of Applied Arts and Technology, Rexdale; Carmine Fabiilii, Economics Department, Business Division, Algonquin College, Nepean; Voyo Kovolski, Department of Economics, Dawson College, Montreal; Rocky Mirza, Vancouver Community College; William Sinkevitch, St. Clair College, Windsor; and Phil Waggett, Thomas Blakelock High School, Oakville.

For the excellent photographic illustrations, I am indebted to Bramalea Limited; Canada Packers Inc.; INCO Limited, Imperial Oil, Limited; Ford Motor Company of Canada; the University of Guelph, Departments of Information and Illustration Services; the University of Calgary, Department of Public Affairs; and the Toronto Stock Exchange.

The text was completed while I was Visiting Professor in economics at the University of Wyoming in Laramie. My thanks go to the Department of Economics at Wyoming for providing a hospitable working environment.

The first complete draft of the manuscript was typed by Mrs. Irene Pereira of the Economics Department at the University of Guelph, and the final version was typed by Ms. Cindi Williams of the Economics Department at the University of Wyoming, and Ms. Sheila Robinson of the Economics Department at the University of Guelph. My thanks go to these individuals both for their effort, and for their patience with the author.

My final debt, and probably the largest, is to my wife, Dale, for her help in proofreading, and for her support during the preparation of the manuscript; and to my daughters, Kelli and Jessica, and my son, Jeremy, for being them.

Bruce A. Forster
Guelph, Ontario
November, 1985

Economics: Its Purpose and Its Scope   **1**

The Importance of Economics and Economic Thought

Although not all of life's problems are economic ones, many are. If we are to understand and search for solutions to some of the most pressing problems in the world today, it is essential to study economics. Inflation, unemployment, poverty, pollution, international monetary problems, the operation of capitalist and socialist economic systems, and many other topics can be adequately explored only by using economic tools, concepts, and theories.

The operation of our economy affects the life of every one of us; and this provides another important reason for studying economics. Each of us is directly affected — our income and employment prospects, the quality of our lives, the taxes that we pay, and the goods and services available to us, all depend on the operation of the economy.

We are also concerned about how the operation of the economy affects others. Most of us are concerned when others are involuntarily unemployed, live in poverty or are denied equality of opportunity, and most of us wish to take constructive social action to remedy such ills. A study of economics provides us with a useful basis for proposing appropriate social actions and assessing the proposals of others.

Economic thought has been a factor in social change. As a rule, not only are the writings of economists influenced by the social trends of their times — they also influence these trends. To realize this, one need only consider the contributions of some of the great economists of the past.

Although economics as a subject did not begin with Adam Smith, his contributions did much to develop the subject, which at this earlier time was known as political economy. Before Adam Smith published his *Wealth of Nations* in 1776, scholars commonly believed that the true wealth of a nation depended on its holdings of gold and precious metals. Smith pointed out that money does not represent the wealth of a nation, even though an individual who has more money is wealthier because he can buy more goods and services with it. The amount of commodities (goods and services) available within a nation to meet the wants or desires of its citizens represents the true wealth of that nation. A nation that deprives its people of other commodities and uses most of its resources to amass gold reserves, which in themselves satisfy few human wants, can be regarded as poor. *The wealth of a nation is to be judged by the extent to which the wants of its inhabitants are satisfied.* Although other factors may also need to be taken into account, Smith's main point is clear.

At the time that Smith was writing, government restrictions on trade and commerce were common, and were believed to be necessary to maintain and increase national wealth. Smith argued in favour of the opposite policy. In his view, a country's resources are used to best advantage, the wealth of the nation is maximized, and human wants are satisfied to the greatest extent possible when trade and commerce are free of government restrictions. Politicians in nineteenth-century Britain generally accepted Smith's policy recommendations, and trade and commerce were freed, to a large extent, from government intervention.

In the twentieth century, however, with further development of capitalist economics, this *laissez-faire* trend has been reversed. In this century, a number of economists have argued in favour of particular types of economic intervention by government. But the debate about how much government interference in the operation of the economy is justified is not settled. In Canada, the Trudeau government increased government intervention in various areas, one being energy development. The New Democratic Party (NDP) favours even more government intervention. In the United States, the Reagan administration espouses the belief that there is too much government intervention in the operation of the economy.

Other outstanding economists who have had influence include David Ricardo, Thomas Robert Malthus, Karl Marx, Alfred Marshall, and John Maynard Keynes. In more recent times, economists such as Milton Friedman and John Kenneth Galbraith have influenced economic thinking and government policy.

Ricardo, Malthus, and Marx, writing in the nineteenth century, were concerned with the possible long-term evolution of the economic world. Ricardo and Malthus were especially concerned about the possible consequences for the economic welfare of rising populations, a matter that still requires our attention. Marx was interested in the development of the capitalist system. He argued that the capitalist economic system leads to exploitation of workers, and that its development will result in workers' becoming progressively worse off. Along with Engels, he predicted that communist or socialist revolution is inevitable in capitalist countries and, in exhorting workers to revolt, he indirectly influenced communist revolutions in Russia, China, and other parts of the world.

Alfred Marshall's economic writings are different in character from Marx'; they are more concerned with social and economic harmony and equilibrium than with social conflict and change. Marshall, a Cambridge economist, writing toward the end of Queen Victoria's reign, developed or refined economic theory to consider the operation of markets. He tended to favour gradual policy changes, and policy changes of a partial rather than of a widespread nature. A number of cost-benefits techniques used today to evaluate alternative economic policies have their origin in Marshall's approach.

In 1936, Keynes published *The General Theory of Employment, Interest and Money* in which he analyzed the kinds of economic factors that can lead to widespread and persistent unemployment such as occurred in the Great Depression of the 1930s. Earlier accepted economic theories failed to explain such unemployment, and maintained that in capitalist systems there is an automatic tendency for full employment of the work force to be ensured. Keynes claimed that there is no such tendency, and that a capitalist economy can permanently stagnate in unemployment unless the government intervenes by buying goods and services, and strengthening demand when unemployment levels are high and demand for commodities is weak. The level of employment and economic activity in a capitalist economy fluctuate, and according to Keynes, it is necessary for the government to intervene and "iron out" such fluctuations in economic activity; otherwise, there can be considerable misery and loss of production as a result of unemployment. Since World War II, all governments have accepted responsibility for regulating the overall level of economic activity and employment in their countries. Keynes' theory resulted in a considerable increase in the extent of government intervention in capitalist societies.

Milton Friedman is the most well-known spokesman for a group of economists referred to as *monetarists*. In the monetarist view, the key factor causing inflation in most countries today is government increases in the supply of money. In its simplest terms, the rate of inflation equals the rate of growth in the money supply. In order to reduce the rate of inflation, the rate of growth of the money supply must be reduced. Friedman also argues that minimal government intervention in the operation of the economy is in the best interests of society. Friedman's prescriptions are reflected in the policies of the Reagan administration in the United States.

The views of Canadian-born John Kenneth Galbraith stand in marked contrast to those of Friedman. Galbraith believes that the best way to control inflation is through government-imposed wage-and-price controls. Galbraith's influence was felt in the Trudeau government's decision to impose wage-and-price controls in Canada from 1975 to 1978. Galbraith, unlike Friedman, advocates increased government intervention in the economy in the pursuit of improving social welfare.

The Basic Economic Problem: Scarcity

Most of the subject matter of economics relates to one basic problem: human wants for goods and services cannot be fully satisfied by using the available resources such as land, labour, minerals, and equipment. Most of us want more than we have, and together we want more than can be produced. Goods and services are scarce *relative* to our desire for them.

In order to make citizens as economically well off as is possible, it is important to organize the use of our *limited* resources so that economic waste is avoided. Economics is a science that studies the social organization or social administration of scarce resources. It looks at the efficiency of alternative social systems or relationships in ensuring the satisfaction of human desires for goods and services. It asks such questions as:

- How efficient is our modified market system?
- How efficient is a nonexchange peasant system?
- How efficient is a centrally planned system?

FIGURE 1.1 **Basic economic problem. Scarcity exists because the quantity of commodities wanted by individuals exceeds the amount that can be supplied using the available limited resources.** *Because scarcity occurs, choice about the use of resources and commodities is necessary.*

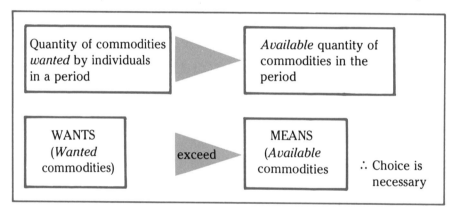

Because the means for satisfying human desires are limited relative to these desires, *choices* have to be made about possible alternative uses of resources. In an economy operating at its attainable capacity, a desire for more of one commodity, such as better hospitals and medical services, can be achieved only at the expense of another commodity or commodities, such as better schools, roads, and communication systems or an increased supply of cars and sweets. This "expense" is called the *opportunity cost.* The opportunity cost of a given economic choice is the foregone alternative economic possibility. Thus, the opportunity cost of producing more hospitals may be fewer schools or roads. It may be well worth foregoing these alternatives to obtain better hospitals and medical services, or other objectives; but, there is a real cost, or sacrifice, involved — the opportunity cost.

Economics is a systematic science, and theories or conceptualizations (images) of the economic world form the basis for systematizing or organizing economic thought. Theories also provide concrete predictions or assertions for possible checking against observations of the real world. When observations do not accord with the prediction of the theory, this may be evidence that the

FIGURE 1.2 **In an efficient economy, more of one commodity can usually be obtained only at the expense of another.** *The opportunity cost of a given choice is the alternative not chosen.*

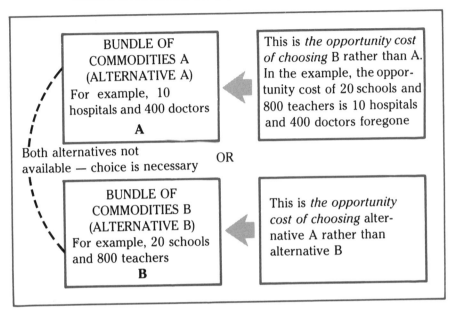

theory is inappropriate as a picture of the world, and it may need modifying. Theories also provide the basis of policy advice.

As Bronowsky has said, one of the greatest assets of the human faculty is the ability to anticipate and visualize the future, and plan for it. To do this, we must build images or theories of the world. There can be no science, and no economic science, without theory. Of course, not all economics consists of pure theory or abstraction; but most of it does, to varying degrees. Even economic history and descriptive economics involve theorizing about how the world was or is.

Analyzing Economic Scarcity

By analyzing the problem of economic scarcity, we will be able to see how the concern of economists about:

1. economic efficiency in the production and exchange of goods and services,
2. the maintenance of full employment,
3. the growth and development of economies, and
4. the distribution of income or the relative availability of goods and services to individuals

relates to the basic problem.

Our previous discussion indicates that an economic theory of scarcity should take account of:

1. human wants, and
2. the quantities of goods and services that are attainable, given the limited resources available to the nation, to the world or to some other appropriate social economic unit.

We now consider a simplified theory that takes account of both considerations.

Representing Wants

One way of representing wants is by means of *indifference curves*, or preference contours. Each indifference curve links alternative combinations of commodities that are rated as equally desirable by the individual or group whose wants are under consideration.

Thus, to take the example in Figure 1.3, the community indifference curve marked I_1I_1 represents quantities of manufactured goods and services (such as clothing and cars), and various quantities of agricultural goods and services, that are regarded as equally desirable by the community. The negative slope of the curve indicates that the community would be willing to give up some manufactured goods for more agricultural products. For example, the community derives the same satisfaction from combination Q as it does from combination R. The community is prepared to give up SR of manufactured goods in order to have QS of extra agricultural goods.

The community indifference curves marked I_2I_2 and I_3I_3 also represent combinations that are equally desired, and we could draw in other curves corresponding to all possible combinations. All combinations on each contour are equally desired, but those on curve I_3I_3 are preferred to those on curve I_2I_2. This is so because, if we take any combination on curve I_2I_2, say the one shown at S, there are combinations on curve I_3I_3, such as combination T, that provide the community with more manufactured goods and services and more agricultural products. As we move in a northeasterly direction — the direction indicated by the arrow — we encounter higher indifference curves and preferred combinations of economic alternatives. In order to achieve its optimal economic position, the community needs to marshall its available resources to reach its highest attainable indifference curve.

Representing Possibilities for Satisfying Wants

The amount of commodities that can be produced or made available to satisfy wants depends on the quality and quantity of resources available to a community. A community with abundant natural resources, a skilled population, and much capital equipment — as in the U.S.A. and the U.S.S.R. — is able to provide

FIGURE 1.3 **Wants represented by indifference curves. Combinations along the indifference curves are equally desired. The further a combination is to the northeast, the more it is desired.**

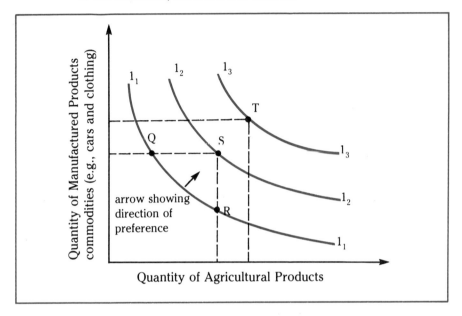

provide more goods and services for its population than are countries such as India, Equador, and El Salvador.

The combinations of economic goods and services that a community can produce using its scarce resources can be represented by a *production possibility set*. In the case of our example, the production possibility set might look like the cross hatched set in Figure 1.4. This set represents all the quantities of commodities that can be achieved using the community's available resources.

The frontier of the set, as indicated by the curve ABC, in Figure 1.4, represents the community's *production possibility frontier* or *economic efficiency frontier*. A community that is not on this frontier is needlessly foregoing opportunities to satisfy the wants of its citizens; it is indulging in economic waste. A community's production may be below this frontier, say at point D, because labourers are involuntarily unemployed or because resources are poorly allocated or combined in the production process. Any economic combination that is not on the frontier of the production possibility set is inferior to at least one combination on the frontier. For example, the combination at D is inferior to that at B because B involves a greater quantity of commodities and an improvement in the quality of the environment. If human wants are to be satisfied to the greatest extent possible, it is *necessary* for the economy to operate in a manner that places it on its production possibility (or economic efficiency) frontier.

FIGURE 1.4 **Production possibility set and frontier. This is determined by available resources. It is inefficient to be below the frontier.**

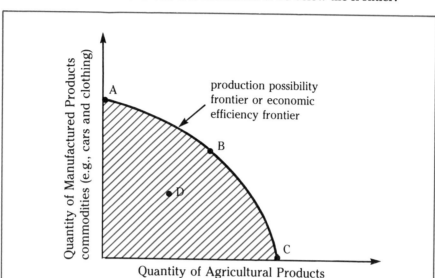

If the economy is below the frontier, it is possible for the community to have more of all the economic objects that it desires. No sacrifice has to be made and no alternative has to be foregone to obtain more of any good or service if the economy is operating below its efficiency frontier. Once the economy is on its efficiency frontier, however, *trade-off* is necessary. More of one commodity such as education can only be achieved at the expense of other commodities such as better roads, and more records and stereo sets.

Minimizing wants

Although it is *necessary* for an economy to operate on its efficiency frontier if want is to be minimized, this in itself is not enough. The composition of production or economic possibilities must also optimally conform with the wants or preferences of the community. The resources in a community may be fully employed and used efficiently, but they may not be used to produce the goods and services that people want. This is an economic waste. Figure 1.5 illustrates the point.

In Figure 1.5, the combination of economic possibilities represented by point B conforms optimally with the preferences or wants of the community. The combination of manufactured goods and agricultural products corresponding to point B is efficient, and enables the community to reach its highest attainable indifference curve, or level of satisfaction.

Although combinations on the production possibility frontier apart from B

FIGURE 1.5 **Efficient and optimal conformance between production possibilities and wants: the economic optimum**

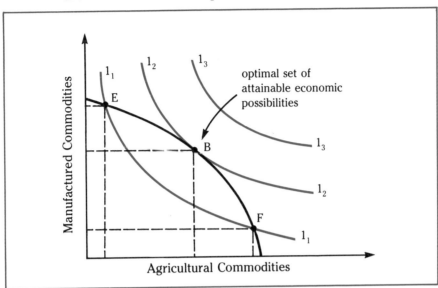

are efficient, all fall on lower indifference curves than B (note that only a small selection of indifference curves is shown); thus, they do not satisfy the wants of the community to the greatest extent possible. The economic possibility at E, for example, is inferior to that at B because, given the preference of the community, it results in too many manufactured goods and too few agricultural products. The opposite is the case at F — too many agricultural products and too few manufactured goods.

Scarcity Dictates a Variety of Trade-Offs

The type of analysis used above may be used to demonstrate that, in an efficient economy, increased production of commodities may require a sacrifice of environmental quality, and that an improvement in environmental quality may require the sacrifice of the production of commodities.

In general, our desires for an increase in environmental quality, or in the production of commodities, will depend upon the cost of the increase. The cost of an increase in environmental quality, for example, is the sacrifice in produced commodities that must be made. The trade-offs that we are willing to make are indicated by the shape and nature of our indifference curves. These, together with the production possibility set, determine the best combination of economic possibilities that we can achieve.

The example of the trade-offs between environmental quality and production of commodities indicates the wide scope of economics. Other trade-offs can also be used to illustrate this. For instance, the trade-off between leisure time and production of commodities represents an economic problem because both use limited resources and both are wanted by the community. This problem can be illustrated by modifying the above diagrams slightly. Leisure time can be measured on one axis of the above figures and the production of commodities on the other, and the previous type of argument repeated.

Other examples that can be used to illustrate the basic economic problem include the production of military goods, such as ships, tanks, and ammunition, versus nonmilitary goods, such as yachts, passenger cars, and sporting goods. Another example is the production of commodities by the government sector, such as roads, bridges, and electricity, versus the production of commodities such as taxi services, food, and clothing by the nongovernment (private) sector of the economy. All of these activities use resources that are relatively scarce — using more resources in producing one set of commodities means using less resources in the alternative set.

International Trade

Countries that do not exchange commodities with foreign countries have what is called a "closed economy". Consumption opportunities for residents of a closed economy are limited to their own production opportunities. Countries that do exchange commodities with foreign countries have what is called an "open economy". This exchange is called "international trade". Open economies are able to escape the restrictions of their country's domestic production possibilities and consume at a point beyond its production frontier, such as point B in Figure 1.6. If the community was initially producing at point A in Figure 1.6 and then reallocated its resources so as to forego ab of manufactured goods, it could at most produce a^1c^1 extra agricultural goods, putting the community at point C. If the community were able to *export* ab of manufactured goods to foreign countries in return for *imports* of more than a^1c^1 (say a^1b^1) of agricultural goods, however, then the community is better off as a result of such international trade.

Canada has an open economy. Sales to foreigners and purchases from foreigners vary between 25 and 30 percent of total national output. Canada's major trading partner is the United States, which accounts for roughly 70 percent of Canada's foreign trade in commodities. This exchange of commodities contributes to the welfare of Canada's residents.

Although Canada is actively involved in international trade, such trade is not without artificial restrictions such as tariffs or quotas levied by Canada to restrict imports from foreign suppliers, or those levied by foreign countries to restrict the exports of Canadian producers. This can be explained by the fact that, although Canadians as a group may gain from international trade, not all Canadians share equally in this gain. Indeed, it is possible that some Canadians may find themselves worse off with unrestricted trade. Those Canadians that

FIGURE 1.6 **International trade allows the community to consume beyond the production frontier.**

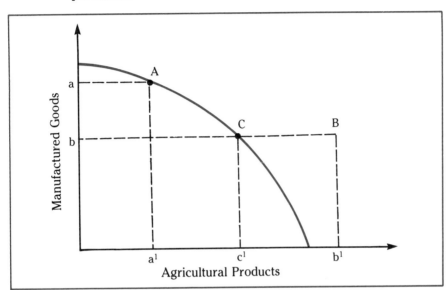

supply factor services (labour, land, and capital) that are most suited to the import-competing sector of the economy will find that international trade lowers the income that they receive from supplying their services, or possibly, in the short-run, results in unemployment of their services. It is not surprising that these Canadians will not only oppose free trade in general, but will push for special measures to protect their own welfare levels.

As a result of the income redistribution or the economic disruption that could occur from trade, it may be necessary for the government to intervene to help those adversely affected by trade. In general, however, it should do so in a way that permits Canadian consumers to benefit from the possibilities of unrestricted trade. Government policies should be designed to ensure that the maximum benefits of international trade are achieved but shared by all Canadians. Chapter 9 discusses these issues in more detail.

Ways of Reducing Scarcity

Scarcity may be greater than it need be:

1. because the economy is operating below its production possibility or economic efficiency frontier, or
2. because the composition of national production does not accord with the wants of the people, or
3. because the benefits of international trade are not fully obtained, or

4. because economic growth and development does not occur at an optimal
rate and in an optimal way.

When labour is involuntarily unemployed, economic opportunities for satisfying wants are not fully exploited. By adopting social measures to ensure that
all who wish to work at the prevailing wage rate are able to do so, it is possible
to make everybody better off. Questions of the employment of labour and
other resources thus form an important part of the subject matter of economics.

When resources are poorly (inefficiently) allocated between their alternative uses, a nation's economic potential for satisfying wants is not fully realized. If land that is relatively more suitable for pork production is used for dairy
production, overall production of pork and dairy products is less than *can* be
attained from the resources employed in these activities. By switching the use
of relatively superior dairy land from pork to dairy production, and the relatively superior land for pork production from dairy to pork production, overall production can be increased. The increase can be achieved without employing any
more resources, and wants can be satisfied to a greater extent than is otherwise
possible.

This can be illustrated by the following example. Suppose that the eastern
part of a province is most suited for dairy cattle and the western part is relatively better for pigs. In the eastern part, dairy cattle give 5 L of milk per head per
day on an average, and pigs produce 50 kg of pork each. In the western part,
dairy cattle produce an average 2 L of milk per head daily and pigs yield 60 kg
of pork each. (In each region, the techniques used to produce pork and milk are
assumed to be the most efficient known.)

Suppose that there are 2,000,000 pigs marketed per year in the western
part and no cattle, and that there are 1,000,000 dairy cattle in the eastern part
and no pigs. This allocation is optimal in the sense that, given the yields mentioned above, production is greatest by having all the dairy cattle in the east
and all the pigs in the west. Given the above allocation, 120,000,000 kg of pork
are produced yearly, and 5,000,000 L of milk are supplied daily.

Now suppose that all the pigs are moved to the eastern part and all the
dairy cattle go to the western part, for example, because eastern pork production and western milk production are subsidized by the government. The total
supply of commodities falls, even though the employed resources are the same
in total. Milk production falls to 2,000,000 L daily, and pork production drops to
100,000,000 kg per year. Even though the best available techniques are being
used, *this poor allocation of resources causes the available supply of commodities to drop.*

In our economy, the prices of commodities, determined mainly by
marketing systems, help to guide the allocation of our resources between alternative uses. These prices act, for instance, as signals to producers seeking
profits. Profit-making producers employ resources in the activities they find
most profitable, and in turn profitability depends on prices. A malfunctioning of
the price system, or certain types of government interference with the

FIGURE 1.7 **Given that land in the eastern part is relatively better suited to milk production and that land in the western part is better suited to pork production, a poor allocation of resources occurs if dairy cattle are run in the west and pigs in the east. When resources are poorly allocated, the available supply of commodities is less than it need be.**

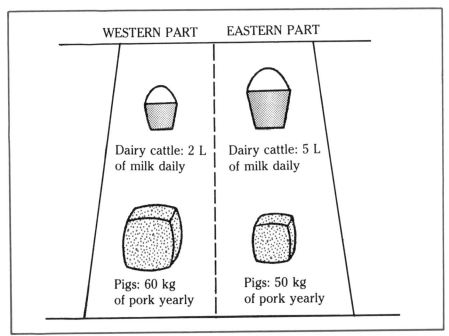

marketing system, such as the payment of subsidies on some commodities, can result in an inefficient allocation of resources, and thus add to economic want. Taking the above example, if dairy producers in regions relatively more suited for pigs paid a subsidy, and if pig producers in areas relatively more suited for dairy production are subsidized by the government, this encourages the inefficient use of land and adds to economic want. Thus, the impact of market systems, and other social means of organization upon the allocation of resources, forms an important part of economics.

So far, our conception of the economic potential of the economy has been rather static. The potential amount of commodities available to the citizens of an economy can expand with the passing of time. Growth and development of the economy can reduce scarcity. Economic growth and development of the economy may occur:

1. because new resources are discovered (consider the oil and gas discoveries in the west and north of Canada recently),
2. because scientific and technical knowledge improves and enables resources to be put to new uses, or to be used with greater technical efficiency (consider the introduction of new man-made fibres, plastic, and colour television

in the last few decades, and more recently, computer- communications
systems),

3. because of greater investment in capital of all kinds.

FIGURE 1.8 **Norman Wells: an island created in the Mackenzie River. The
discovery of new resource deposits or new ways to develop these
deposits can aid economic growth and development.**
Courtesy Imperial Oil Limited

Capital can be regarded as the stored man-made means of further production. It includes tools, equipment, and machinery of all kinds, and also human
capital such as education, and social capital such as roads and railways. The accumulation of capital and the expansion of knowledge have done much to
reduce human want, poverty, and misery.

Economic growth and development can be envisaged as pushing the production possibility or efficiency frontier of the economy outward. In Figure 1.9,
an economy's production possibility frontier is shown as involving a trade-off

between farm and nonfarm commodities. The economy's production possibility frontier is originally ABC, and, as a result of economic growth, it moves out to DEF. Economic growth has made it possible for the economy to produce a greater quantity of both farm and nonfarm commodities. Growth of this kind might occur, for instance, because improved types of pastures are discovered, because more disease-resistant plants, such as rust-resistant wheat, are found, and because machines are redesigned to operate at faster speeds in the manufacturing industry. Everyone in the community can be made better off as a result of economic growth.

FIGURE 1.9 **Production possibility frontier pushed out by economic growth and development**

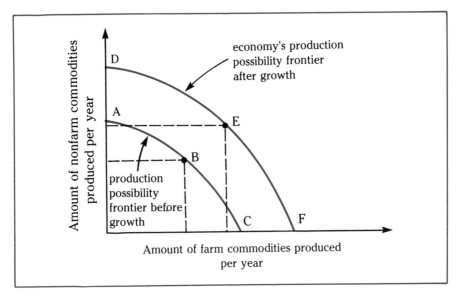

Although everyone in the community, and future generations, can be made better off by economic growth, whether or not they will be depends upon what is done with the new economic potential. For instance, the discovery and exploitation of a new oil field can impoverish future generations unless the present generation uses its greater wealth to devise new technologies to replace the use of oil. Resource opportunities arising from growth can be squandered, or they can be used to assist future generations. If earlier generations had been barred from using nonrenewable resources, we would not have reached the stage of knowledge, economic development, and wealth that we enjoy at present.

The benefits of economic growth need not only be taken out in the form of more material goods. They can be taken out in other ways such as improved environmental quality and more leisure. Take, for example, the trade-off between the production of commodities and the availability of leisure time. In Figure 1.10, the economic efficiency frontier, the trade-off between production and leisure, for a hypothetical economy before growth, is as shown by curve ABC. After growth, because resources become more productive or are added to, the economy's trade-off frontier moves out to DEC. As a result of economic growth, members of the community can have more material goods and more leisure time. In terms of Figure 1.10, the community has an opportunity of moving from a position such as B to a position such as E.

FIGURE 1.10 **Opportunities for leisure and the production of commodities increased by economic growth**

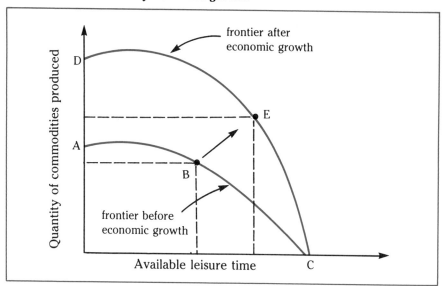

In the last century, Canadians have taken advantage of economic growth in many ways. They have, for instance, reduced the length of their working week, thus taking more leisure time.

In the above discussion of economic development, the level of population in the economy has been assumed to be constant. The possibility of population growth, however, needs to be explicitly taken into account. If population grows at a faster rate than the production of commodities, incomes or the available commodities per person decline, and scarcity rises relative to human wants. In India, for example, the overall level of production has increased substantially since World War II, but because population levels have also risen substantially, income per head in India has risen only slightly. The scarcity of commodities needs to be considered in relation to a country's or region's level of population. Economists must do this.

Again, in considering the existence of scarcity in any region or country, it is important to consider the way in which incomes, or claims on commodities, are distributed among its inhabitants. Even in the richest country, acute poverty, want, and misery may be suffered by some of its citizens if incomes are poorly distributed. It has been estimated that about 10 to 20 percent of the Canadian population lives in poverty, depending upon the criteria used in the calculation. The distribution of income, and the measures to alter the distribution of income, involve important economic issues. As available resources cannot satisfy all of our wants, because of overall scarcity, there is interpersonal conflict or competition for the use of available resources and commodities. Thus, the distribution of income forms an important part of economic studies.

Employment, the allocation of resources between alternative uses, international trade, economic growth and development, and the distribution of incomes are basic topics of interests to economists. Each topic relates to the basic scarcity problem, and involves the social organization or administration of scarce resources.

Economic Waste in Canada

During the last half of the 1970s, the unemployment rate in Canada varied between 6.9 and 7.5 percent of the labour force. This represented between 690,000 and 827,000 people, respectively. In 1982, the unemployment rate rose significantly as a result of a serious recession. The unemployment rate in December, 1982 was 12.8 percent — 1.49 million people.

In addition to those individuals classified as officially unemployed, there were thousands of "discouraged workers" who left the labour force because they had been unable to find suitable employment. For December, 1982, this group was estimated to include 156,000 people who believed that there was no work available.

The economic cost of this unemployment to society is the foregone output of goods and services that could have been produced if the individuals had been employed. In addition to these economic costs, there are social and psychological costs that are borne by the unemployed and their families as a result of personal economic hardships.

The Economic Council of Canada, in its Eighteenth Review, suggested that policies that would lower the unemployment rate by 1 percent would result in national output increasing by $5.9 billion. In its Seventeenth Review, the Council suggested that for 1974-79 the gap between actual and potential growth of the Canadian economy ranged between $7 billion and $10 billion (in 1971 constant dollars) — roughly 6 percent of national output. The foregone income cost to Canadians owing to the economy operating below potential during this time period was $58 billion. In its Eighteenth Review, the Council estimated the annual gap for 1980-85 to be $7.8 rising to $10.8 billion for the last half of the decade. The cumulative loss in output for the 1981-90 period will be $91.5 billion.

KEY CONCEPTS
(FOR REVIEW)

Alternative foregone
Basic economic problem
Capital
Closed economies
Distribution of income
Economic growth
Efficiency frontier
Indifference curves
Inefficient allocation of resources
International trade
Involuntary unemployment

Means
Open economies
Opportunity costs
Optimal allocation of resources
Production possibilities
Production possibility frontier
Resources
Scarcity
Trade-offs
Wants
Wealth

QUESTIONS FOR REVIEW AND DISCUSSION

1. "The wealth of a nation does not consist of its money and gold." Explain.
2. Why is it worthwhile studying economics?
3. "Economic thought has been a factor in social change. As a rule, the writings of economists are influenced by the social trends of their times and also influence these trends." Explain, discuss, and give examples.
4. What is the basic economic problem?
5. What is of interest to economists in studying alternative social systems?
6. "The opportunity cost of choosing one economic alternative is the best alternative foregone." Explain and discuss.
7. Why are economists concerned about economic efficiency, full employment, economic growth and development, and the distribution of income?
8. What is an indifference curve?
9. How can indifference curves be used to represent wants? Illustrate your answer with a diagram.
10. What is a production possibility set and why is it important?
11. What is a production possibility frontier (or economic efficiency frontier) and what bearing does it have on the problem of reducing scarcity or satisfying want?
12. "It is necessary for the composition of production of commodities to conform optimally with wants, if scarcity is to be minimized." Explain.
13. "An increase in the armed forces and the amount of military equipment (ships, aircraft) in a fully employed economy results in a decline in the availability of civilian commodities (merchant ships, private aircraft, cars)." Explain. Use a diagram to illustrate your answer.
14. "The economic problem of trade-off of commodities is not restricted to trade-offs between material goods. The allocation of time and the quality

of the environment must also be taken into account in the basic economic problem." Discuss.

15. "Scarcity can be minimized by ensuring (a) that resources are not involuntarily unemployed (full employment); (b) . . . ." Indicate three other major ways of reducing scarcity.

16. Suppose that the example illustrated in Figure 1.7 is altered so that milk yields are higher in the west and wool yields are higher in the east. What then is the optimal allocation of dairy cattle and sheep?

17. How would you use indifference curves to represent wants between manufactured goods and environmental pollution?

18. What is economic growth, and what factors may cause economic growth?

19. "Economic growth and development push an economy's production possibility frontier or efficiency frontier of 'availabilities' outward." Explain.

20. "Everyone in the community can be made better off by economic growth." Discuss.

21. "Economic growth can lead to the availability of more material goods, a better environment, and more leisure time. There is no guarantee, however, that it will have all of these advantages." Discuss.

22. Show how a shift outward in the production possibility frontier, or other availability frontiers, can be used to illustrate economic growth.

23. In what ways might population growth affect economic scarcity?

24. Why does the distribution of income form an important part of economic studies?

25. What types of economic waste are occuring in Canada? How important are these wastes, in your opinion?

26. How does international trade affect individuals in society?

FURTHER READING

Blomqvist, A., Wonnacott, P., & Wonnacott, R., *Economics*, 1st Canadian ed. Scarborough: McGraw-Hill Ryerson Limited, 1984, chapters 1 & 2.

Lipsey, R.G., Purvis, D., Sparks, G.R., & Steiner, P.O., *Economics*, 4th ed. New York: Harper & Row, Publishers, 1982, chapters 1 & 2.

Samuelson, P.A. & Scott, A.D., *Economics*. Scarborough: McGraw-Hill Ryerson Limited, 1980, chapters 1 & 2.

2 Basic Economic Choices and Alternative Economic Systems

Basic Economic Choices or Problems

Because the resources or means available to any community for satisfying its wants are scarce relative to the wants of its citizens, every community has to make important economic choices about the use of its resources. In different communities or economic systems, the way in which these choices are made may be different. In some countries, custom and tradition play a large role in determining economic choices; and in others, such as some communist countries, control and regulation by a central committee or group of individuals is important. In communities such as our own, market mechanisms are of considerable significance in determining the allocation of resources.

No matter which social mechanism or combination of social mechanisms is used, every society makes decisions or choices about its production of commodities, about the exchange of commodities by members of the society, and about the way that individuals share in the output and wealth of the community. In short, *every society makes decisions about production, exchange, and the distribution of income* (the entitlement of individuals to available commodities).

The Basic Economic Choices to Be Made

By some social means, every society resolves:

1. *what* is to be produced;
2. *how* commodities are to be produced, for instance what methods of production will be used and what resources will be used in their production;
3. *by whom* commodities will be produced;
4. *when* new commodities are to be produced and used up;
5. *where* commodities should be produced; and
6. *for whom* the production is intended.

Similar types of choices and decisions are made about the exchange of commodities and the sharing of these.

Take a commodity such as cheese, and consider the choices that need to be made about its production. It is necessary to decide whether or not cheese will be produced rather than an alternative commodity, such as condensed milk, and how much cheese should be produced. The type of cheese to be manufactured must be determined, and the method of manufacture must be chosen from the alternative methods available. By whom will the cheese be produced? Will it be produced in large factories, as in Canada, or by individual farmers, as was once the case in Europe? In what districts or parts of the country is it to be produced, and should it be manufactured throughout the year, or only when milk is in bountiful supply? Should some of the cheese be stored or held in stock for future consumption? Is the production intended for local consumption or for export, or for both? These are just some of the many choices that need to be made about the production of a commodity such as cheese.

Social Mechanisms or Means of Making Economic Choices

The *social rules* that govern or affect the production, exchange, and distribution of commodities may vary from community to community, and alter with the passage of time. The relative importance of (1) custom and tradition, (2) dictatorship or central control, and (3) market mechanisms (combined with a great deal of personal freedom) as regulators of the use of resources is not the same in all communities, and has changed historically. Consider some examples.

In medieaval times, it was customary for a son to follow the occupation of his father; but this is no longer the case. In mediaeval times, custom resulted in certain resources (types of labour, for instance) being traditionally allocated to produce particular goods. More recently, in India, an individual's caste determined the occupations open to him or her. It has been the accepted custom in Japan for employees not to leave their company (for example, to earn a higher income elsewhere) without first obtaining the approval of the company. These customs may reduce the flexibility of resource allocation.

In some tribal communities, the chief plays a large role in determining what is produced, for instance, when to hunt and what to hunt. In centrally planned economies, such as that of the Soviet Union, central political bodies and central planning authorities largely determine the composition of production, that is, the available amounts of different goods and services.

Although market forces are of considerable importance in determining the nature of production and economic activity in our economy, nonmarket forces, such as government intervention in economic activity, are also significant. Our economy has therefore been called a *mixed economy*. Much of the economy is controlled by market forces that result in production being adjusted to the wants or demands of consumers as signalled by their willingness to pay for commodities. Nevertheless, a significant part of our economy is not steered, regulated or controlled in this way, but is controlled by the government.

Markets, Exchange, Barter, Money

Markets

A market exists when a commodity can be and is traded among a group of individuals, each of whom is motivated by his own gain in making transactions, that is, in buying and selling. The fewer the barriers or difficulties involved in arranging the trading of commodities, the larger or wider are markets.

Trading is facilitated when potential buyers and sellers find it easy to communicate with one another — for instance, when they find it easy to discuss the terms of trade and inspect the goods involved in a transaction. This is why traders sometimes meet at a common place, a market place, and why an invention such as the telephone widens the market. Trading is also facilitated when it is easy to transport goods and effect the easiest exchange of commodities from sellers to buyers. Improved communication and transport systems have done much to widen the operations of markets.

As the markets for commodities become larger, the way in which the commodities are produced may change. Individuals and firms may specialize in the production of particular commodities and build up their skills in producing these, and producers may be able to take advantage of the economies of large-scale production. As a result, the total output and welfare of the community may rise.

Exchange a Necessity in Modern Societies

In some peasant communities, there is little exchange, and each family provides for almost the whole of its needs from its own produce. This is also the ideal of a few communes that have formed in recent years.

In modern societies, however, self-sufficiency of this form is rare because it is usually uneconomical. As individuals, we specialize in production in modern societies, and must exchange our production to obtain the balance of commodities that we wish to consume. Thus, our income is much greater than it otherwise would be. Systems of exchange that have developed in modern societies, in both capitalist and socialist ones, have added considerably to our wealth and income.

Money versus Barter as a Means of Exchange

The exchange systems of modern societies are based on the use of money as a medium of exchange. In some peasant and isolated communities, a *barter* system of exchange still operates. Barter refers to an exchange system in which some commodities are directly exchanged for others. For instance, bread may be directly exchanged for meat, instead of for money.

A barter system of exchange is a poor one, from an efficiency point of view. The system does not make it easy to calculate and compare the relative prices of a range of goods. It can also result in valuable commodities being tied up in the exchange process. For instance, one or both parties to an exchange may be forced to buy a commodity that they themselves do not want to consume or use; this may happen because they cannot easily find a trading partner who wants the commodity that they have to offer and who in return is offering the commodity they want. It is not easy to find a trading partner with the required *coincidence of wants*. They *hold* these unwanted commodities in anticipation of trading them later for something they do want. Thus, we may have meat to offer and require bananas in exchange, but we may not be able to find persons offering bananas who want meat. We may have to exchange the meat for apples, hold these, and then exchange them later for bananas.

The advantage of *money*, especially paper money, is that it ties up virtually no resources in itself — few resources beyond a little paper and some ink. It is very portable, and its use allows the relative prices of goods to be quickly determined. Money is a convenient medium of exchange, and, in normal times, it is a store of value and a suitable unit for keeping accounts. In Canada, the supply of money consists of coins and notes in circulation and bank deposits. The Bank of Canada is responsible for printing and issuing our bank notes and coins. The Canadian financial system is discussed in Chapter 8.

Economic Systems

There are a number of different economic systems (that is, collections of the social mechanisms determining the use of scarce resources) in the world. That of the Soviet Union, for example, differs from our own in several important respects and, in turn, our economic system and that of the Soviet Union deviate from the Yugoslavian system. The economic systems of few, if any, nations are identical, although some systems are more alike than others.

The Canadian economic system is very similar to the systems of the United States, the United Kingdom, and various other developed noncommunist countries. The majority of resources in our economy are privately owned and, subject to normal legal safeguards, individuals are free to use the resources they own in the manner that they prefer. They may also exchange them freely for other resources. Individual resource-holders have considerable freedom of choice. Not all resources are privately owned, however; some resources are owned by the government, and other resources are redistributed by the government. Indeed, in Canada, slightly less than 25 percent of annual output is accounted for by government activity. Thus, our economy is not entirely a free-enterprise economy. It is sometimes maintained that our economy differs greatly from a free-enterprise system. It is best described as a mixed or quasi-captialist economy. Nevertheless, free enterprise accounts for the major part of economic activity in Canada.

In the Soviet Union, by contrast, most of the means of production (productive resources) are owned by the government. The government, through the political process and central planning, directs the use of most of the nation's productive resources. A similar situation exists in communist countries such as East Germany, Hungary, and Czechoslovakia. Such economies can be described as centrally planned, socialist economies. Not all socialist economies in which most of the productive resources are owned by the state, operate in the same way. Some, such as the Yugoslavian economy, make greater use of market mechanisms to guide production than do others. All advanced socialist countries, however, use markets extensively to sell, clear or ration goods intended for consumption.

Sometimes, the classification of economies allows for a third type of economy, namely, subsistence economies. We now consider those "Third World" economies, and then discuss free-enterprise and socialist economies in more detail.

Subsistence and Developing Economies

About two-thirds of the world's population lives in "developing countries". Many of the economies of Africa and Asia, and some in Latin America, fall into this category. Most individuals in these countries must continually struggle with their resources to earn a subsistence, that is, to earn the basic necessities of life. Most of the population in these economies is engaged in hunting, in fishing, in gathering, in agriculture or in grazing; their economic fortune depends very much on the vagaries of nature. To a considerable extent, they are at the mercy of natural occurrences such as droughts, floods, and pestilence.

In subsistence economies, the family or the tribe is the main productive unit. That is, social groups produce commodities. Most production is intended for the consumption of the family, and is not exchanged or sold. Each family hunts or cultivates to meet its own immediate needs, and specialization in production is limited. Specialization in some primitive tribal societies is limited to division of work between the sexes, e.g., the men may hunt, and the women may cultivate and gather crops.

In such societies, income per head remains low. This is so partly because primitive technologies of production are used, and these technologies change slowly. Most production must be consumed in order to ensure survival, so that little or none is left to improve productive processes — to add productive equipment and durable aids to production (capital) to raise educational levels and to improve community health. Consequently, it is difficult for these economies to raise living standards. Many are caught in a *poverty cycle*, or trap. They are too poor to be able to increase their standard of living or can only increase their standard of living through great sacrifice. Their poverty keeps them in continuing poverty.

Life expectancy in subsistence economies is lower than that in developed countries because nutrition is sub-optimal, advanced medical services are beyond the reach of many, sanitation tends to be poor, and people are often

FIGURE 2.1 **Children collecting water in a squatter's settlement in Bogota, Columbia. Many developing countries cannot cope with the influx of population to urban areas because capital is in short supply. Housing, sanitation, water supplies, and roads are inadequate in many of these areas.**

ignorant about hygiene. Many individuals in such economies are illiterate and few are able to obtain formal advanced education.

The wide gap in incomes, in life expectancy, in adult literacy, and in medical services between developed and developing economies can be seen in Table 2.1.

There is always a danger in subsistence economies that increased production will be absorbed by increases in population. If total production rises, total population may increase so that income per head fails to rise. Unfortunately, this has been largely the experience of developing countries such as India and Indonesia. This keeps people trapped at a subsistence level. The trap may be overcome if income per head can be increased substantially and sharply because, beyond a threshold level of income, families tend to be smaller. Again, industrialization seems to be associated with smaller families. Hence, if economic growth is accompanied by industrialization, this may place a brake on population growth. Industrialization, however, is difficult in developing countries. Thus, population pressures create significant barriers to growth in subsistence economies.

The size of markets in subsistence economies is usually limited because transport and communications are poor. In some developing countries, there are few roads suitable for motor transport, and some parts of these countries are accessible only by tracks. Consequently, the operation of market systems is hindered, and national production suffers.

Free-Enterprise, Private-Property Economies

In contrast with the operation of subsistence economies, free-enterprise economies are dominated by the operation of markets. Price mechanisms play a large role in determining what is produced, how it is produced, when and where, and for whom.

Private Property, Freedom, and Self-Interest

The institution of private property is basic to the operation of free-enterprise economies. In this system, individuals are free to purchase resources and use these, subject to general community safeguards, for whatever purpose they desire. They may use them for production and profit, they may exchange them freely, and they may accumulate resources. Individuals in a free-enterprise economy, apart from owning goods for personal use, may own productive resources: there is a great deal of individual freedom in economic choice. Consumers are free to choose, as are producers and resource-holders, and their choices influence the use of resources.

In a free-enterprise economy, individuals can be expected, as a rule, to attempt to maximize their own gains, subject to the general restraints imposed by the system. Consumers or householders, on the whole, use their limited income to buy the commodities that give them the greatest satisfaction. Producers try to produce the commodities that give them the greatest profit. Individuals in the economy are guided in their economic actions by their own self-interest; but they are subject to the discipline of competition from others, and this competition brings order into the system. Thus, the operation of free economic choice does not lead to chaos. On the contrary, it has the important role of ensuring that the goods produced are those that consumers want.

TABLE 2.1 Income per head, life expectancy, adult literacy, and the relative number of physicians in selected industrial-market economies and low and middle-income countries.

	Income Per Capita in U.S. Dollars Per Year 1980	Life Expectancy at Birth in Years 1980	Adult Literacy (Percent) 1977	Population Per Physician 1977
Industrial-Market Economies				
Switzerland	16,440	75	99	510
West Germany	13,590	73	99	490
Sweden	13,520	75	99	560
Norway	12,650	75	99	540
France	11,730	74	99	610
U.S.A.	11,360	74	99	580
Canada	10,130	74	99	560
Japan	9,890	76	99	850
Australia	9,820	74	100	650
United Kingdom	7,920	73	99	750
Italy	6,480	73	98	490
Low and Middle-Income Countries				
Paraguay	1,300	65	84	2,190
Equador	1,270	61	81	1,570
Philippines	690	64	75	2,810
Thailand	670	63	84	8,220
El Salvador	660	63	62	3,600
Indonesia	430	53	62	13,670
Kenya	420	55	50	11,630
Tanzania	280	52	66	17,550
India	240	52	36	3,630
Chad	120	41	15	41,940

SOURCE: World Bank, *World Development Report 1982* (New York, Oxford University Press). Reprinted with permission.

Consumer Sovereignty

It is sometimes said that in a free-enterprise market system *consumers are sovereign.* The system adjusts to their demands. Suppose that consumers' demands for some product, or products, increases — for example, the demand for health foods. This, at least initially, results in a rise in the price of these goods. This in turn raises the *profitability* of producing and retailing such goods. Therefore, in order to improve their profits, more producers may begin producing health foods, and a greater number of retailers may commence selling these. Existing producers and handlers of health foods may also expand the volume of their supplies. Thus, the supply of health foods expands in response to increased demands by consumers for these products. More resources are allocated to supplying these products. A fall in the demand for a product has the opposite effect.

The Price Mechanism

The price mechanism registers the relative demands of consumers for commodities, and the costs to producers of supplying them. In a competitive economy, market prices mirror the relative demands of consumers and the relative costs of supplying commodities.

If the demand for a commodity rises, its price increases, and the supply normally expands as producers try to increase their profit. Also, if the costs of producing a particular commodity fall, say because of improvements in technology, production of the commodity becomes more profitable, and its supply will expand until the value that consumers place on additional production (as indicated by the price they are willing to pay) is equal to the cost of extra supply. Thus, the relative value of extra production and the relative costs of extra production are kept in balance by the price mechanism.

Table 2.2 provides an illustration of the operation of the price mechanism. In the illustration, consumer demand shifts from wheat to rye bread. Resources are therefore switched from whole-wheat-bread production to rye-bread production, as bakers and farmers, guided by profits, follow their own self-interest. This reallocation of resources comes about without any central direction or command.

Competition and the Price Mechanism

Competition is important in the effective operation of this system. If competition is impeded, the system does not adjust adequately to the demands of consumers. For instance, if there are barriers to new firms' entering an industry, prices in the industry may exceed costs of production, and supplies may not be sufficiently increased. Again, new and improved technologies may be adopted more slowly when competition between firms is weak.

TABLE 2.2 **An example of the price mechanism in action. The increased
preference of consumers for rye bread rather than whole-wheat
bread, as reflected in their choices (consumer sovereignty), results
in more resources being allocated to the production of rye bread
and less to whole-wheat bread**

Less Whole-Wheat Bread Chosen	More Rye Bread Chosen
Price of wheat bread ↓	Price of rye bread ↑
Profits of bakers of wheat bread ↓	Profits of bakers of rye bread ↑
Bakers reduce production of wheat bread and lower their purchases of wheat	Bakers expand production of rye bread and increase their purchases of rye
Some bakers switch to or increase their production of rye bread	Number of bakers of rye bread increases
Price of wheat ↓	Price of rye ↓
Profitability of wheat production ↓	Profitability of rye production ↑
Farmers reduce their output of wheat	Farmers increase their output of rye

An adequate or workable degree of competition is not assured in a *laissez-faire* market system (that is, a system in which the government does not interfere). Many governments, including our own, have, therefore, passed legislation aimed at maintaining market competition. For instance, in certain cases conspiracy by firms to maintain prices by common agreement is illegal.

Advantages of the Free-Enterprise System

A free-enterprise system has a number of advantages and disadvantages. A major advantage of the system is that it leaves considerable scope for individual initiative; within the limits of the individual's resources, *everyone* has an opportunity to pursue his or her own economic plans. This freedom is not exclusive to any individual or selected individuals, even though competition can be keen, which limits the effective exercise of the freedom. In some societies, however, such freedom is reserved only for a selected few. When this freedom is coupled with inventiveness, enterprise, and a traditional virtue such as thrift, it can be very effective in reducing scarcity, that is, in solving the basic economic problem.

Another substantial advantage of a market system relying on the price mechanism is that it economizes on the amount of information needed for relatively co-ordinated decision-making in the economy. As information gathering and processing on a large scale can be extremely costly, this is a significant advantage. No central commands are needed to ensure that the products we want are produced. For example, the cereals or other breakfast foods that we eat are frequently supplied without us knowing who has produced the ingredients and without the producers' having any knowledge that we are the ones who will consume the food.

If you have eaten bread recently, where was the wheat produced and by whom? Where were the salt and other ingredients manufactured and by whom? The chances are that you do not know. It is really not important for you to know in order to ensure that your bread is supplied. More importantly, it is not necessary for any one person to know *all* of these facts in order to ensure that you are supplied with the commodities that you demand. Each individual within his or her own limited area of decision-making reacts to price signals that, under various competitive conditions, ensure that his or her demands are satisfied. The price mechanism or market system operates relatively effectively on the basis of individuals' seeking their own gain and reacting to limited sets of information.

Shortcomings of the Free-Enterprise System

The free-enterprise market system does not work perfectly. Indeed, some economists believe that it works poorly, and they would like to see it replaced by, say, a socialist system. Some problems of a completely free-enterprise market system are:

1. It does not always produce commodities that are wanted as some commodities cannot be easily marketed, even though they may be wanted. An example is a program to eradicate malaria-carrying mosquitoes in areas where malaria is a problem. People who do not contribute to the cost of the program will nevertheless benefit if the program goes ahead. Their benefits cannot be made dependent upon their payment, and therefore the program cannot be marketed. Goods of this nature, called public goods, can be effectively supplied only by the government or by collective action.
2. The free-enterprise system does not always make adequate allowance for environmental spillovers such as pollution. This is very often the case, however, because not all resources in the economy are private property.

Some, such as air and water, are common property. Because the use of these is sometimes free (no price is charged for their use), they are sometimes utilized by producers to dispose of socially excessive amounts of pollutants, and this disposal adversely affects the welfare of others in the community. Government intervention may be needed to deal with problems of this nature.

3.   A free-enterprise system does not always ensure full employment of labour; it does not ensure that all of those who want to work are able to find work. Furthermore, the overall level of economic activity in such an economy can fluctuate considerably, and lead to unanticipated disruption.

4.   A free-enterprise system need not result in an equitable or socially acceptable distribution of income.

5.   Workable or effective competition is not always ensured in a free-enterprise system. It is possible, for instance, for some industries to be monopolized (to fall into the hands of one seller, who may exploit this situation to its own advantage). The price mechanism is then impeded in its operation.

6.   The price mechanism may fail to bring about desirable large-scale global changes in an economy. For example, it may fail to promote desirable regional or decentralized economic growth. Operation of the price mechanism results in an economic system adjusting in small variations.

Although adjustments of this kind can lead to a social optimum, they need not do so. They may lead to an optimum that is not the global one, and governmental interference may be needed to shunt the system toward the global optimum.

Government Economic Intervention in Free-Enterprise Economies

Because of difficulties of this nature, no economy in the world today is completely operated by free enterprise. In our economy, although the major part of production is accounted for by private enterprise, the extent of government production and interference is substantial. Governments in Canada operate a number of public enterprises. Some of the services that these enterprises supply are: postal services (Canada Post), rail transport (Canadian National Railway), air travel (Air Canada), and electricity (Ontario Hydro, B.C. Hydro and Power Authority, Hydro-Québec). Indeed some of the enterprises owned by Canadian governments are among the largest industrial companies operating in Canada. Table 2.3 presents the top ten industrial companies ranked by assets with their ownership indicated.

The government also provides for services such as education, defence, justice, law and order, health (hospitals), and various types of scientific research. Roads and port facilities are also supplied by the government. Thus,

TABLE 2.3 **Top 10 Industrials: Rank by Assets 1982**

Rank	Company (head office)	Assets ($ thousands)	Major Shareholders
1.	Hydro-Quebec (Montreal)	23,169,000	Quebec gov't, 100%
2.	Ontario Hydro (Toronto)	20,720,832	Ontario gov't, 100%
3.	Canadian Pacific Ltd. (Montreal)	17,273,034	Power Corp. of Canada, 11%
4.	Bell Canada Enterprises (Montreal)	13,421,800	Wide distribution
5.	Dome Petroleum (Calgary)	9,916,600	Dome Mines Ltd., 26%
6.	Alcan Aluminium Ltd. (Montreal)	8,212,981	Wide distribution
7.	B.C. Hydro & Power Authority (Vancouver)	7,790,226	B.C. gov't, 100%
8.	Petro-Canada (Calgary)	7,552,115	Federal gov't, 100%
9.	Canada Development Crop. (Vancouver)	7,525,890	Federal gov't, 48%
10.	Imperial Oil Ltd. (Toronto)	7,486,000	Exxon Corp., 70%

SOURCE: *Financial Post 500,* June 1983.

the activity of government in Canada is vitally important in the operation of our
present economy.

Apart from its role as a producer of goods and services, the government
sector plays an active role in attempting to manage the level of overall
economic activity in an economy. In a market economy, the level of employment and the rate of inflation can fluctuate considerably. As will be discussed
later, a government, in certain circumstances, can control such fluctuations,
and may try to do so. In our economy, governments also concern themselves
with the distribution of incomes. For instance, the government provides pensions for the aged, invalids, and other groups likely to be in need. To do this, the
government transfers income from some individuals in the community to
others.

In addition, the government not infrequently regulates the operations of
markets and business enterprises. At present in Canada, there is legislation
dealing with the restrictive business practices and consumer protection, and
various prices are regulated by various government agencies such as the
agricultural marketing boards. There are also regulations specifying minimum
wages and conditions of work. Many other regulations — for instance, health
regulations — have an effect on the operation markets. Few markets in Canada
are free of some form of government control. The economy is a *regulated
mixed-economy*, that is, an economy in which there is regulated free-enterprise

and a considerable amount of government activity. Government agencies have entered into various joint-ventures with companies in the private sector. Most of these are in the area of natural-resource developments. Petro-Canada is involved in many such joint ventures. In the manufacturing sector, the Canada Development Corporation (CDC) had been involved in joint ventures. The government, however, decided to sell its shares of ownership in the CDC to the public. Although this convergence may be occurring, there is still a substantial difference between the method by which the economy of a country such as the Soviet Union operates and the method by which the Canadian economy operates. The scope for free enterprise in the Canadian economy, despite the role of government, is still substantial.

Planned Socialist Economies

Socialist economies vary considerably in the way in which they operate. In the Soviet Union, central planning and central direction largely determine the allocation of resources. In Yugoslavia, decision-making is much more decentralized, and markets play a larger role in the allocation of resources. In all socialist or communist systems, however, most of the means of production are collectively owned and are directed toward "socialist objectives". Practically all land and capital is collectively or state owned in communist countries.

Centrally Planned Socialist Economic Systems: The Soviet Union

Consider the Soviet Union as an example of a centrally planned socialist economic system. Since 1929, the Soviet Union has had *Five-Year Plans* that, as each year comes along, are specified as detailed *Annual Plans*. The general goals and features of annual and longer-term national economic plans are set by the Presidium of the Communist Party and the Presidium of the U.S.S.R. Council of Ministers, or Supreme Soviet. The membership of these political bodies overlaps to a considerable extent. These political bodies are the general policy-makers. Routine and detailed work on the plan is done by an administrative body known as Gosplan, or the Central Planning Board.

During the first half of a planning year (the year in which plans are worked out for the following year in which they are to be implemented), the Central Planning Board (Gosplan) collects information about the state of the economy. It reports to the presidiums of the Communist Party and of the Council of Ministers on the performance of the economy, and any bottlenecks. After studying this information, these bodies decide on the general economic objectives that are to be sought during the following year (the plan year). The objectives are stated in broad terms. It may be stated, for instance, that attempts should be made to increase wheat production to a level where imports are no longer necessary; that the expansion of the steel industry should be slowed

down and special emphasis placed on the development of the chemical or elec-
tronics industries. It might also be decided that a greater proportion of total production should be made available for consumer goods.

During the latter half of the planning year, Gosplan, taking account of the
general aims as set out by the presidiums of the Communist Party and of the
Council of Ministers, works out a consistent and workable plan. It does this by
passing suggested production targets down the organizational hierarchy to individual state-enterprises. This being done, plant officials may suggest changes
in the plan and comment on the possibility or otherwise of achieving various
targets. This information is then passed back up through the planning hierarchy to Gosplan. At each stage in the planning process, pressure is brought to
bear on those responsible for implementing plans to make sure that any claim
that the plan cannot be fulfilled has foundation. After taking account of all such
difficulties, and after adjusting the initial plan appropriately, Gosplan sends the
finalized plan to the Supreme Soviet to become law.

The only operational plans in the Soviet Union are annual ones. These are
the plans around which action is centred. The longer-term plans for five, seven,
ten, and twenty years are intended to provide a perspective on future
economic development. To make the annual plans operational, Gosplan uses a
balance method. It specifies how much of the main commodities should be
available, how this supply will be provided for, and how such supplies will be
used. The annual plan shows the intended sources of supply and destinations of
more than 20,000 commodities. For each of these commodities, a planned
materials balance is drawn up, that is, a statement of the planned physical supplies and their destination. The original estimates of these are called control
figures. They are sent by Gosplan to the various production ministries, which
allocate the production among the Soviet Republics or other geographical
units, and send regional planning authorities details of their intended part in
carrying out the plan. In turn, these authorities add details to the plan and pass
it down to smaller geographical administrations; finally, plans reach individual
plants or firms. Each administrator in the chain of control checks whether it is
possible to carry out production as planned. Any difficulties are reported back
to Gosplan, which may then revise the control figures before arriving at the
final plan to be submitted to the Supreme Soviet to become law.

The fundamental plans of the Soviet Union are in terms of quantities of production and quantities of inputs. Financial and monetary relationships in the
economy are adjusted to make the physical plans possible. Financial plans
cover such matters as the extension of credit by the State Bank, the determination of prices to balance demand and supply in retail markets, and the levying
of taxes.

Retail prices are set by the government to clear, or dispose of, or ration
available supplies. Consumers are free to choose among the goods that are
available, but they have little (direct) sovereignty. If the demand for a particular
product, say television, rises, production of television sets need not necessarily

increase. The price of television sets may be raised to keep demand in line with available supply, but supply may not be altered. Whether or not this increased demand will eventually be reflected in increased production depends on whether or not the presidiums of the Communist Party and of the Council of Ministers decide to raise the planned level of production of television sets when the next annual plan is determined.

The Soviet Union does not allocate labour directly, but regulates wage rates to promote the growth of industries and skills considered to be of most value by the Presidium of the Communist Party. Wage rates are unequal (much more so than in Canada), and reward is according to effort, and to the social value of the task performed, the social value being determined by the Presidium of the Communist Party. Incentive schemes are widely used in the Soviet Union. Managers and workers obtain bonuses for exceeding their planned, or target, level of production or performance. The size of the bonus depends on the social priority placed on the industry concerned.

Some companies from socialist countries operate in Canada. More than half of these companies were established in the 1970s. Most are relatively small in terms of capital invested. The details are summarized in Table 2.4.

Advantages of the Centrally Planned Socialist Economic System

One of the advantages of the Soviet centrally planned system is its ability to maintain full employment with only moderate inflation. The system has also been able to enforce high levels of savings and capital accumulation; this has resulted in considerable growth in the production of goods and services in the Soviet Union. The system permits large-scale changes to be made in the structure of the economy, if necessary, at a faster rate than might occur in a free-enterprise system, or it enables the system to be shunted into desirable lines of economic development to which a free-enterprise market system might not gravitate (as its adjustment processes tend to be localized).

Shortcomings of the Centrally Planned System

A problem of the system is the high cost of central planning. Many people are employed in drawing up economic plans. As the economy becomes more and more advanced, and the range and sophistication of available goods increase, the required amount of planning increases.

Another problem is that freedom is limited. Individuals are not free to launch their own productive enterprises, and they cannot of their own volition produce products that consumers want. The nature of the rewards and economic possibilities open to the individuals of the Soviet Union is largely dependent on the views of leading members of the Communist Party.

A central planning system such as that of the Soviet Union is not always

TABLE 2.4 **Soviet and East European Companies in Canada**

Company	Head Office	Year Estab-lished	Socialist Partner	Socialist Equity	Issued Share Capital	Principal Activity
Omnitrade Ltd.	Montreal	1947	Transakta (Czechoslovakia)	100%	$1,000,000	Sells and services wide range of industrial products.
Pekao Trading Company Canada Ltd.	Toronto	1956	Bank Polska Kasa Opieki (Poland)	99%	$ 25,000	Sells consumer and manufac-tured products.
Dalimpex Ltd.	Montreal	1965	DAL (Poland)	95%	$ 150,000	Sells and services wide range of consumer and industrial products.
Cebecom Ltd.	Toronto	1965	Bulgarkonserv (Bulgaria)	50%	$ 47,600	Sells fruits, conserves, and other food products.
Motokov Canada Inc.	Montreal	1966	Motokov (Czecho-slovakia)	100%	$ 725,000	Sells and services Czech motor-cycles, bicycles, and mopeds.
Superlux Canada Ltd.	Montreal	1967	Glassexport (Czecho-slovakia)	100%	$ 100,000	Sells products of Czech glass industry.
Morflot Freightliners Ltd.	Vancouver	1971	Sovinflot (USSR)	95%	$ 100,000	Agent for Soviet shipping to Canadian West Coast
Belarus Equip-ment Ltd.	Toronto	1972	Traktoroexport, Zap-chastexport (USSR)	100%	$ 500,000	Sells and services Soviet agricul-tural equipment in Canada.
Stan-Canada Machinery Ltd.	Toronto	1972	Stankoimport (USSR)	100%	$ 900,000	Sells and services Soviet machine tools in Canada and the United States.

Company	Head Office	Year Established	Socialist Partner	Socialist Equity	Issued Share Capital	Principal Activity
EMEC Trading Ltd.	Vancouver	1973	Energomachexport (USSR)	95%	$ 414,000	Sells and installs electrical generators and turbines.
Omnitrade Industrial Co. Ltd.	Montreal	1973	Transakta (Czechoslovakia)	100%	$ 50,000	Sells and services textile machinery and other products in the United States through operating divisions in New York and North Carolina.
Hungarotex-Canada Ltd.	Montreal	1974	Hungarotex (Hungary)	50%	$ 50,000	Sells Hungarian textiles in Canada and abroad.
Terra Power Tractor Company Ltd.	Saskatoon	1974	Universal Tractor (Romania)	100%	$ 100,000	Sells and services Romanian agricultural equipment in Western Canada.
Socan Aircraft Ltd.	Calgary	1975	Aviaexport (USSR)	67%	$ 50,000	Sells and services Soviet aircraft.
Ascott Equipment Ltd.	Sherbrooke	1976	Universal Tractor (Romania)	49%	$ 150,000	Sells and services agricultural equipment in Eastern Canada.

SOURCE: C.H. McMillan, "Soviet and East European Direct Investment in Canada," *Foreign Investment Review*, II, 2 (Spring 1979), p. 16. (Taken from information on file in the East-West Project, Institute of Soviet and East European Studies, Carleton University.)

flexible. If unexpected shortages occur, say of a particular type of raw material, this may strain the whole system and dislocate the plan.

A planning system based on physical targets, as is basically the case in the U.S.S.R., can give rise to a number of problems. Managers may understate the capacity of their plant and be allocated low production targets that can be readily achieved or over-fulfilled. They can then earn bonuses easily. Again, managers may achieve their physical targets by producing products of poor quality or of inadequate variety. For instance, if a plant canning vegetables is given a production target of 500 t of canned vegetables per year, the manager may decide to meet the target by producing only large cans of vegetables; or he may decide to can only one type of vegetable, say peas — and it may not matter if these are old and starchy. Consumers may really want a wider variety of packs, and a greater variety of vegetable types and qualities.

In a centrally directed socialist economy, barriers to invention and innovation can be considerable. No individual can "go it alone" in inventing or innovating, as is possible in a free-enterprise system. Social support is needed in a socialist system for any venture of this type. A good deal of red tape may be involved before any support is obtained. Furthermore, managers who adopt new inventions may profit little from them. Their production targets may be increased to take account of any increase in productivity resulting from the invention, and they may fail to meet their target during the period of installation and "running-in" of the innovation. Thus, some Soviet managers prefer to work with known techniques rather than to experiment with new ones.

It should be noted that the Soviet model of socialism is not the only possible one. Models of competitive, or market, socialism have been devised in which all land and capital is owned by the state, but managers of state-owned enterprises are encouraged to operate like free-enterprise managers to maximize profit.

In the socialist system as envisaged by Oscar Lange, there is a Central Planning Board that determines how much of national output will be invested, and how much used for the provision of public, or nonmarketable, goods. All marketable goods are traded in markets and produced by state enterprises in response to the profit motive. Prices of these goods are adjusted by the Central Planning Board to ensure that supply and demand are balanced, and that production responds to the demands of consumers. Consumers are sovereign in determining the composition of production of consumer goods. The Yugoslavian economy roughly approximates this model. Other socialist economic-systems can also be envisaged.

This chapter has indicated that there are a variety of economic systems in the world today. All have to face the same basic economic choices or deal with the same basic economic problems. They make these choices in different ways. In economies such as that of the Soviet Union, central direction, or control, primarily determines the response of the economy to the basic problems. In an economy such as our own, the response depends on a combination of actions by individuals, free enterprises, and the government.

KEY CONCEPTS
(FOR REVIEW)

Barter

Centrally planned socialism

Coincidence of wants

Decisions and choices to be made
  in an economy

Economic system

Environmental spillovers

Exchange

Free-enterprise, private-property
  economies

Functions of any economy

Government economic activity and
  regulation

Competition in markets

Competitive or market socialism

Consumer sovereignty

Markets

Money as a medium of exchange

Poverty cycle, or trap

Price mechanism

Public goods

Regulated mixed-economy

Social means, or mechanisms, and
  economic choice

Subsistence economies

QUESTIONS FOR REVIEW AND DISCUSSION

1. Why must any economy make important choices about the use of its resource?
2. What basic decisions have to be made in every economy about the use of its resources? Illustrate your answer by an example.
3. "Custom or tradition, dictatorship or central control, or market mechanisms can be used to allocate resources." Explain.
4. What is money in Canada?
5. What is a market and a market place? What factors are likely to facilitate trading in a market?
6. How may the size of markets be related to the extent of specialization in production, and to the occurrence of economies of large-scale production?
7. Why is exchange necessary in modern societies? Is it advantageous?
8. Compared with barter, what are the main advantages of using money as a medium of exchange?
9. There are a number of economic systems in the world. In a general way, distinguish between them.
10. State the main economic characteristics of subsistence in developing economies. Give some examples of developing countries.
11. How well developed and used are markets in developing countries?
12. Why do population pressures create special problems for developing countries?
13. What is a poverty cycle, or trap?

14. Discuss the role of markets and the price mechanism in free-enterprise economies.
15. "Private property, freedom and self-interest are the cornerstones of free-enterprise economies." Explain and discuss.
16. What is meant by saying that consumers are sovereign? How do their choices affect the allocation of resources?
17. What is the price mechanism, and how does it operate?
18. Update the information in Table 2.3 for the Top 10 Industrials in Canada.
19. How can the lack of competition impede the operation of the price mechanism?
20. What are the advantages of a free-enterprise economic system?
21. What are the shortcomings of a free-enterprise market system?
22. Do governments intervene to a considerable extent in the operation of free-enterprise economies? To what extent has this occurred in Canada?
23. "The Canadian economy is a regulated mixed-economy." Explain.
24. What are the main ways in which the Soviet economic system differs from the Canadian economic system?
25. Outline the method of resource allocation and economic planning adopted in the Soviet Union.
26. "In the Soviet Union, consumers are free to choose between goods that are available, but they have no sovereignty as in the Canadian system." Explain.
27. Outline the advantages of a centrally planned socialist system.
28. Paying particular attention to the Russian system, what are the main shortcomings of a centrally planned socialist system?
29. Do socialist companies operate in Canada? What are their characteristics?

FURTHER READING

Blomqvist, A., Wonnacott, P., & Wonnacott, R., *Economics*, 1st Canadian ed. Scarborough: McGraw-Hill Ryerson Limited, 1984, chapters 3 & 37.

Lipsey, R.G., Purvis, D.D., & Steiner, P.O., *Economics*. New York: Harper & Row, Publishers, 1982, Chapter 4.

McMillan, C.H., "Soviet and East European Direct Investment in Canada." *Foreign Investment Review* (Spring, 1979).

Samuelson, P.A., & Scott, A.D., *Economics*. Scarborough: McGraw-Hill Ryerson Limited, 1980, chapters 2 & 3.

Swedlove, F., "Business-Government Joint Ventures in Canada." *Foreign Investment Review* (Spring, 1978).

Resources: Factors Determining Economic Potential

3

Introduction

A nation's or a region's possibilities for producing commodities and for satisfying the wants of its inhabitants depend on the quality and quantity of its resources and the nature of its environment. The natural environment occasionally provides for some of our wants, and we do not need to engage in an elaborate productive process to satisfy these wants. For instance, some people may be fortunate enough to live in a warm, sunny area where no artificial heating and little clothing is needed, or in an area where berries or coconuts or other fruits grow naturally and can easily be gathered. But for nearly all of us (possibly for all of us), the natural environment is unable to satisfy our wants fully; we can more adequately satisfy these by engaging in productive activity, that is, in action designed to increase the quantities and types of commodities available to us.

The extent to which we can expand the quantities and types of commodities available to us depends on the resources that are at hand, on our knowledge, and, in some instances, on the environment. Our success in overcoming scarcity depends largely on our available resources and our ability to transform these into commodities. The economic ascent of the human race has depended largely on its ability to harness and control nature.

Classification of Resources

The resources available for productive purposes can be classified or grouped in several different ways. One traditional classification is to divide resources into land, labour, capital, and entrepreneurship. This classification was the one adopted by Alfred Marshall at the beginning of this century.

Land is defined to include much more than a land mass. It includes all natural resources: agricultural land, minerals, wildlife, natural forests, fish, and, indeed, all the gifts of nature.

Labour refers to the availability of human effort. The available amount of labour in an economy depends on the level of population, the ages of the members of the population, and their health and well-being.

Capital can be looked upon as the produced means of further production or as the produced means of future consumption. It includes items such as bulldozers, factory equipment, houses, stocks of wheat, and cars.

Entrepreneurship, as a factor, is more difficult to define; but it refers to the ability and willingness to put into commercial practice new productive ideas, that is, the ability to innovate and engage in creative economic change. Uncertainty and risk are associated with creative economic change; but the rewards for successful innovation can be great.

Corresponding to each of these grouping of resources just mentioned are different types of income. Even though the correspondence is far from exact, *rent* is associated with land, *wages* and *salaries* are payments for labour, *interest* stems from capital, and (pure) *profit* is the reward for successful entrepreneurship. The association, however, is by no means watertight.

For some purposes, resources can be classified in other ways. It is sometimes useful to classify resources according to their economic value. For example, it may be helpful to classify mineral deposits such as coal according to whether they are of commercial value, of marginal commercial value, or of sub-marginal commercial value. Again, from a conservation point of view, it may be relevant to divide resources into those that are renewable and those that are nonrenewable. Classifications of this type will be discussed later in this chapter.

Resources in the Circular Flow

Resources are the bases of production, and they help to determine the amount of commodities produced to satisfy wants. In our market system, resources are used by business firms to produce products (goods) to sell to households. Resources are owned by households, which in turn obtain incomes from firms by supplying the services of resources to firms. In turn, the incomes received by households are used to purchase commodities from firms.

Markets for resources (the building blocks of production) and markets for products (the end result of production) are linked by a *circular flow*. This circular flow is illustrated in Figure 3.1. The figure indicates:

1. Firms purchase the services of resources supplied by households.
2. The payments of firms for these (wages, rent, interest, and profit) provide the incomes of households.
3. Firms use the services of these resources to supply products to householders, who pay for them from their incomes.
4. Householders' payments provide receipts for firms and thereby the means to continue purchasing the service of resources.

In Figure 3.1, the outer circle represents *money* flows, and the inner circle (with arrows in the opposite direction to the outer circle) represents *real* flows, that is, physical flows of products and resources. The circular flow of the economy will be discussed in more detail in Chapter 7. It is introduced at this stage to indicate the link, or interdependence, between markets for products and markets for resources.

FIGURE 3.1 **Circular flow of an economy that indicates the links between markets for resources and markets for products**

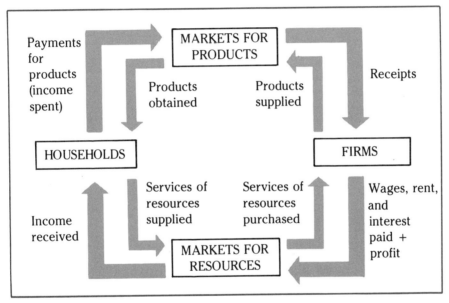

Land, Labour, Capital, and Entrepreneurship in Canada

We will now consider some general features of the resources land, labour, capital, and entrepreneurship in Canada.

Land

Canada is the second largest country in the world with a territory of 9,900,000 km^2. Eighty-nine percent of this area is without permanent settlement, however. The harsh northern climate means that agriculture is restricted to the southern region with most of the approximately 300,000 farming units being within 484 km of the American border. Nevertheless, more than 25 percent of Canadian economic activity is based upon agriculture (including processing, wholesale, and retail activities).

FIGURE 3.2 **Experimental cropland at a Canadian university. Roughly 7 percent
of Canada's land mass is engaged in agricultural production.**
Courtesy University of Guelph Illustration Services

Looking at the utilization of land holdings in Canada, only about 68,000,000 ha are cultivated. Thus, roughly 7 percent of Canada's land mass is used for agricultural production. Another 44,000,000 ha are improved land. Cattle and calves are the most valuable category of agricultural commodities. Wheat is the most valuable crop.

Roughly 37 percent of the land area in Canada is forested. The leading timber-producing provinces are British Columbia, Ontario, and Quebec. In 1978, 66 percent of all Canadian lumber was produced in British Columbia. Processing beyond the raw material stage contributed nearly 18 percent of all value added for goods-producing industries. Given the traditional economic approach to classifying resources, fishing resources can be regarded as a part of land. In 1978, Canada was the world's largest exporter of fish, with exports of $1.1 billion.

Canada's mineral industry has been a major factor in its economic development. Exports of minerals account for more than a third of Canada's total foreign sales of merchandise. The largest industry in this sector is petroleum and natural gas production and refining. Other important minerals are iron ore, copper, zinc, coal, and nickel. Minerals such as manganese, chromium, bauxite, and tin are imported.

As is the case with many other natural resources, the value of mineral resources depends on capital investment. The value of mineral resources located near existing railways or ports is likely to be greater than the value of those in remote areas, as the exploitation of these resources can involve a considerable amount of capital investment. The commercial value of "land" really depends upon the capital investment that is combined with it.

Labour

Labour, too, is a resource. As of June 1, 1982, the population of Canada was 24.6 million. Some of the population were too young, too old, or too handicapped, to work. Others, such as homemakers, were involved in domestic duties, and some were full-time students. Less than half of the total population was classified as being in the labour force in 1982. In that year, there were 11.9 million people in the civilian labour force. This figure represents 64 percent of the civilian noninstitutional population over 15 years of age. Of the 11.9 million, 10.6 million were employed.

Of the 10.6 million people employed, 6.2 million were male and 4.4 were female. An interesting feature of the Canadian labour market is the increase in the proportion (participation rate) of females in the labour force since the 1960s. The participation of males aged 15 to 24 also increased during the 1970s. The participation rate of males over 25 years of age has decreased slightly during this period. The main trends can be seen in Table 3.1.

The labour force as a resource depends on the composition of the population — its size and ages of the workers — on community attitudes, and on the

FIGURE 3.3 **Nickel Mine in Thompson, Manitoba. Canada's mineral industry has
been a major factor in its economic development.**
Courtesy INCO Limited

TABLE **3.1**   **Canadian Labour Force Participation Rates 1970-82**

	Male		Female	
	15-24	25+	15-24	25+
1970	62.5	83.3	49.5	34.5
1971	62.7	82.7	50.8	35.4
1972	64.0	82.3	51.8	36.2
1973	66.0	82.3	54.2	37.6
1974	68.9	82.2	56.0	38.5
1975	68.8	81.9	56.8	40.0
1976	67.9	81.1	56.8	41.1
1977	68.8	80.9	57.5	42.1
1978	69.7	81.0	8.9	44.0
1979	71.4	80.9	61.0	44.9
1980	72.0	80.5	62.6	46.2
1981	72.5	80.3	63.2	47.9
1982	69.5	79.3	62.3	48.3

SOURCE: *Economic Review,* Department of Finance, April 1983.

remuneration received. The fact that there is now a greater participation in the labour force by females may reflect a change in community attitudes. The generosity of the *Unemployment Insurance Act* in the 1970s may have increased the participation rate of young people and women by increasing the effective remuneration received for (temporary) employment. The income earned from (temporary) employment includes not only the income earned directly from employment, but the stream of U.I.C. benefits collected during the subsequent period of unemployment.

The size of the labour force is also affected by immigration. In 1981, Canada received 128,000 immigrants, of which 57,000 were destined for the labour force. The level of immigration depends upon Canadian unemployment conditions and the tightness of immigration rules. In the past, immigration has been an important source of skilled labour for Canada. When unemployment conditions are slack (high unemployment) in Canada, foreigners are less likely to want to immigrate, and/or immigration rules are likely to be more stringent than if unemployment is low, and employment prospects are good.

The potential labour resources of the Canadian economy, as in most economies, are not fully exploited. Most individuals want leisure time; it is not socially acceptable to work long hours in order to maximize the total level of national productivity. It is not the most important end of economic activity. The prime purpose of most economic activity is to satisfy the wants of individuals efficiently. They value both leisure time and produced goods for consumption;

but beyond a point, they do not desire to give up more leisure time for more
productivity.

It is worthwhile illustrating this point. Trade-off between production and
leisure time was first discussed in Chapter 1 (see Figure 1.10). The curve ABCD
in Figure 3.4 represents the efficiency frontier of trade-off between national
production and the amount of leisure time taken by the community. Points on
this frontier indicate the (maximum) level of national production that *can be
attained* when various amounts of leisure time are taken. The curves marked
I_1I_1, I_2I_2, and I_3I_3 are indifference curves representing the preferences of the
community for produced commodities and leisure time. The nature of these
curves was discussed in Chapter 1.

FIGURE 3.4 **Production is not the sole aim of economic activity. Individuals' wants
may be most desirably met by lower than maximum-attainable levels of
production and more leisure time.**

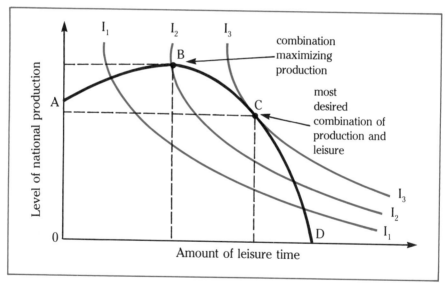

The amount of leisure time (and, indirectly, work time) corresponding to
point B maximizes the level of national production. But to maximize national
production is not paramount, given the wants of the community for commodities *and* for leisure time. The most desirable level of national production is
the one corresponding to point C. This gives the community more leisure time
than choice B.

In Canada, the normal work week is forty hours or less. Most employees
receive paid annual vacations as well as statutory holidays. The actual amount
of time for vacation and holidays varies according to province as well as to
occupation.

Capital

Although capital is sometimes defined as consisting of those produced resources that are means for further production, fixed assets, such as houses, that provide a service over a long period can also be regarded as part of capital. In Canada, houses are regarded by the statistician as being a part of capital, but cars, unless used in a business, are not. Buildings, plant and machinery, and constructions of various types, such as roads, form part of a nation's capital.

The economist's concept of capital should be distinguished from the accountant's concept, and from that of the layman. The economic concept refers to real resources. An accountant regards the amount of money subscribed to a company by its shareholders as the company's capital. The value of a company's fixed assets (excluding land) and its stock — its capital in the economic sense — may exceed, or be less than, the amount of capital subscribed by shareholders to the company.

In Canada in 1982, approximately 22 percent of total expenditure was either for additional fixed capital or for replacement of existing fixed capital. The main sources of Canada's gross fixed-capital expenditure for 1982 are shown in Table 3.2.

TABLE 3.2 **Components of Gross Fixed Capital Formation in Canada, 1982**

Component	Value ($ millions)
Business	53,039
Housing	12,734
Government	10,620
Total	76,393

SOURCE: *Economic Review,* Department of Finance, April 1983.

Additions to a nation's capital can be an important source of economic growth and an important means of reducing scarcity. This is especially so if new capital embodies the latest techniques and advances in scientific knowledge. There can be little doubt that capital has played an important role in making work easier for us and more productive. Approximately $60,000 worth of capital is required by a worker in Canadian manufacturing in order to perform a job.[1]

A nation's expenditure on capital and stocks is financed out of savings, and from allowances for depreciation of fixed capital (that is, sums set aside by enterprises for replacement of capital as it wears out). Potential levels of con-

[1]P. Fuhrman, *Business in the Canadian Environment* (Scarborough: Prentice Hall, 1982).

sumption must be foregone in order to allow capital accumulation to take place. Some of the potential rewards of capital accumulation are higher levels of consumption, more varied types of goods, and a greater amount of leisure in the future.

Capital accumulation can, however, also bring problems. For instance, assembly-line workers may find that their jobs are repetitive and boring. The organization of a capitalistic enterprise may also leave them with a sense of alienation — a lack of job satisfaction, a lack of self-esteem, and a feeling that their jobs are not socially significant.

Another problem from an employment point of view is that the rate of capital accumulation (investment) in an advanced economy such as Canada's can fluctuate greatly, and this can cause the level of employment in the economy to fluctuate.

Entrepreneurship

The factor of business enterprise (or *entrepreneurship*) is extremely difficult to measure; but it is a very important ingredient in economic growth. It refers to the willingness and ability of enterprises to adopt new ideas and to create commercially successful new ones. It is frequently alleged that Canadian businessmen are more conservative than their American counterparts. This may explain why various sectors of the Canadian economy are characterized by intensive American participation.

The organization of business enterprise can aid or hinder entrepreneurship. Joseph Schumpeter, a famous economist writing during the first part of this century, believed that the growth of modern large companies might in the end hinder entrepreneurship. Large companies involve a complex organization, in much the same way that government departments do. Individuals operating such companies usually own little of the capital, and top management may prefer security rather than risky innovation, which may bring them little personal reward if it succeeds but disgrace and loss of position if it fails. Much more evidence, however, is required to determine whether or not the growth of big companies is leading to a decline in entrepreneurship.

Ownership, Organization, and Control of Canadian Resources

Labour

The resource that obtains the greatest share of national output is labour. In recent years, wages and salaries have accounted for 56 to 57 percent of national income. Most Canadian employees have individual contracts with their employers. Some employees, however, belong to unions that negotiate terms of employment for all members with their employer. At the start of 1983, about

3.6 million people were members of unions. This represented 40 percent of nonagricultural paid workers, and 30.6 percent of the civilian labour force. Membership in the ten largest unions is shown in Table 3.3.

TABLE 3.3   **Union Membership in the 10 Largest Unions in Canada, 1983**

	Name	*Membership*
1.	Canadian Union of Public Employees	281,242
2.	National Union of Provincial Government Employees	242,321
3.	Public Service Alliance of Canada	159,646
4.	United Steelworkers of America	148,000
5.	United Food and Commercial Workers	141,400
6.	International Union: United Automobile Aerospace, and Agricultural Implement Workers of America	98,000
7.	International Brotherhood of Teamsters: Chauffers, Warehousemen, and Helpers of America	91,500
8.	Central de l'enseignement du Québec (Quebec Teaching Congress)	86,615
9.	United Brotherhood of Carpenters and Joiners of America	85,000
10.	Fédération des affaires sociales (Social Affairs Federation)	83,246

SOURCE: Directory of Labour Organizations in Canada, 1982, Labour Canada, 1983.

Of total union membership, 56.5 percent was affiliated with the Canadian Labour Congress, and 41.3 percent were members of international unions with headquarters in the United States.

Land

It should be noted that more land in Canada is owned by the Crown than is owned privately: 90% to 10%. The number of farming units is comparatively large with more than 300,000 such units.

Mining Establishments

In contrast with agriculture, the number of mining establishments in Canada is not large. In the late 1970s, there were 14 companies mining iron ore; the largest three are the Iron Ore Co. of Canada, Quebec Cartier Mining Co., and

Wabush Mines. Copper is produced at 25 mines; Inco (International Nickel), Falconbridge Mines, and Noranda Mines are major companies.

As of December 31, 1975, 54 percent of the petroleum and natural gas industry, and 58 percent of the "other minerals" industry were foreign-owned.

Manufacturing

The number of manufacturing establishments in Canada is much greater than the number of mining establishments but considerably smaller than the number of farming units. In 1978, there were approximately 31,963 manufacturing establishments, employing nearly 1.8 million people. Although there are a large number of manufacturers in Canada as a whole, some industries are dominated by a few firms. For example, in 1975 the top four firms in the tobacco-products industry controlled 88.1 percent of it. For petroleum and coal products, 75.4 percent of the industry was controlled by the top four firms — 88.0 percent was controlled by the eight largest. The largest four firms control 70.1 percent of the transport-equipment industry. In terms of overall manufacturing, the ten largest industries in 1978 accounted for 43.5 percent of the total value of manufacturing shipments, indicating a high degree of concentration of output in certain industries. The top ten were petroleum refining, motor vehicles, pulp and paper, slaughtering and meat packing, iron and steel, sawmills and planing mills, and motor-vehicle parts and accessories.

Some sectors of the manufacturing industry also exhibit a high degree of foreign ownership or control. Many of the dominant firms are multinationals, that is, companies with business operations in several countries. Foreign-owned firms dominate the Canadian motor-vehicle industry, the rubber-products industry, the chemical industry, and other smaller manufacturing industries. Table 3.4 presents the relevant statistics on foreign ownership for selected industries.

In 1972, 60 percent of value added in Ontario manufacturing was controlled by foreign interests. In British Columbia, the Prairie Provinces, and Quebec, roughly 40 percent of manufacturing was controlled by foreign interests. In the Atlantic Provinces, the proportion was roughly 35 percent. In all instances, the United States was the major foreign investor. In 1982, 141 of the top 500 Industrials ranked by the *Financial Post* were wholly foreign owned, and another 74 had at least 40 percent foreign ownership.

In order to safeguard Canadian welfare the Canadian government enacted the *Foreign Investment Review Act* in 1973, which took effect in two phases in 1974 and 1975. The *Act* created the Foreign Investment Review Agency (FIRA), which was given the responsibility of reviewing foreign takeovers of existing businesses and new investment proposals made by foreign-owned firms (termed noneligible persons). The main criterion employed by FIRA was whether or not the proposal would be of "significant benefit to Canada."

During its existence under the Trudeau Liberal government

TABLE 3.4 **Foreign Ownership and Control in Selected Manufacturing
Industries (as a percentage of capital employed in 1979)**

	Ownership (%)	Control (%)
All manufacturing	47	51
Rubber products	76	98
Textiles	27	31
Pulp and paper products	52	42
Motor vehicles and parts	83	92
Electrical products	59	71
Chemicals	61	71

SOURCE: Statistics Canada, *Canada's International Investment Position*, Catalogue no. 67-202 (July, 1984), Table 44.

(1974/75-1984), FIRA was a subject of controversy in Canada. It has been argued that FIRA was largely ineffectual, as it approved roughly 80 percent of the proposals that it received. Foreign businesses complained that the procedures increased the cost of setting up business in Canada. The 80 percent-approval figure may contain a bias, however, as many businesses that might have failed the test were likely discouraged from applying to the Agency. It is also possible that some proposals that would have been of "significant benefit to Canada" were discouraged because of the additional cost and frustration imposed by FIRA.

When elected in September 1984, the Mulroney Conservative government announced its intention to change the name of FIRA to Investment Canada. Investment Canada will take a more positive view of foreign investment than did its predecessor. For example, a foreign investment proposal would be approved if it provided "net benefits to Canada" (rather than the more stringent "significant benefit" required by FIRA).

SERVICES

The service sector includes those industries for which the production of material goods is a minor part of production. The main function is the service provided to the customer. Labour may be the most important resource used by firms that operate in the service sector. The major categories in the service sector are:

- Public administration and defence
- Community, business, and personal services
- Finance, insurance, and real estate

- Wholesale and retail trade
- Transportation, storage, and communication

In the service sector, there is considerable government involvement. The obvious example is in transportation, storage, and communication. The government owns a railway and an airline. In communications, the government supplies postal services. The C.B.C. operates radio and television networks. Canadian banks operate under a parliamentary charter, and operations are regulated by the *Bank Act.*

The government is not involved to any considerable extent in the wholesaling and retailing of goods, (provincial government liquor stores and Petro Can service stations are notable exceptions). Well-known companies in this sector include Dominion Stores Ltd., Simpson-Sears Ltd., the Hudson's Bay Co., and the T. Eaton Co., which are all large chain stores. In Canada, *chain stores* dominate in combination (groceries and meats), department, general merchandise, and variety stores, whereas *independent stores* dominate in grocery stores, motor-vehicle dealers, service stations, household-furniture stores, sporting-goods stores. In 1978, sales by independent stores amounted to almost $40 billion compared to $29 billion by chain stores.

The Business Firm:
The Form of Its Legal Ownership

The form of its legal ownership influences the nature of the control over a firm, and possibly its objectives. Of the principal forms of organization, sole proprietorship and partnership are the oldest. Only since the nineteenth century has it become relatively easy to form companies, which is now a common form of business organization.

Sole Proprietorship

Any person who is capable of entering into a binding agreement is capable of engaging in a business activity as a single proprietor. If the individual desires to use a name other than his or her own, or add the words "and Company", he or she must file a declaration stating the name and residence of the person involved, the intended business name, that no other individual is in partnership, and that he or she is twenty-one years of age.

The sole proprietor of a business is fully responsible for the debts of the firm. If the proprietor is unable to meet its debts, creditors may require him or her to sell personal assets to meet them. Advantages of sole proprietorship are that it is easy to commence business, and that anyone has an opportunity to do so if he or she desires. Most single proprietors are also managers of their own business, and have a personal interest in it.

Disadvantages of this form of ownership are that it involves unlimited liability for the owner, and it hampers the growth of large-scale enterprise. Large-scale production is necessary in many modern manufacturing and manufacturing-related industries if costs are to be kept low. The growth of large-scale operations is hampered because the availability of funds to individuals may be restricted. Most lending institutions are not prepared to lend venture or risk capital to an enterprise. An individual is, as a rule, forced by institutional restraints on lending to maintain a minimum equity in the business, and the required equity is likely to become too large to finance from personal funds once the contemplated size of the business becomes large.

Partnership

To a limited extent, these difficulties may be overcome by forming a partnership. A partnership may consist of two or more people, often from the one family. Additional partners in a firm may bring with them extra equity capital or funds, or intangible assets such as business connections and good will.

In a *general partnership*, each partner has unlimited liability for the debts of the partnership, and any partner can act as an agent for all the partners and commit the whole partnership. Thus, members may encounter personal risks, especially as the number of partners increases. Other disadvantages of a partnership are that any partner can dissolve it whenever he or she wishes, and no new partner can be admitted to the partnership without the consent of all existing partners. The disadvantages of this form of organization are such that it is common only in small businesses.

A *limited partnership* has at least one general partner who is responsible for operating the business, and at least one other person who contributes financially to the enterprise. The latter individual is called a "limited partner", and this individual or group of individuals is liable only to the extent of their financial commitment to the firm. Limited partners must not take part in the management of the firm; if they do they become general partners. Individuals who establish a limited partnership must file a declaration stating the terms of the partnership including a list of general and limited partners, and the amount of financial capital contributed by each limited partner.

Corporate Forms of Business Operation

Corporate forms of business are more complex and more expensive to organize than are other forms. The corporation may be a private company or a public company. In a *private company*, the number of shareholders is limited to 50 and there is a restriction on the right to transfer shares. The private company also has a clause prohibiting the offer of securities for public subscription. These prohibitions restrict the growth and flexibility of private companies. In the case of private companies, shareholders either form part of the management of the company or are in close contact with the management.

Many large-scale enterprises in our economy (apart from public enterprises) are organized by means of *public companies*. Unlike the case of a private company, the number of shareholders of a public company is not limited, and shareholders are free to transfer their shares to any other person. Directors may issue prospectuses and invite members of the public to subscribe capital to the company. Large amounts of capital can be raised in this way, and the risks of business enterprise can be shared among a large number of people, because the liability of shareholders is limited but not the number of shareholders.

Public companies have played an extremely important role in the growth of mixed economies. Such companies are able to take a long-term stance as they are legal entities with a perpetual life. Public companies have been able to raise huge amounts of capital required for new ventures needed to ensure that full advantage is taken of economies of scale. On the debit side, this form of organization has enabled large and politically powerful companies to form, which has given some firms considerable market power — power to raise their prices well above costs and make above-average levels of profit, for instance.

A company can finance itself in a number of ways. First of all, it issues ordinary shares, and it may increase the number of these at any time. Holders of ordinary shares are the prime risk-takers in the company. Whether or not they receive a dividend, or return on their capital, usually depends on whether there is a profit and on whether a dividend is declared. The dividends paid to ordinary shareholders are usually paid out of residual profit, and such shareholders receive a dividend only after dividends are paid to holders of preference shares, a less risky form of share that may also be issued by a company to raise capital. A public company may, in addition, raise funds by issuing notes or debentures to companies or individuals who are willing to lend it money, or a company may obtain loans from banks and other financial institutions. The shareholders of a company, however, can be regarded as its owners.

Control of Public Companies and the Aims of Their Managers

The extent to which the shareholders (owners) control public companies is open to debate. It is now generally agreed, however, that shareholders have little control over the operations of most large public companies. Most such companies are managed by professional managers, most of whom hold little or no capital in the company. Most shareholders do not attend annual general meetings. Instead, they most often appoint management-suggested directors as proxies, they seldom organize to reject directors' proposals, and they have access to a limited amount of information about the company.

Does the separation of ownership and management in modern large public companies mean that the latter does not pursue the aim of shareholders to maximize the return on their shares through dividends and capital gains (that is, capital gains as reflected in increases in the traded value of their shares)? Some economists believe that management may carry out policies that improve their own prestige, such as expanding the sales and growth of the company at a rate faster than is most profitable. Alternatively, management may decide to "take it easy" — not take advantage of profitable opportunities and instead provide themselves with advantages such as more secretarial staff and equipment than is needed, extra "business" trips, and other "perks".

There are constraints limiting management in following purely its own interest, however. If management does not use the assets of the company in the most profitable way, other companies, if they realize this, may try to take it over. This they can do by buying a majority shareholding in the company. The threat of takeover acts as a constraint to some extent. Furthermore, although profit may not be the most important prestige or status consideration for management, it is still an important one. Furthermore, if the management of a company wishes to raise additional funds from its shareholders for the purpose of expansion, as a rule it must be able to ensure them of a reasonable return on their capital.

The above example indicates that in our society, and in others, the individuals who are the ultimate owners of resources may have little control over their use. This is true for large public companies and for resources managed by public enterprises and government departments. There may be no workable alternative on efficiency grounds to owners delegating many of their powers to professional managers. *Ownership, control, and power do not necessarily go hand in hand.*

Co-operative Forms of Business Organizations

Co-operatives are owned by members. In 1979, there were more than 2500 co-operatives in Canada. They are usually agricultural in nature, although there are also financial co-operatives such as credit unions. The top ten co-operatives (not including financials) in 1981 are presented in Table 3.5.

Figure 3.5 shows the change in percentage distribution of business form, from 1946 to 1976. Corporations are becoming the predominant form of business.

Crown Corporations

Another form of business enterprise is the Crown Corporation, which is wholly owned by Canadian governments. Table 3.6 presents the top ten Crown corporations for 1982. A majority of these corporations operate in the energy-supply sector. Most of these are provincial rather than federal enterprises.

FIGURE **3.5 Percentage Distribution of Establishments by type and size,
1946-76**

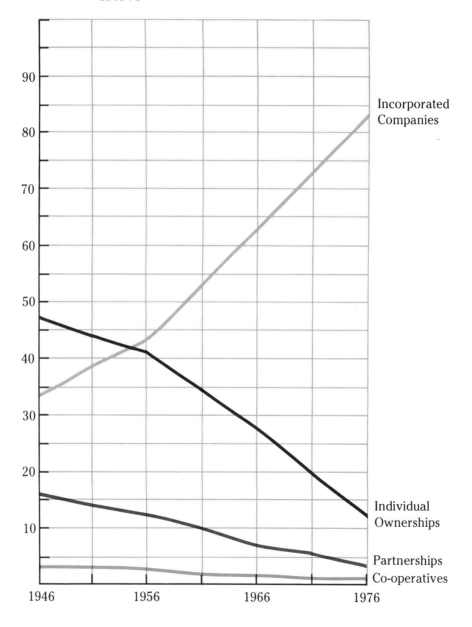

SOURCE: Manufacturing Industries by Type of Organization and Size of Establishment (Ottawa:
Statistics Canada), Cat. 31-210.

TABLE 3.5   **Top 10 Co-operatives in 1982**

		Sales ($ thousands)
1.	Saskatchewan Wheat Pool	2,253,220
2.	Groupe Metro Richelieu	1,570,000
3.	Alberta Wheat Pool	1,455,639
4.	Federated Co-operatives	1,371,808
5.	United Grain Growers	1,245,694
6.	Co-opérative Fédérée de Québec	1,219,168
7.	Agropur, Co-operative Agro Alimentaire	616,834
8.	Manitoba Pool Elevators	603,753
9.	United Co-operatives of Ontario	545,752
10.	Fraser Valley Milk Producers' Association	308,261

SOURCE: Financial Post 500, June 1983.

TABLE 3.6   **Top 10 Crown Corporations, 1982**

		Assets ($ thousands)
1.	Hydro-Quebec	23,169,000
2.	Ontario Hydro	20,720,832
3.	B.C. Hydro & Power Authority	7,790,226
4.	Petro-Canada	7,552,115
5.	C.N.R.	6,335,971
6.	Canadian Wheat Board	4,109,000
7.	Manitoba Hydro-Electric Board	2,725,814
8.	New Brunswick Power Commision	2,657,955
9.	Alberta Gov't Telephones	2,311,877
10.	Saskatchewan Power	2,054,156

SOURCE: Financial Post 500, June 1983.

Quality of Resources, Technology, Education, and Economic Growth

Studies in the United States by Edward F. Denison indicate that almost half of the increase in American national output in the last three or four decades can be attributed to increased education and improved technology. These forces have been powerful sources of economic growth in developed countries.

Investment in Human Beings

In general, increased investment in human capital — investment in human beings by way of better and more education, sanitation, and health programs, improvements in public safety, and so on — has done much to reduce scarcity and overcome want. Considerable increases in productivity (output per employed person) can stem from greater investment in human beings.

Education can have two aspects: a productive aspect and a consumption aspect. One may learn in order to do productive things with the greater knowledge, or one may learn for learning's sake and out of pure interest or curiosity. An engineer or a physician, for instance, principally learns in order to do productive work, work of practical value. On the other hand, an historian may learn to satisfy curiosity more than anything else. Society wants both these kinds of knowledge.

In 1981-82, there were roughly 5,000,000 young people attending primary and secondary schools in Canada. Full-time enrollment at post-secondary institutions amounted to 652,000 with 265,000 attending community colleges and 387,000 attending universities. A further 255,000 people were attending university on a part-time basis. There were 271,000 teachers in the primary and secondary-school system, and 54,600 full-time post-secondary school teachers. Expenditures on formal education accounts for roughly 8 percent of national output of goods and services.[2]

Skills are learned not only through formal education programs at schools. Many occupations have apprenticeship or training programs where skills are learned on the job. In many instances, people who have completed their formal training or education requirements continue to learn and acquire human capital in a process called "learning by doing".

Expenditure on public health, social welfare, and law and order, can also be productive. Immunization programs and adequate sanitation facilities reduce the incidence of disease and poor health in the community, and add to the productivity of the labour force. They reduce absenteeism and loss of productivity owing to illness. Social-welfare payments, even though their prime objective is to redistribute income in favour of the needy, may in part be a productive community investment. Those on inadequate incomes may, for example, become grossly undernourished and absorb a greater amount of medical and hospital resources than if they are given an adequate social-service allowance. An adequate system of law, order, and justice is necessary for the efficient running of an economy. For instance, it is important that private property be reasonably secure from theft, that it be reasonably easy to transfer assets legally, and that contracts for the sale of goods be enforceable at low cost. If these conditions are not satisfied, production and trade will be hampered. For example, if considerable legal and other transfer costs must be paid by sellers

---

[2] *Advance Statistics of Education, 1981-82*, Statistics Canada, 1982.

of houses, this makes sellers reluctant to sell houses, and trading in houses may decline.

Technological Progress

Nothing has been so important to our economic progress as technological progress, that is, our discovery of new ways to produce commodities and our discovery of new commodities. Many new products have been produced in this century. These include aeroplanes, television sets, synthetic fibres, plastics, electronic calculators and computers, and aluminium. Electricity is being produced from the new sources of atomic energy; hybrid corns and improved types of grain plants have been introduced into agriculture; new pesticides and fungicides have been discovered that have enabled the productivity of rural industry to be raised. In the field of medicine, new drugs and techniques such as the fitting of artificial limbs and organ transplants have increased our possibilities for maintaining our well-being. It would be easy to add to this list of technological and biological accomplishments.

It should, however, be noted that economic progress can also stem from new ways of socially organizing the use of resources. For instance, the self-service form of retailing (supermarkets and gasoline/service stations) that has become widespread in the last twenty years has reduced the costs of retailing commodities.

The Canadian government is concerned with the Canadian performance in the R and D (Research and Development) area. Roughly 1 percent of Canadian output is accounted for by R and D spending. This compares with 2.3 percent for the United States, 2.2 percent for Switzerland, 2.1 percent for West Germany, 1.8 percent for France and Sweden, and 1.7 percent for Japan. Canada has a target of 1.5 percent of total final national expenditure for R and D.

There is also concern that, although for the above comparison group at least 60 percent of R and D is performed by the business sector, only 40 percent of Canadian R and D is performed by the business sector. The top ten R and D firms for 1981 are shown in Table 3.7. Half of the companies listed are owned by Canadian governments.

The returns or productivity from R and D expenditure vary greatly; but even when the research is for military purposes, it sometimes has a "spin-off", everyday application. For instance, the United States' space program has resulted in rapid advances in computer technology with commercial and everyday applications.

The Process of Technological Change

Research needs to be followed through and applied if it is to be of real economic value. In the process of introducing new technology, there are usually four stages. These are:

1. research,
2. development,
3. innovation, and
4. diffusion of the new technology.

Research refers to the initial phases of the process. Much of the research may be of a basic, or fundamental, nature. This may then be followed by the development of prototypes, for example, a pilot orbital engine, and various working models may be tested. If it is decided that one of these prototypes has a possibility of commercial success, a decision may be made to innovate, that is, to begin the commercial production and sale of the invention. If the innovation is successful, other firms may decide to produce the new product, and thus diffusion occurs. Production and economic growth within a nation will be affected by how well this whole *chain* in the process of technological change operates.

TABLE 3.7   **Top 10 R & D Firms, 1981**

		Expenditures ($ millions)
1.	Bell Canada	245
2.	AECL	168.4
3.	Pratt & Whitney	113
4.	Gulf	75
5.	Petro-Canada	66
6.	Imperial Oil	60.5
7.	Canada Development Corp.	58
8.	Alcan	51.7
9.	Hydro-Quebec	38.1
10.	Ontario Hydro	35.6

SOURCE: Financial Post 500, June 1982.

FIGURE 3.6   **The chain of technological change. The whole process affects techno-logical change.**

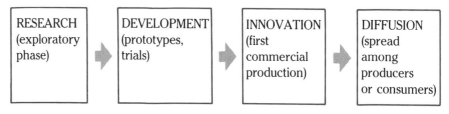

Renewable and Nonrenewable Resources

In recent years, there has been a great deal of concern about the depletion of natural resources such as oil, which are nonrenewable. Resources have been divided into those that are renewable (such as forests, domesticated animals, and their products such as wool, and cultivated plants and trees), and those that are not renewable but are in fixed supply or availability (such as crude oil, coal, and iron ore). The ultimate limit on the availability of these resources is the stocks embedded in the earth.

When nonrenewable resources are used in the productive process, it may be either impossible or difficult to re-use them. Coal and oil used for energy purposes are clearly not available for re-use. Iron ore used in building machinery and other equipment may be available again to some extent for re-use, or recycling. There will be loss of iron in the process, however, and the material, say in car bodies, may be so scattered that it is not very economic to recycle it.

Just how long it will take to exhaust the earth's resources of nonrenewable resources is uncertain. The problem is that the extent of reserves is often not known, and as depletion proceeds new reserves may be discovered. Furthermore, as resources become scarcer their price may rise and result in their increased conservation and an increased use of substitutes. Thus, as oil prices rise, gasoline may be conserved, new reserves of crude oil discovered, and alternative energy sources, such as solar energy, exploited. Nevertheless, it has been estimated by the American Academy of Science that by the beginning of the next century most of the world's supply of crude oil will be exhausted.

Energy plays an important role in contributing to economic growth and maintaining high levels of national output. Mechanization and industrialization, electricity generation and transport, use a great deal of power. Individuals with a higher standard of living consume a great deal of energy in their homes and in transport. The higher a nation's income or output, the higher generally is its energy use. The rich and developed nations of the world are presently using up the world's energy reserves at a rapid rate.

Table 3.8 indicates the level of per capita energy consumption in selected countries. Although the level of per capita energy consumption is positively related to the level of income per year, it is also influenced by other factors such as the composition of the nation's industry (some industries use much more energy than others), the climate, and the efficiency with which fuels are turned into energy.

As economic development, industrialization, and mechanization become more widespread in the world, the demand for the world's energy resource is likely to intensify, and a serious shortage of traditional fuels is likely to emerge. To maintain high standards of living, it will be necessary to develop and use alternative sources of energy such as solar and nuclear energy. At the present time, many developed countries rely heavily on imports of fuels and raw materials from developing countries. When the latter countries develop, if they do, such supplies will not be so readily available for export.

This chapter has made it clear that resources can be classified in different ways and that they are important determinants of what can be produced. Society's ability to overcome scarcity depends on available resources. Our success in reducing scarcity, however, depends on how well we use our available resources.

TABLE 3.8 **Energy consumption per capita and income per capita for selected countries in 1979**

Country	Income Per Capita ($ U.S. Per Year)	Energy Consumption Per Capita (kg of Coal Equivalents)
Chad	110	24
India	190	242
Tanzania	260	53
Indonesia	370	237
Kenya	380	180
Thailand	590	376
Philippines	600	356
El Salvador	670	351
Ecuador	1,050	654
Paraguay	1,070	251
Italy	5,250	3,438
United Kingdom	6,320	5,637
Japan	8,810	4,260
Australia	9,120	6,975
Canada	9,640	13,453
France	9,950	4,995
U.S.A.	10,630	12,350
Norway	10,700	11,919
West Germany	11,730	6,627
Sweden	11,930	8,502
Switzerland	13,920	5,138

SOURCE: World Bank: *World Development Report 1981* (New York, Oxford University Press).

KEY CONCEPTS
(FOR REVIEW)

Capital	Labour
Capital expenditure	Land
Circular flow	Multinationals

Company (public and private)
Depreciation
Diffusion of technology
Entrepreneurship
Foreign Investment Review Act (FIRA)
Human capital
Innovation
Interest
Investment
Investment Canada

Nonrenewable resources
Partner (general, limited)
Process of technological change
Profit
Renewable resources
Rent
Sole proprietor
Technological progress
Wages and salaries

QUESTIONS FOR REVIEW AND DISCUSSION

1. Why are the quality and quantity of a nation's resources important?
2. "The resources available for productive purposes can be classified or grouped in several different ways." Explain.
3. Explain the meaning of the following terms as used in economics: land, labour, capital, entrepreneurship, rent, wages and salaries, interest and profit.
4. Show in what ways the markets for resources and the markets for products are interrelated. Use a circular flow diagram to illustrate your answer.
5. How considerable and valuable are Canada's land resources? Why are forests, fisheries, and minerals included in an assessment of Canada's land resources?
6. Is it appropriate to describe land resources as natural resources? To what extent do other than natural factors (such as investment) affect the apparent value of Canada's land resources?
7. Education has a production and a consumption aspect. Explain.
8. "An adequate system of law, order, and justice is necessary for the efficient running of an economy." Discuss.
9. List the usual processes involved in technological change. Try to apply these to the introduction of a new product with which you are familiar (for example, home computers and video games).
10. Distinguish between renewable and nonrenewable resources, and give examples of each. Do you believe that the nonrenewable resources of the earth will soon be exhausted?
11. Why are energy resources of particular importance to modern societies? How does the quantity of energy used in developed countries compare with that used in developing countries? Do you believe that in the future we will be able to rely on alternatives to fossil fuels (coal, petroleum, natural gas, etc.) for most of our energy supplies?
12. Update the information on Canadian participation rates in Table 3.1.
13. What are the ten current largest unions in Canada?

FURTHER READING

Abdel-Malek, T., & Sarkar, A.K., "An Analysis of the Effects of Phase II Guidelines of the Foreign Investment Review Act." *Canadian Public Policy* (Winter, 1977), pp. 36-49.

Blomqvist, A., Wonnacott, P., & Wonnacott, R., *Economics*, 1st Canadian Ed. Toronto: McGraw-Hill Ryerson Limited, 1984, chapters 6 & 31.

Coleman, J., & Swedlove, F., "New Incentives for Industrial Research and Development." *Foreign Investment Review* (Autumn, 1978), pp. 4-6.

Denison, E.F., *The Sources of Economic Growth in the United States and the Alternatives before Us,* Committee for Economic Development. New York, 1962.

Denison, E.F., "Sources of Postwar Growth in Nine Western Countries." *American Economic Review* (May, 1967).

Fuhrman, P.H., *Business in the Canadian Environment.* Scarborough: Prentice-Hall Canada Inc., 1982, chapters 2 & 3.

Lipsey, R.G., Purvis, D. D., Sparks, G.R., & Steiner, P.O., *Economics*, 4th ed. New York: Harper & Row, Publishers, 1982, Chapter 11.

Samuelson, P.A. & Scott, A.D., *Economics.* Scarborough: McGraw-Hill Ryerson Limited, 1980, chapters 3, 6, & 7.

Production and the Firm

4

Production: Its Purpose and Its Measurement

The Purpose of Production

The purpose of production is to satisfy, or to more adequately satisfy, human want than would not be possible in its absence. Production is not an end in itself, and is only socially useful to the extent that it improves human welfare. Adam Smith believed that production is only socially useful to the extent that it efficiently meets the needs of consumers. Although the general thrust of his view can be accepted, human welfare also depends on other considerations, one being job satisfaction of individuals involved in the productive process. Most individuals in paid employment in Canada spend at least one-third of their nonsleeping hours at their place of employment. Clearly, their well-being depends partly on conditions at their workplace, or whether they find their job interesting and worthwhile, and not merely on how economically they can obtain consumer goods.

Production is the process of transforming resources or semi-processed commodities into output, or products. The process requires the exertion of energy toward the end of turning out products. In its simplest form, the productive process can be represented by Figure 4.1. This representation highlights the importance of energy in the productive process, and the importance of energy resources as discussed in the last chapter.

Economists, however, do not regard all activity as productive. The only activity that is productive is that which adds value or utility to commodities or

FIGURE 4.1 **A simple "flow chart" representation of the productive process. Inputs are transformed into output using energy.**

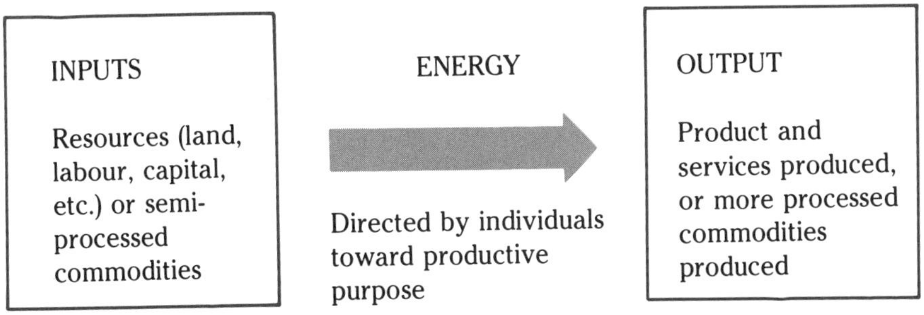

INPUTS	ENERGY	OUTPUT
Resources (land, labour, capital, etc.) or semi-processed commodities	Directed by individuals toward productive purpose	Product and services produced, or more processed commodities produced

resources. Thus, the destructive activity of vandals, although it uses energy and resources, cannot be regarded as productive. An activity, however, may be productive even though it does not result in the production of material goods. Transport services are productive because they provide a service that has value: goods need to be transported to the place where they are to be used, and individuals are prepared to pay for this service.

Measuring the Value of National Production

Some earlier economists, e.g., Adam Smith, considered the only productive labour to be that which results in the supply of material goods. The provision of services was not regarded as productive. This is fallacious. Most services have value, or utility, and many individuals are prepared to pay more than the cost of providing these. In Canada's official statistics of national production, the only commodities that are counted are (except for an allowance for the rent that might be earned by owner-occupied dwellings) those that are marketed.[1]

Government statisticians seek to measure the total final value of marketed goods and services produced in an economy during a specified time period, usually one year. There are a number of ways in which the total value of production can be assessed. Three major methods are:

1. by computing the value added at each stage in the production of goods and services and summing all these net additions,
2. by summing the expenditures made on final produced goods and services, and
3. by summing the income received as a result of the production of final goods and services.

This is illustrated by the example in Figure 4.2. The figure depicts the market value of daily production stemming from the operations of a wood-chip industry (one not producing chips for pulp to be used in paper production).

In determining the value of production, we must be careful to avoid *double counting.* If total values at each stage in Figure 4.2 are summed, the value obtained would be $100,000, which overstates the real value of production.

The real value of production of particle board may be obtained by taking the sum of *net value added at each stage of production.* This approach can be discussed more simply using Figure 4.3.

The sum of the net value added at each stage is $5000 (timber) + $5000 (chips) + $22,000 (particle board) + $1000 (retailing services) + $30,000 (furniture) = $63,000.

---

[1]But government services, e.g., defence, are included in the estimates as the cost of the labour and other resources used.

FIGURE 4.2 **Gross value and final value of production associated with the production of particle board. Figures next to arrows are total values at each stage.**

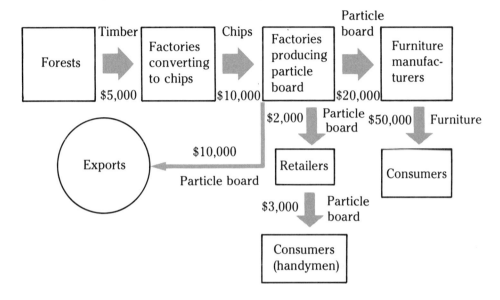

FIGURE 4.3 **Net value added to each stage of production**

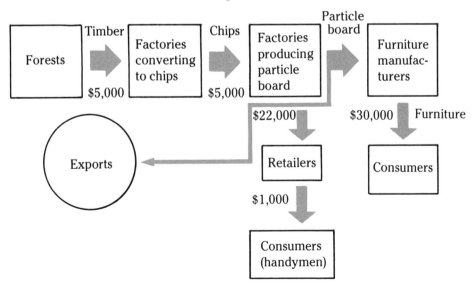

This may also be determined by summing the expenditures by purchasers of particle board. Referring back to Figure 4.2, this value can be determined as $10,000 (exports to foreign residents) + $3000 (handymen) + $50,000 (furniture for consumers) = $63,000. When computing the value of national production, the statistician usually considers four major groups of purchasers: Canadian households, Canadian business firms, Canadian governments, and foreigners. The purchases are called consumption expenditures, investment expenditures, government expenditures, and exports, and these are usually denoted C, I, G, and X for simplicity. The values for these expenditures are estimates made by government statisticians, who include expenditure by these groups on all final goods and services — both domestically produced and foreign produced. Thus, if the values for C, I, G, and X were merely added, this would overestimate the value of Canadian produced goods and services by the amount supplied by foreigners. To correct for this the estimated value of goods and services imported from abroad, M, is subtracted. Thus, a measure of the national value of final goods and services (gross national expenditures, or GNE) is given by:

$$GNE = C + I + G + X - M$$

The third approach to valuing output is to sum the income received for the production. Whenever we spend a dollar on a commodity, someone receives it and uses it to pay those individuals who were responsible for making goods available. The $50,000 paid by consumers for furniture will be used by furniture manufacturers to pay the sales people, the cabinet makers, the owner of the factory, interest on loans needed to operate the business, and the supplier of particle board (who in turn must make payments). Anything left over after everyone else has been paid (including indirect taxes to governments) is profit received by the owners of the business. In general, the income received can be classified as wages, interest, rent, indirect taxes, and profits. The resulting value is called Gross National Product (GNP). In principle, GNE and GNP are equal; however, as they are obtained as statistical estimates, they could differ. The statisticians resolve this by taking the difference between the two estimates and splitting it in half, with a half allocated to each estimate to establish equality. This adjustment is called the Residual Error of Estimate.

In estimating GNP or GNE, note that as a rule only commercial transactions are counted. Thus, in the above example, the production by handymen for their own use is not counted. Similarly, domestic services provided for a family by members of the family are not counted; domestic help, however, is counted. Thus, estimated GNP would suddenly rise if homemakers started to work for wages. Similarly, the produce of the backyard gardener who grows vegetables for the family's use is not counted.

GNP as an Indicator of Welfare

This raises the question of whether GNP as measured by the government statistician is a suitable index of welfare. In the past, there has been a tendency to use GNP per head of the population as an indicator of welfare. The measure has a number of deficiencies as an indicator of the economic welfare of the community. Welfare can be affected by the availability of nontraded goods (for instance, goods provided by a family for itself), and by the quality of the environment (such as the purity of air and water). Indeed, it is ironic that GNP, as officially measured, can rise when welfare declines.

Suppose, for instance, that pollution increases and that factories causing this pollution add an extra $1 million to the net value of production. As a result of the pollution associated with this increased production, it is possible that illness may increase and additional medical expenses of $1.5 million may be incurred. Cleaning expenses may also rise by $0.5 million, say. Consequently, an increase in GNP of $1 million (extra net production from factories) + $1.5 million (extra medical services) + $0.5 million (extra cleaning services) = $3 million will be recorded. This is the increase in the value of market transactions. But the net social value of this extra factory production is clearly negative. The community is worse off by any reasonable reckoning. It is worse off by at least $1 million (that is, the value of extra factory production less extra medical and cleaning expenses) because the extra medical and cleaning expenses should be recorded as a *social cost*. Again, the concept of GNP takes no account of the amount of leisure available to individuals. If members of the community decide to work a shorter working week and take longer holidays, GNP *may* fall. Nevertheless, the community may consider this sacrifice to be worthwhile, and its welfare may rise.

Thus, it can be seen that we must be wary about using GNP as a measure of economic welfare. Some economists have proposed that more weight be placed upon alternative indicators of welfare, such as *Net Economic Welfare* (NEW), that make allowance for environmental deterioration, leisure, and so on. NEW is designed as an indicator of a community's standard of living. Although community's standard of living depends on its material welfare, other factors, such as the leisure opportunities available to its citizens, are important. The fact that there is more than one telephone for every two Canadians, one passenger car for every three Canadians, and so on, is only a partial indicator of our welfare, although such indicators are sometimes used.

Contributions to Production from Various Sectors of the Canadian Economy

Comparative Importance and Size of Various Sectors

François Quesnay, a French physician writing about political economy in the early 1700s, took the view that the only productive labour is labour employed in the cultivation of land. As indicated earlier, however, this is clearly not so. For instance, the effort involved in manufacturing tractors and implements for agriculture must be considered productive because these capital goods increase the productivity (output per person) of individuals cultivating the land. Indeed, all labour and economic effort that increase the net value of resources or commodities can be regarded as productive. Thus, all sectors of the economy are productive. If the economy is divided into the *goods-producing* sector (consisting of agriculture and nonagricultural primary industries such as manufacturing, and construction) and the *services* sector (consisting of transportation, storage, communication, and utilities; trade; finance, insurance, and real estate; community, business, and personal services; and public administration), both can be considered to be productive.

In Canada, the service sector makes the largest contribution to real domestic output. In 1982, if accounted for 67.8 percent of real domestic output. The goods-producing sector accounted for only 32.2 percent. Manufacturing accounted for 20.2 percent. Agricultural output accounted for less than 3 percent. These relative contributions of the sectors to national output do not show that one sector is more important than another in the productive process. Our prosperity depends upon the productivity of all sectors, and the activities of the sectors are interdependent.

Changes in the Importance of Different Sectors with Economic Growth

The contributions of various sectors to Canadian output has changed over the years. For instance, the service sector has shown an increasing trend as a proportion of output whereas the agricultural sector has shown a decline. In the service sector, community, business, and personal services have shown an increasing trend. These trends are shown in Figure 4.4. The relative sector shares of output, employment, and new capital investment in 1982 are given in Table 4.1.

The service sector is also the largest sector in terms of employment. In 1982, 69.3 percent of employment was in the service sector. The service sector also accounts for the bulk of new capital investment with 56.7 percent of the total for all industries in 1980. The bulk of this investment was in transportation, storage, communications, and utilities category.

The goods-producing sector is sometimes divided into the *primary sector* (consisting of agricultural and pastoral industries, forestry, fishing, and mining), and the *secondary sector* (consisting of manufacturing industries). In this terminology, the service sector is referred to as the *tertiary sector*. The shares of industry sectors in employment are shown in Figure 4.5 for selected developed and developing countries.

Why has the pattern of production in the Canadian economy changed? Partly it is because productivity in primary industry has risen greatly as a result of mechanization and the application of scientific advances to agriculture. This development has released labour from agriculture for employment elsewhere in the economy. Recent productivity increases in manufacturing industry have

FIGURE 4.4 **Percentage output supplied by sector for 1949, 1961, and 1971**

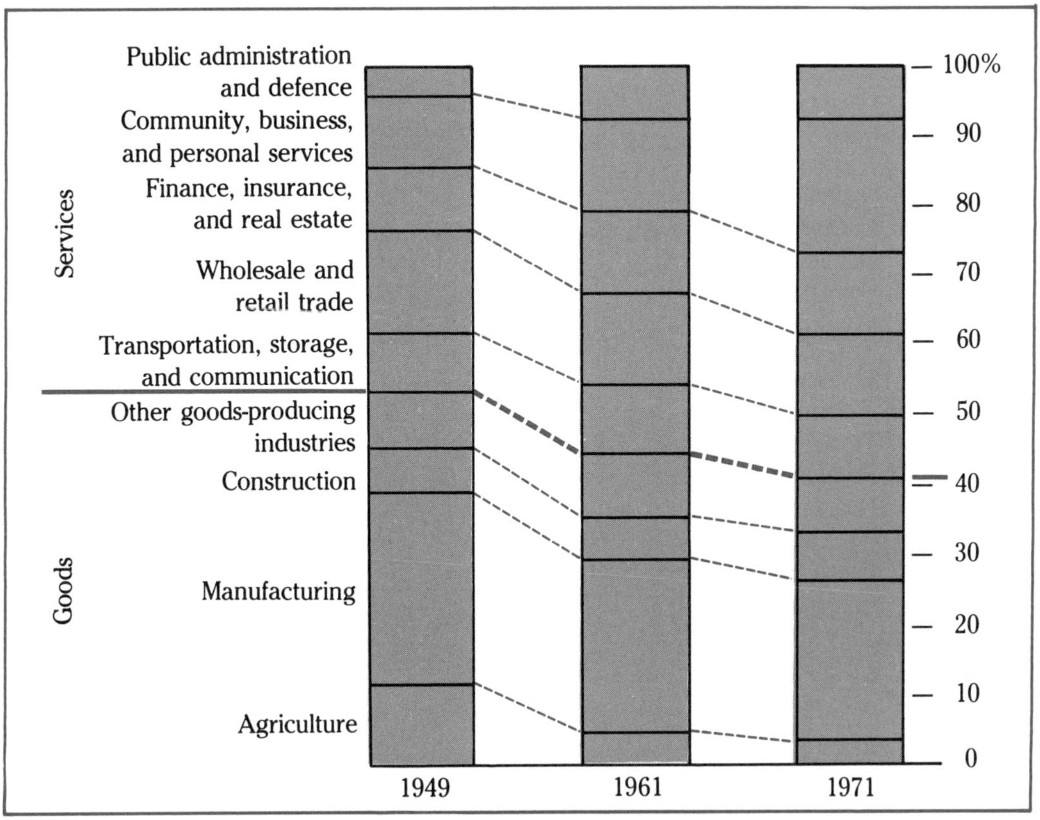

SOURCE: *Canada Handbook* (Ottawa, Statistics Canada, 1979), p. 200.

also made more labour available for the tertiary sector. Apart from this, however, the demand for agricultural products has not expanded as quickly as the rise in incomes. Although agricultural goods are essential, the demand for these does not rise in proportion to income. As consumers' incomes rise, they tend to demand relatively more services. The way in which the demands of consumers change as their incomes rise helps to explain the changing shares of industry sectors in Canadian output. Conditions in export markets are a further contributing factor.

In general, the proportion of employed persons engaged in the service sector is relatively larger in developed countries (that is, in countries with high incomes per capita) than in developing countries (that is, in countries with low incomes per capita). This is a reflection of differences in productivity between these countries, and the emerging pattern of demand for goods and services as incomes rise.

TABLE 4.1   **Percentage of output, employment, and new capital investment by sector, 1982**

Sector	Output	Employment	New Capital Investment (1980)
Agriculture	2.9	4.4	7.8
Nonagricultural primary industries	3.2	2.5	16.1
Manufacturing	20.2	18.2	17.5
Construction	5.9	5.6	2.0
Total: goods-producing sector	32.2	30.7	43.3
Transportation, storage, communications, and utilities	14.5	8.2	24.0
Trade	11.8	17.4	3.0
Finance, insurance, and real estate	13.7	5.7	6.8
Community, business, and personal services	20.5	30.8	10.9
Public Administration	7.3	7.2	11.9
Total: services sector	67.8	69.3	56.7
Total: all industries	100.0	100.0	100.0

SOURCE: *Economic Review*, Department of Finance, April, 1983.

Input–Output Relationships

The Production Function and Marginal Physical Productivity

The relationships between inputs – the materials or resources used for production – and output – the product or result of productive activity – can be represented in a number of ways. A simple representation was given in Figure 4.1, emphasizing the importance of energy in the productive process. For many purposes, however, it is important to represent the relationship between inputs and output by means of a *production function*. A production function represents the relationship between the quantity of physical output of a product, and the quantity of the inputs – resources or materials – used to make or produce it.

For instance, let us suppose that a bakery has its baking equipment installed and has a large stock of flour on hand. Given all facilities of this type, its daily production of bread may depend on the amount of labour that it employs. Assuming that each labourer works a standard number of hours each day, the relationship between the number of labourers employed per day and the output of bread (the number of loaves of bread produced daily) might be like that shown in Table 4.2. Note that, in this example, each additional labourer adds

FIGURE 4.5 **In developed countries, employment in the primary sector is propor-**
tionately smaller, and employment in the tertiary sector is relatively
larger than in developing countries.

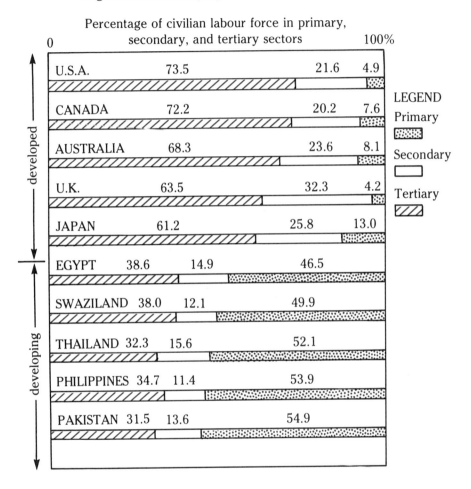

Percentage of civilian labour force in primary,
secondary, and tertiary sectors

110 loaves to the daily output of bread. This is the *marginal* (or additional) *pro-*
ductivity of each extra labourer.

We can also graph the production relationship outlined in Table 4.2. The
dots in Figure 4.7 show the output of bread that results if the quantities of
labour shown on the X-axis are employed by the bakery. Note that all these
points lie along a straight line.

If, in fact, the hours of work could be varied continuously, the production
function might form a straight line like that shown by OA in Figure 4.8. The
production function shown as OA is based on the assumption that the bakery
uses its existing machinery and techniques. If the bakery installs new

FIGURE 4.6 **Ploughing with bullocks in the Punjab, Pakistan. The percentage of the labour force employed in primary industry in a developing country such as Pakistan is much higher than in a more developed economies such as those of Canada and the United States.**

machinery and adopts new techniques, a different production relationship between labour and output is likely to emerge. For instance, the production function shown by OB could emerge. This indicates that, with adoption of new machinery and techniques by the bakery, output per labourer (when each works 8 hours per day) rises from 110 loaves of bread to 150 loaves.

TABLE 4.2   **Production relationship between the number of labourers employed per day by a bakery and its daily output of bread**

Variable input (number of labourers employed per day)	Output (number of loaves of bread baked daily)
0	0
1	110
2	220
3	330
4	440
5	550

FIGURE 4.7   **Production relationship between the number of labourers employed by a bakery and its output bread**

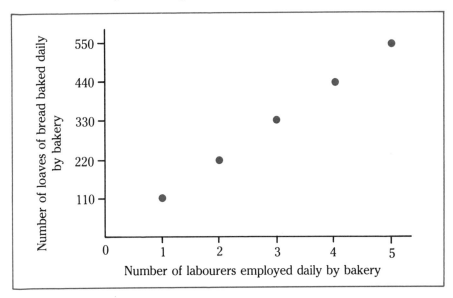

The above discussion of production has glossed over a number of issues that we must now consider. First, it is necessary to make a distinction between inputs, or factors of production, that are *fixed* and those that are *variable*. In the example considered above, factors of production such as buildings, land, and machinery were assumed to be fixed and labour variable. The variability of a factor depends on the particular production situation being considered; in general, the longer the period for altering production, the greater the number of inputs that are variable. Although, in the short run, factors of production such as labour and raw materials used by a firm may be variable, and land,

FIGURE 4.8 **Shift in the production function owing to the installation of new machinery**

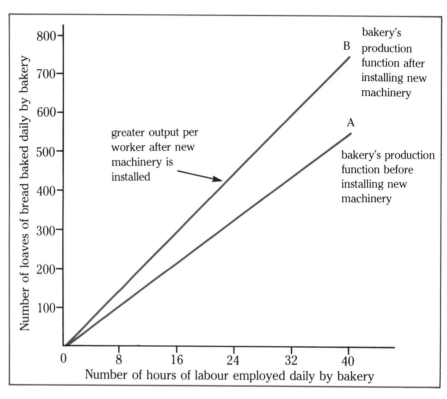

buildings, top management, and machinery may be fixed, in the long term, a firm can vary its employment of all these factors of production.

Second, we need to consider the typical shape, or nature, of production functions. In the bakery example considered above, the marginal physical productivity of labour, and the additional production resulting from the employment of an additional unit of labour, were assumed to be constant. The total product function is a straight line. Each additional worker in the bakery produces the same extra amount of loaves. But this is unlikely to be typical when some of the factors of production are fixed.

Declining Marginal Physical Productivity

When some of the factors used in production are in *fixed supply*, increased use of variable factors in an attempt to raise production is likely to become less effective after a point; production becomes subject to the *law of diminishing (marginal) returns*, and may indeed fall. Consider the example of manufacturing wooden cabinets. The size of the factory and the number of machines are fixed. As the number of cabinet-makers hired increases, the number of cabinets produced may, at first, increase at a decreasing rate. Once the factory becomes too crowded, however, additional cabinet-makers milling around may slow down the production rate of other workers, so that fewer cabinets are produced. The relationship between cabinet-makers and the output of cabinets may be like the example shown in Figure 4.9.

FIGURE 4.9 **The marginal physical productivity of cabinet-makers is declining in this example.**

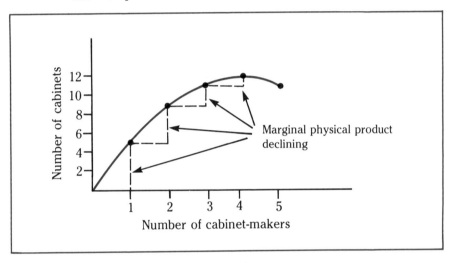

As illustrated, the marginal physical productivity of each cabinet-maker declines as the number of cabinet-makers hired increases. The first cabinet-maker produces five cabinets per month, the second cabinet-maker adds four cabinets, the third adds two cabinets, and the fourth cabinet-maker adds one additional cabinet per month. A maximum number of twelve cabinets is produced when four cabinet-makers are hired. Additional cabinet-makers only reduce the number of cabinets produced.

It should be noted that it is usually optimal, from an economic point of view, to hire or use less than the quantity of the variable factor of production that maximizes physical output – in the example above, less than four cabinet-makers. A profit maximizing firm will only hire cabinet-makers up to the point where the cost of hiring an extra cabinet-maker is equal to the extra revenue it obtains by selling the extra cabinets produced. As the maximum number of cabinets is approached, then fewer additional cabinets are produced, and the extra revenue obtained is likely to fall short of cost of hiring extra cabinet-makers. Thus, it will not be profitable for a firm to produce the maximum number of cabinets possible.

Increasing Marginal Productivity

The marginal productivity of a factor of production need not decline continuously. Indeed, the most common situation may be for it to increase initially, and then to decline as the volume of use of the factor rises. This can be illustrated by the example of a firm packing shampoo for retail sale. For simplicity, assume that its operations consist:

1. of pouring shampoo into bottles,
2. of placing the caps on the bottles,
3. of fixing the labels on the bottles,
4. of placing the bottles in cartons, and
5. of sealing the cartons.

The firm's production function may be like the one shown in Figure 4.10.

The production relationship shown by the production function in Figure 4.10 can also be represented in tabular form, as in Table 4.3. This table also indicates the marginal physical productivity of packers, that is, the extra or additional number of boxes of shampoo packed by extra packers.

TABLE 4.3 **The total number of boxes of shampoo packed, and the marginal number of boxes packed as a function of the number of packers employed**

Number of Packers Employed (per hour)	Total Number of Boxes Packed (per hour)	Marginal or Additional Number of Boxes Packed		
0	0			
		→ 5 that is 5 - 0		marginal productivity rising
1	5			
		→ 10 that is 15 - 5		
2	15			
		→ 15 that is 30 - 15		
3	30			
		→ 10 that is 40 - 30		marginal productivity declining
4	40			
		→ 5 that is 45 - 40		
5	45			
		→ 2 that is 47 - 45		
6	47			

FIGURE 4.10 **Typically, the marginal productivity of a factory may initially increase and then decline as more of it is employed, the employment of other resources remaining constant.**

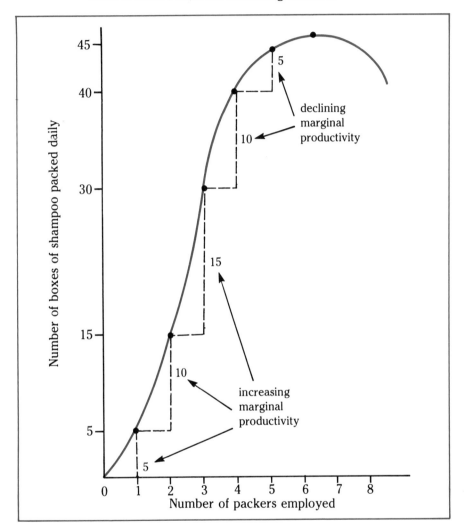

In the example shown in Table 4.3 and Figure 4.10, the marginal physical productivity of packers increases until three packers are employed, and then it declines. The first packer packs five cartons of shampoo daily, an additional packer enables an extra ten cartons to be packed and a third packer adds an extra fifteen cartons to the daily output.

The marginal physical productivity of the packers may increase up to a point because greater employment enables the workers to specialize in their tasks. The workers may engage in *division of labour*. For instance, once two

packers are employed, one may do tasks 1. and 2. mentioned above and the
other may do tasks 3., 4., and 5. When three packers are employed, one may do
task 1., another tasks 2. and 3., and the third tasks 4. and 5. This specialization
makes assembly-line production possible, saves the time that may otherwise be
wasted in switching from one task to another, and enables the simplified task to
be learnt quickly and to become "second nature" to the operator. Workers can
also be allocated the task for which they are best fitted.

After a point, however, the advantages of the division of labour may begin
to be lost as more resources are employed. In the shampoo-packing example,
boredom may occur because tasks become too simple, and crowding in the
packing area and problems of shortages of machinery may arise once the
number of workers is increased beyond a certain level; then diseconomies may
become evident. Marginal productivity may eventually diminish, and, after a
point, total output may fall.

If the firm installs additional machinery and facilities, it may be able to
employ a large number of packers and expand its total output. In that case, its
employment of labour *relative* to packing facilities will not be as great, and it
may be able to expand production profitably. The extent to which the firm can
profitably expand its production, if it can vary all of its resources (or several of
these), depends partly on the nature of its costs of production.

Production and the Structure of Costs

The structure of the firm's cost of production can be determined once the production function and factor-input-prices are known. Suppose that the firm's production function is that described by the schedule in Table 4.3. Further, suppose that the hourly wage rate is $10. The hourly cost of production is deter-
mined simply by multiplying the hourly wage rate by the number of packers
employed per hour. The firm's cost function as a function of output is determined by examining total costs for the level of output produced. The firm's cost
curve for the present example is shown in Figure 4.11.

Economists are interested not only in the firm's total cost of production C,
but also in two related cost concepts. The first of these is *average cost*. The
average cost, AC, of producing a given level of output, Q, is the total cost of producing that level of output divided by that level of output. That is,

$$AC = \frac{C}{Q}$$

The second related cost concept is *marginal cost*. The firm's marginal cost,
MC, is the additional cost of producing a given increase in output divided by the
given increase in output. That is,

$$MC = \frac{\Delta C}{\Delta Q} \left(i.e., \frac{change\ in\ C}{change\ in\ Q} \right)$$

FIGURE 4.11 **Cost function based upon Table 4.3. Productivity and a $10 hourly wage rate.**

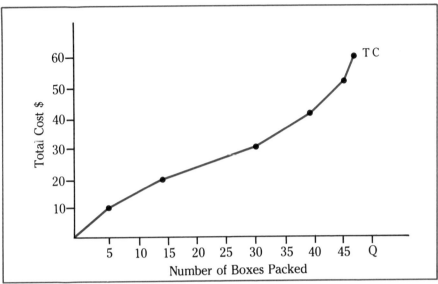

The values for the three cost concepts based on Table 4.4 and a $10 hourly wage rate are presented in Figure 4.12. Notice that it is assumed that the cost of producing 0 boxes is $0. This means that there are no *fixed* costs. The only cost item is the variable number of packers employed. Notice also that when *MC* is below *AC*, the *AC* curve is falling; when *MC* is above *AC*, the *AC* curve is rising. The two curves cross each other when *AC* is at its lowest point.

Costs, Economies of Scale, and the Expansion of the Firm

Average Costs of Production and Economies of Scale

Most production in our economy is directed by firms that may be owned by single proprietors, by partners, or by a private or a public company. As firms expand their scale of operations, they *may* experience economies of scale at first (that is, a reduction in their per-unit costs of production), and then, as they grow larger, diseconomies of scale.

The nineteenth-century economist Alfred Marshall believed that a relationship of this kind would be typical. If the firm is producing only one product, the Marshallian relationship implies that its costs per unit of production fall and then rise as the firm expands its quantity of output. This can be illustrated by a U-shaped average-cost curve (Figure 4.13).

TABLE 4.4 **The firm's cost structure**

Number of Packers Employed (per hour)	Number of Boxes Packed (per hour)	Total Costs (per hour) C ($)	Average Costs C/Q ($)	Marginal Cost ΔC ΔQ ($)
0	0	0	—	—
1	5	10	2	2
2	15	20	1.3	1
3	30	30	1	-0.7
4	40	40	1	1
5	45	50	1.1	2
6	47	60	1.3	5

FIGURE 4.12 **Average cost and marginal cost for Table 4.4, assuming $10 hourly wage**

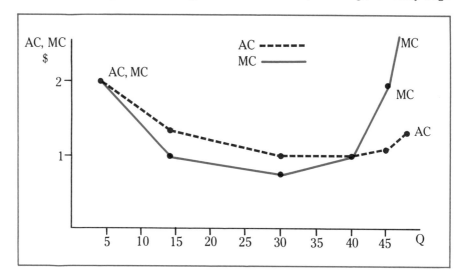

A hypothetical example of average costs of production is given in Figure 4.13 for a dairy farm. As the daily production of the farm increases, owing, say to an increase in the size of the dairy herd, the average cost of producing each litre of milk falls until 500 L of milk are produced daily. The cost of producing each litre of milk then averages 8¢. Further expansion in daily production can only be achieved by incurring greater per-unit costs of production. If the farmer produces 800 L of milk daily, for instance, his cost per litre averages 15¢.

TABLE 4.13   U-shaped average cost curve resulting from economies of scale
followed by diseconomies of scale as the firm expands its level of
production

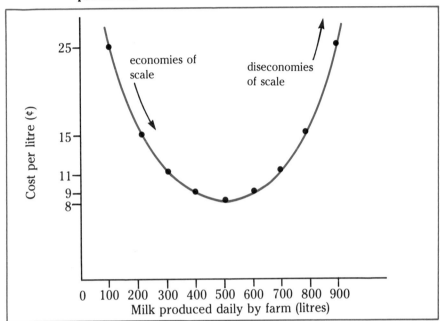

Although U-shaped average-cost curves may be the norm in agriculture, many economists doubt whether this is so in manufacturing industry. A manufacturing firm may find that its average cost of production falls until its level of output becomes a significant proportion of the output of its whole industry. A manufacturing firm may experience continually falling average costs of production as it expands its volume of output. For instance, a car manufacturer may find that its average cost of producing cars falls continually as its annual volume of car production rises. Its average cost of production may be as shown in Figure 4.14. The per-unit cost of producing cars falls sharply at first as the manufacturer's volume of car production rises, and then at a slower rate. If a manufacturer is producing 500,000 cars per year, its average cost of production per car is $8000. If a manufacturer produces 2,000,000 cars annually, its average cost of production per car falls to $4500.

Size of Market and Economies of Scale

Firms in countries that provide a large market for manufactured goods are likely to have large volumes of production and lower average costs of production than firms in countries with a small market. Thus, manufacturing firms in

FIGURE 4.14 **The average cost of producing cars falls continually as car production rises. Falling average costs may be common in manufacturing
industry.**

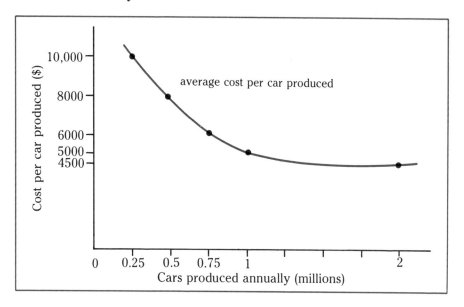

Canada, such as car manufacturers, are unable to obtain the economies of scale
enjoyed by American, European, and Japanese manufacturers, and, consequently, average costs of production tend to be higher in Canada. Indeed, the
survival of industries such as the Canadian textile industry and shoe industry is
largely dependent upon the imposition of tariffs and nontariff barriers against
competing imports. Tariffs are taxes on imported goods; and they tend to raise
the price of imported goods and so protect the local industry. Quotas and
Voluntary Export Restraint (VER) Agreements are examples of nontariff barriers. These are restrictions on the quantity of imports that is permitted to enter
the country. VER agreemeents have a long history in international textile
trade, and, in recent years, North American car manufacturers have pressed
for restrictions on Japanese car imports.

Causes of Economies and Diseconomies of Scale

It is interesting to consider some of the reasons why firms experience
economies or diseconomies of scale as they expand the level of their operations. Economies of expansion may be *internal* to the firm – a consequence
merely of its own expansion – or *external* to the firm – a consequence of the
expansion, say, of industry in its own locality. The former type of economy is
discussed in this section.

Internal economies may arise from expanding the operations of a single plant, factory or sales outlet, or from operating an increased number of plants, factories or outlets. These two sources of economies are sometimes called *plant economies* and *multiple plant economies* respectively.

A firm may experience internal economies of scale because some of its factors are "lumpy", and the costs of these can be spread over greater volume of output. For instance, much the same type of press for pressing out car bodies is required whether the volume of production is high or low. The greater the number of car bodies pressed, the lower the average cost of pressing these out. Furthermore, as the size of a firm's operation expands, it may achieve economies because members of its work force and its machinery may be able to specialize to a greater extent. Labourers can specialize in accordance with their aptitude, and can more easily become knowledgeable and skilled in a specialized job.

In a small firm, the owner-manager is frequently the production manager, sales manager, and bookkeeper, and may even do some of the labouring work. He or she is in effect a "jack of all trades". As the firm grows, it is usually possible to appoint specialists in each of these areas. This is likely to raise the firm's productivity and lower the firm's average costs of production. The process of production may also be divided into simple tasks as the volume of production expands. Machinery is then designed specifically to deal with each task, and individuals are assigned to particular tasks. The final outcome of such development may be continuous assembly-line production. Although this may add to productivity, it has a drawback in that labourers on the assembly line may be under pressure to keep up with the general flow of work, and their jobs may be repetitive and boring.

Apart from "plant specific" economies owing to the division of tasks, specialization, and the greater or more efficient use of "lumps" of resources, physical relationships may give rise to important internal economies of scale. As the diameter of a pipe is increased, for instance, its volume rises more than proportionately, and the same is true of most storage vessels. It is possible to take advantage of such physical relationships to reduce costs per unit of output as volume of output rises. Savings of this type can be very important in industries such as the chemical and petro-chemical industries. This is an example of "product specific" economies of scale. Product-specific economies include those reductions in unit costs arising from longer production runs, larger output or a faster rate of output.

Plant-specific economies are important for the following industries:[1]

- chemicals
- beer
- bakeries
- detergents
- cement
- bricks
- bicycles
- petroleum refining

[1]Gorecki, P., "Economies of Scale and Efficient Plant Size in Canadian Manufacturing Industries," Consumer and Corporate Affairs, 1976.

Product-specific economies are important for the following industries:

- machine tools
- dyes
- shoe making
- bottle blowing
- hosiery
- book printing
- fabric weaving and finishing

Which of these types of economies is more important for a given industry has important implications for policy aimed at industrial organization.

A firm that operates a *number* of plants, factories or outlets may also achieve economies in a number of ways. For instance, chain stores such as Woolworths, Simpsons-Sears, and Eaton's may find that the cost of advertising nationally distributed goods at an additional outlet is negligible. The same advertisement in a national newspaper serves all or most outlets. Also, by expanding and operating a number of plants, a firm may be able to obtain extra economies of management. The top management, overseeing all plants or divisions, may be specialized to a greater extent in a large multiplant firm, and any information that this management obtains about marketing conditions and so on can frequently be used to the advantage of all plants or divisions. Costs of some centralized activity, such as research and development, and warehousing, can be spread over a greater volume of output in a large multiplant firm. Successful new products developed in a company's research-and-development section can be applied to many of its plants and divisions. For instance, if the research-and-development section of the Ford Motor Company or of General Motors in the U.S.A. discovers a new and commercially viable car engine, the production of this engine can be introduced to their plants, not only in the U.S.A., but in Europe, Canada, and other countries. This may make their research-and-development activity more profitable than otherwise would be the case.

A firm may eventually experience diseconomies, however, if it becomes too large. The size at which diseconomies become important varies from industry to industry. In agriculture, diseconomies are important when firms are comparatively small; but in manufacturing and distributing industries, they may not become significant until firms become very large. Physical constraints and problems in managing large firms may give rise to diseconomies. After a point, firms may become so large that it is difficult to co-ordinate their activities: top management may get out of touch with operations, and a costly bureaucratic structure may emerge that reduces flexibility. A firm that attempts to expand very quickly may experience diseconomies as expansion usually requires additional management and personnel, and it takes time for a "new team" to learn to work together and adjust to change.

Expansion of the Firm by Horizontal Integration, Vertical Integration, and Diversification

A firm that expands by adding new plants or establishments may do so:

1. by horizontal integration, or
2. by vertical integration.

To do this, it may buy out existing firms or build additional plants, outlets or establishments of its own.

In *horizontal integration*, the establishments added by the firm operate at the same stage of production and are in the same line of business. Thus, a retail grocery firm that purchases the retail outlets of another retail grocery firm is expanding by horizontal integration.

In *vertical integration*, the firm adds operations that produce inputs for the existing operations or carry its present operations farther forward in the production chain. Thus, an oil producer that expands by exploring for new oil deposits, or by refining the crude oil that it produces, or by operating retail establishments, is engaging in verticle integration. Many large well-known oil companies in Canada such as Imperial Oil Ltd. are vertically integrated in the petroleum industry.

A company or firm may grow by *diversification*. When a firm has exhausted its market possibilities for any particular product, it can only continue to grow by adding new products to its range, that is, by diversifying. Canadian Pacific (CP) is a diversified firm. In the transportation industry, CP has a railway, an airline, shipping operations, and trucking operations. It is also involved in telecommunications. Its subsidiary Canadian Pacific Enterprises Ltd., (CPE), has interests in oil and gas, mines and minerals, forest products, iron and steel, finance, real estate, and agriproducts.

Diversification can be advantageous to a firm. It enables a firm to spread its risks. A slump in demand for one of its products, or a disruption in its production, will be less serious to the firm when it has alternative income from other sources. Thus, a slump in demand for rail transportation is less serious for CP as it has income from other transportation services, and from the nontransportation enterprises of CPE.

As the firm expands, the form of its legal ownership is liable to change. As discussed in the last chapter, it may alter its legal status from a sole trader to a partnership, to a private company, and then to a public company, as it grows in size. Some of the earlier stages in this possible chain of legal status may, however, be missed out. The public-company form of ownership has many advantages for a large firm, as discussed in the last chapter.

FIGURE 4.15 **Imperial Oil is a *vertically integrated* firm. These photographs show two stages of production: a refinery at Dartmouth and a retail outlet.**
Courtesy Imperial Oil Limited

(a) Dartmouth Refinery

(b) Retail Outlet

Other Aspects of Production

Although firms are the main organizing units of production in our economy, they do not control all their costs; their costs can be affected by *external* factors. If industry and population expand in an area or region where a firm is located, the firm may experience external economies, that is, lower costs of producing each unit of output. For instance, a firm fabricating steel products may gain if more industry locates in its area. It may gain:

1. internal economies from a larger local market for its product,
2. greater and speedier availability of specialists, for instance, specialists able to repair its machinery,
3. greater availability of spare parts and materials,
4. a larger local labour force, which makes it easier to vary the extent of its production activity,
5. improved communications, such as more frequent rail, air, and shipping services, all of which may help the local firm by reducing the amount of stock it has to store, widening the market for its products, and making outside assistance more readily available.

In a larger community, new ideas may be more quickly introduced from outside, and this may improve productivity at a faster rate than would otherwise be the case.

FIGURE 4.16 **The larger a firm, the more likely that it has the legal status of a
public company.**

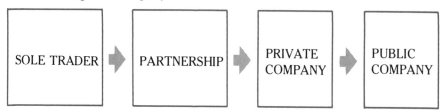

Neighbourhood Economies of Production

The growth of cities and towns is partially explained by the occurence of external economies. Firms tend to "conglomerate" to reduce their transport costs
when they are using inputs from one another, and to take advantage of the
types of external economies mentioned above. Such external economies may
cause cities to grow beyond a socially optimal size, and may retard the growth
of small towns as firms locate in metropolitan areas. Thus, Toronto, Montreal,
and Vancouver have possibly grown beyond an optimal size. Unless some
country towns can be pushed beyond a critical, or threshold, size, they may fail
to grow, and may even decline and lose their population to metropolitan areas.

Specialization in Production

In modern societies, production tends to be specialized. Different regions and
different countries tend to specialize in the production of different goods.
Sometimes this depends on natural endowments. For instance, it is clearly not
very economic to grow bananas in Sweden, whereas the climate of Colombia is
very suited to their cultivation. It therefore pays Colombia to specialize in the
production of bananas and export them to Sweden, importing manufactured
products in return. Even if the resource endowment of one country is better in
every respect, however, it can benefit it to specialize in the production of goods
in which it has a *comparative* advantage.

Again, countries may specialize in production to take greater advantage of
economies of scale. If economies of scale are important, greater production
may result if one country concentrates on producing a large volume of one product, and another country on a large volume of another product, and both
trade these products. In addition, differences in technological knowledge and
skills can also help to explain differences between production in different
countries.

Just as regions and countries tend to specialize to some extent in production, this is even truer of individuals. Very few individuals in modern societies
are self-sufficient. Most specialize in production, and some consume none of the
commodities they produce. Given the existing degree of specialization in production, trade and exchange are vital to the operation of modern societies. In

our society, trade or exchange is effected by means of markets, the operation of which is discussed in the next chapter.

KEY CONCEPTS
(FOR REVIEW)

Average cost of production
Diseconomies of scale
Diversification
Division of labour
Double counting
Economies of conglomeration
Economies of scale
External economies of expansion
Fixed input
Gross National Expenditure (GNE)
Gross National Product (GNP)
Horizontal integration
Inputs
Internal economies of expansion
Law of diminishing returns
Marginal cost
Marginal physical product
Marginal physical productivity of
   a resource
Multiplant economies
Net economic welfare

Nontraded goods
Neighbourhood economies
Output
Primary sector
Plant-specific economies
Production
Production function
Productive resources
Product-specific economies
Returns to scale
Rural industry
Secondary industry
Size of market
Social cost
Tertiary sector
Total cost of production
Value added
Variable Cost
Variable input
Vertical integration

QUESTIONS FOR REVIEW AND DISCUSSION

1. What is the purpose, or end, of production?
2. Outline the process of production. What value does energy play in the process?
3. What types of activity are productive?
4. What is Gross National Product (GNP)? Indicate at least two other ways in which national production may be measured.
5. "In determining the level of national production, we must be careful to avoid double counting." Explain. Give an example of double counting.
6. Why is GNP an inadequate indicator of the welfare of a country? What factors should be taken into account in determining Net Economic Welfare (NEW)?
7. What are the relative sizes of the main economic sectors of the Canadian economy? How have these changed during this century? Why have these alterations occurred?

8. In what ways do the relative sizes of the main economic sectors of developing economies differ from those of more developed ones? Why do the patterns differ?
9. Explain carefully what is meant by a production function.
10. What is meant by the phrase "marginal physical productivity of a resource"?
11. The production relationship between the number of labourers employed by a bakery and the number of loaves of bread baked daily is shown in the following table. Complete the third column of the table to show the marginal physical productivity of labour. Is marginal productivity increasing or decreasing?

Number of Labourers	Number of Loaves of Bread Baked Daily	Marginal Physical Productivity of Labour
0	0	
1	60	
2	100	
3	120	

12. What is the marginal physical productivity of labour in the example shown in Table 4.2? Is it declining, constant or increasing?
13. Assuming a daily wage of $60, calculate the cost structure for Question 11.
14. Set out, in a similar form to Table 4.2, the production relationship corresponding to production function OB in Figure 4.8. Assume that each labourer works 8 hours per day.
15. Distinguish between fixed and variable inputs, and give examples of both.
16. "When some factors of production are fixed, the marginal physical productivity of a resource is unlikely to be constant." Explain.
17. What is the law of diminishing returns? Give an example of its operation.
18. It usually does not pay a firm to maximize its possible level of production. Why?
19. "The increased employment of a resource may raise its marginal physical productivity because increased employment allows greater specialization and division of labour." Explain and discuss.
20. How are changes in average costs of production related to the occurrence of economies and diseconomies of scale?
21. What types of average-cost curves of production may be:

      a. typical for agricultural businesses?
      b. typical for manufacturing firms?

      Draw examples of each.

22. How does the size of the Canadian market affect the competitive position of Canadian manufacturers compared with their American, European and Japanese counterparts?

23. What types of factors may cause economies or diseconomies of scale as a firm expands in size?

24. Indicate some alternative ways in which business enterprises can expand in size. Give some examples of firms that have expanded by horizontal integration, vertical integration or diversification.

25. Distinguish between economies internal to the expansion of the firm and economies external to the firm.

26. What are some of the advantages to a business of locating its productive activity in a large community or city?

27. How do external economies affect the growth of cities?

28. What factors lead to production being specialized in different regions and countries? Why do individuals tend to specialize in their productive activities?

FURTHER READING

Blomqvist, A., Wonnacott, P., & Wonnacott, R., *Economics*, 1st Canadian ed. Scarborough: McGraw-Hill Ryerson Limited, 1984, Chapter 21.

Fuhrman, P., *Business in the Canadian Environment*. Scarborough: Prentice-Hall Canada Inc., 1982, Chapter 7.

Gorecki, P.K., *Economies of Scale and Efficient Plant Size in Canadian Manufacturing Industries*. (monograph) Consumer and Corporate Affairs, 1976.

Lipsey, R.G., Purvis, D.D., Sparks, G.R., & Steiner, P.O., *Economics*, 4th ed. New York: Harper & Row, Publishers, 1982, chapters 11, 12, & 13.

Samuelson, P.A. & Scott, A.D., *Economics*, Scarborough: McGraw-Hill Ryerson Limited, 1980, chapters 24 & 27.

5 Demand and Supply

FIGURE 5.1 **Bramalea Limited Outlet Centre, Brampton. Demand and supply in action: markets consist of buyers and sellers exchanging goods or services.**
Courtesy Bramalea Ltd./Photo by Jac Jacobson

Price Mechanism, Markets, and Competition

As previously discussed, markets play a large role in determining the allocation and use of resources in our economy. Markets also help to determine our incomes. If we are to gain a better understanding of the way in which our economy works, we need to know more about the effects of market forces on economic activity.

To a considerable extent, economic activity is determined by conditions of demand and supply; however, it is not entirely determined by the free play of these forces because governments intervene in the operation of our economy. For instance, the government may restrict the imports of goods into the country, or encourage the production of particular goods by paying a subsidy or bounty to their producers. Even when such intervention occurs, it is useful to know about supply and demand conditions. Such knowledge can help us assess the impact of government intervention.

More than a rote understanding of the dependence of prices and traded quantities on supply and demand is needed. A model or analysis of the way in which supply and demand help to determine prices and traded quantities is needed as this can be used to make predictions about what will happen to economic activity as conditions change. This chapter contains a model, an abstraction, of the way in which supply and demand determine prices and traded quantities of commodities.

In our society, the price mechanism operates through market forces. The efficiency of the price mechanism in guiding the use of resources depends on the strength of competition between buyers and sellers of commodities. In certain circumstances when such competition is intense or perfect, the price mechanism leads to *an optimal allocation of resources*. Even when competition is not perfect, however, but a market system is in operation, prices and traded quantities are likely to change in the direction indicated by the theory of supply and demand outlined in this chapter.

As observed in Chapter 2, the price mechanism operates by suppliers responding to the demands of consumers for commodities. Should the relative demand of consumers for a particular commodity increase, this will in the first instance be reflected in an increase in its price, and a rise in the profitability of producing the commodity. The increased profitability of producing the commodity will encourage producers to produce more of it; so, supply expands in response to demands of consumers. A fall in the demand of consumers for a particular commodity has the opposite chain of consequences. In a socialist economic system, however, there is frequently no close connection between the demands of consumers and supply, because supply may be controlled by a central body of people such as members of the Planning Bureau or the Communist Party.

Basic Market Model

The basic market model for any commodity relies on the concepts of a market, or aggregate, demand curve for the commodity, and a corresponding market, or aggregate, supply curve for the commodity. Together these two curves largely determine the price of a commodity and its traded quantities. The market demand curve takes into account the demands of *all* potential buyers of the commodity, and the market supply curve takes into account the willingness of *all* potential sellers to supply the commodity.

Market Demand Curve

To illustrate the theory, let us consider the market for shoes. Let us look at the relationship between the price of shoes and the quantity of shoes that buyers wish to buy, that is, the demanded quantity of shoes. To isolate the effect of the price of shoes on the quantity of shoes demanded, we must hold all other factors constant. The factors held constant include:

1. the tastes or preferences of consumers,
2. their incomes,
3. the population,
4. the prices of other commodities, and, in appropriate cases,
5. the availability of goods that can be substituted for, or used in conjunction with, the commodity under consideration.

The effect on demand of a change in some of these factors will be discussed later in this chapter.

As a rule, we expect the quantity demanded of a commodity to increase as its price is lowered. In the cases of shoes, the relationship between the price of shoes and the quantity of shoes demanded daily may be like that shown in the first two columns of Table 5.1. In this instance, the quantity of shoes demanded yearly rises by 1 million pairs each time the price of shoes is lowered by $10 per pair.

TABLE **5.1**   **Demand and Supply Schedules for Shoes in a Region**

Price of Shoes Per Pair ($)	Quantity of Shoes Demanded Daily (Millions of Pairs)	Quantity of Shoes Supplied (Millions of Pairs)
80.00	0	8
70.00	1	7
60.00	2	6
50.00	3	5
40.00	4	4
30.00	5	3
20.00	6	2
10.00	7	1
0.00	8	0

The relationship between the quantity of shoes that buyers wish to purchase and the price of shoes can be graphed as shown in Figure 5.2. The circled points along the straight line marked DD in Figure 5.2 correspond to the prices and quantities demanded of shoes shown in columns one and two of Table 5.1.

The prices shown in Table 5.1, however, are only some of the possibilities. Prices can be varied by small amounts. When this is taken into account, the demand curve — the curve showing the quantity of the commodity demanded at each possible price (other determinants of demand being constant) — is the straight line DD.

Market Supply Curve

The demand schedule, or curve, takes account of the buying side of the market for shoes. The selling side is taken into account by means of a supply schedule, or curve, showing the quantity of the commodity that is supplied at each possible price (other determinants of supply being constant). For most commodities, their supply — the quantity of the commodity that suppliers are willing to exchange — rises as their price is increased. For example, the supply schedule for shoes might be like that indicated by the relationship between column one and column three in Table 5.1. This relationship indicates that for every $10 rise in the price per pair of shoes, the supply of shoes rises by 1 million pairs daily. As the price of shoes rises, shoemakers find it more profitable to make them. They may hire more shoemakers and/or work longer hours. In addition, if the making of shoes becomes very profitable, new suppliers may be attracted to the making of shoes. Supply thus expands as price rises. As price increases, it becomes profitable to make shoes in more costly areas and by more costly means. As the price falls, production by marginal means and in marginal areas (means and areas affording a bare profit) is no longer profitable, and so supply contracts.

The supply relationship may be graphed. The circled points along the line marked SS in Figure 5.2 correspond to the prices and quantities of shoes supplied shown in columns one and three of Table 5.1. Allowing for the fact that the price of shoes can be varied by small amounts, the supply curve of shoes is the straight line marked SS. *The supply curve of a commodity shows the quantity of the commodity that will be supplied at each possible price of it, other influences apart from its price being held constant.*

Market Equilibrium Price and Traded Quantities

An examination of Table 5.1 indicates that, as shown in the elongated rectangle, there is one price for shoes that balances or equates the quantity of shoes that buyers wish to buy with the quantity that sellers wish to supply. This is called the *equilibrium price*, and in this instance it is $40.00 per pair. In Figure 5.2, the equilibrium price corresponds to the price at which the supply and the demand curves cross. The equilibrium point is marked by E in Figure 5.2.

The equilibrium market situation in which the equilibrium price occurs and the equilibrium quantity of the commodity is demanded and supplied is of in-

Figure 5.2 **Example of demand and supply curve for shoes. As is typically the
case, the demand curve slopes downward and the supply curve
slopes upward. The point at which the two curves cross, E, determines the equilibrium price and market quantity of shoes.**

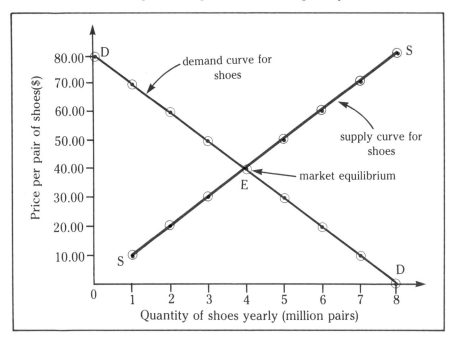

terest from a number of points of view. It represents a position of perfect
balance that, if it occurs, repeats itself period after period *if the conditions of
supply and demand do not change.* In many circumstances, actual prices and
quantities traded in a market tend to the equilibrium price and quantity. For instance, in the above example, if the market price of shoes is initially $20.00 per
pair, the quantity demanded (6 million pairs) will exceed the quantity supplied
(2 million pairs), and competition for this limited supply will force the prices of
shoes up. The price will continue rising until it reaches $40.00, at which level
demand no longer exceeds supply. Again, disequilibrium occurs if the price of
shoes is initially $60.00 per pair. At this price the quantity supplied (6 million
pairs) exceeds the quantity demanded (2 million pairs). Competition between
sellers because of excess supply will force the price of shoes down. The price
will continue to fall until the equilibrium price of $40.00 per pair is reached.

Although actual market prices and traded quantities are not always
equilibrium ones, equilibrium prices and quantities provide useful reference
points for market prices and traded quantities. Market values are likely to
change in the same direction as equilibrium values. We will study changes in
equilibrium values later in this chapter.

Applications of the Basic Market Model Developed So Far

The model considered so far can be used to illustrate some of the difficulties involved in regulating prices.

Regulation of Maximum Prices

If the government fixes the maximum price of a commodity at a price less than the equilibrium price, this results in some demands being unsatisfied. For instance, if the government sets the maximum price of shoes at $20.00 per pair, in the above example 6 million pairs of shoes are demanded yearly and 2 million pairs supplied; so, the unsatisfied demand amounts to 4 million pairs of shoes yearly. Just how will the limited supply be rationed out if price is not allowed to serve this role? Sellers may arbitrarily determine a quota for each customer or operate on the principle of "first come first served", and queues may form. It is also possible that an illegal market or blackmarket in shoes may arise, in that individuals with unsatisfied demands may buy at higher than the legal price.

It might also be observed that price regulations do not always help those whom they are designed to help. Take the case of a regulation on the maximum level of house rent, a measure designed to help the poor. If the maximum rent is set below the market equilibrium level, this reduces the amount of housing available for rental. Because of the reduced availability of housing space, some of the poor may be denied housing, or may be forced to live in more crowded and squalid conditions. The theoretical effect of a regulation of this kind is illustrated in Figure 5.3.

In Figure 5.3, the demand curve for housing is indicated by DD and the supply curve by SS. The equilibrium rental for housing is $10.00/m² weekly, and 15,000,000 m² of housing are supplied for rental in market equilibrium. Suppose that politicians decide that the price of housing is too high, and pass a law regulating the rental to a maximum of $5.00/m². As a result, the amount of housing available for rental falls from 15,000,000 m² to 10,000,000 m². Less housing space is available for rental as a result of the regulation. The social cost of this price regulation is a reduction in the volume of housing space available for rental.

There are other instances where regulation of prices can have unwanted social effects. For example, widespread controls on rates of interest on loans for purchasing houses have been advocated in recent years in Canada because of high rates of interest. These high rates of interest reflect the recent high rates of inflation in Canada, and of course, the rate of interest can be regarded as the price of a loan. But it is by no means clear that controls on the rate of interest would overcome the difficulty that many people face in obtaining finance. At a lower rate of interest, a smaller quantity of funds may be available for lending.

FIGURE 5.3 **A regulation on the maximum price of a commodity usually reduces
its supply, and if its maximum price is less than its market
equilibrium price, it is reflected in a shortage of supply. In the
example below, a ceiling price of $5.00 m² for housing rental is
reflected in a shortage of housing space. At the ceiling price of $5.00,
20,000,000 m² of housing space are demanded, but only 10,000,000
m² are supplied.**

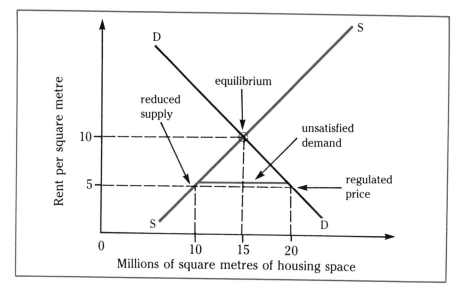

It might also be noted that a policy of regulating prices on a broad front, say
to control inflation, can result in shortages of particular commodities if prices
get out of line. During the period 1975-78, the Anti-Inflation Board (AIB) in
Canada attempted to control the rate of increase of prices and wages. In 1982,
the Federal Government announced that it would limit the growth of wages
and prices in the federal public service and in Crown Corporations.

Regulation of Minimum Prices

Apart from controlling maximum prices, governments or interested parties
sometimes attempt to control the minimum prices for commodities. For instance, provincial governments specify minimum wage rates for certain occupations; a minimum price is set for the sale of agricultural commodities such as
eggs by an agricultural marketing board. When the minimum price is set above
the equilibrium price, demands are not satisfied to the extent possible, and
unless restrictions are placed upon supply, excess supplies may emerge.

As an example, suppose that the equilibrium wage rate for tool and die
makers is $10.00/hour, but the union pushes for a minimum $15.00/hour.
Compared to the equilibrium situation illustrated in Figure 5.4, the demand for

tool and die makers falls from 100,000 to 50,000. Although on the one hand the employed tool and die makers gain by the higher wage, there is a social cost reflected partly in a lowering of the number of tool and die makers employed.

Quotas or Limitations on Production

In the case of products such as eggs, governments, through marketing boards, sometimes attempt to enforce a minimum price exceeding the equilibrium one. To do this, they may impose quotas or upper limits on production by individual producers of the products in question. For example, suppose that the demand and supply relationships for eggs are like those shown in Figure 5.5, and the government wishes to raise the price of eggs from $1.00 per carton to $1.50 per carton. At the price of $1.50 per carton, buyers wish to buy 1,500,000 cartons of eggs daily, but producers would like to supply 2,500,000 cartons daily. Supply would therefore exceed demand.

FIGURE 5.4   **A minimum wage rate above the equilibrium results in unemployment.**

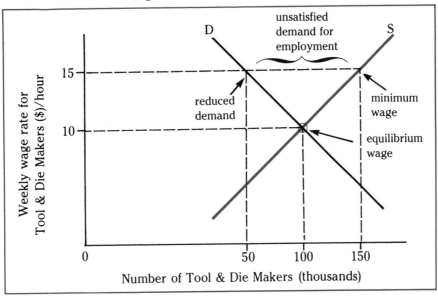

Some means of restricting or rationing supply to the amount demanded is needed. The government may ration the supply of 1,500,000 cartons among producers by giving each producer the same proportionate share in production as he had in the equilibrium situation. Alternatively production quotas may be based on average past production or other factors. Another method, not often used, is for the government to sell or auction rights to supply the restricted amount of production. Certificates or coupons may be issued giving the bearer a right to supply a particular quantity of the product (eggs in this case), and

FIGURE 5.5   **An attempt to raise prices may need to be backed up by limitations on
the production of individual producers. In this example, it is necessary
to restrict overall supply to 1.5 million cartons daily to maintain a price
of $1.50 per carton.**

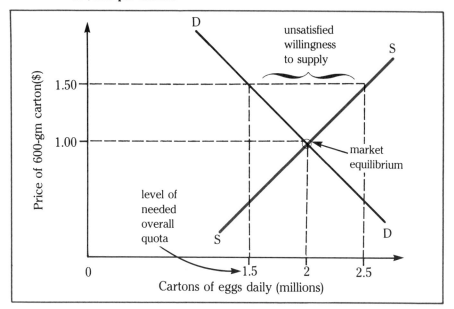

these may be sold by the government to suppliers. Depending on the system,
suppliers may be allowed to resell these certificates. Although all limitations on
supply are liable to add to economic scarcity, some methods of limiting supply
increase scarcity more than others.

Shifts in Supply-and-Demand Curves and of Market Equilibrium

In the above discussion of economic activity, the only determinant of demand
and supply of commodities allowed to vary was their price. Price is not the only
determinant of demand and supply, however, and other determinants may
vary in practice. *If these other determinants vary, they cause the demand or
supply curve of a product drawn as a function of its price to shift.*

Shifts in Market-Demand Curves

Some of the factors that are held constant when the demand for a commodity is
expressed only as a function of its price are:

1. the population, that is the number of potential buyers of the commodity,
2. tastes or preferences for the commodity,

3. the availability of substitutes for the commodity,

4. the price of substitutes for the commodity, or the price of complementary commodities, that is, commodities that tend to be used in conjunction with the commodity (such as swimming pools and water), and

5. the level of incomes.

Normally, at any given price for a commodity, the demand for it is increased by a rise in population, by a swing of preferences in favour of it, by the reduced availability of substitutes for the commodity, by a rise in the price of substitutes or by a fall in the price of the complementary commodities, and by a rise in incomes. The effect of any of these changes is to shift the demand curve for a commodity (expressed as a function of its price) to the right. The opposite changes shift the demand curve for a commodity to the left (see Figure 5.6).

Figure 5.6 is a hypothetical example of the market demand for oysters. Suppose that this demand under initial conditions is as shown on the demand curve marked DD. DD indicates the relationship between the price of oysters and the demand for oysters, given the initial conditions. A change in these initial conditions is likely to shift the demand curve. For instance, the demand curve may shift to the right to D_2D_2 as population increases and more people demand oysters. It may also shift to the right because incomes rise and individuals find that they can more easily afford oysters, or it may shift to the right for any of the other reasons mentioned above. At any price, more of the commodity is demanded than before. For instance, in Figure 5.6, when oysters cost $1.00 per bottle, 10,000 bottles are demanded daily under initial conditions. But with the shift in the demand curve to D_2D_2, the demand for oysters at $1.00 per bottle rises from 10,000 bottles daily to 15,000 bottles daily. A shift of the demand curve to the left is illustrated by a shift in the demand curve from

FIGURE 5.6   **A shift to the right in the demand curve for a commodity implies that more of the commodity is demanded at each price for the commodity. A shift to the left in the demand curve implies the converse.**

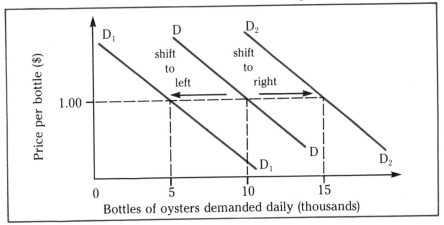

DD to D_1D_1. With the shift of the demand curve to the left, fewer oysters are demanded at any price. For instance, at a price of $1.00 per bottle, 5000 bottles of oysters are demanded daily after the shift in demand, whereas 10,000 bottles were previously demanded.

Shifts in Market-Supply Curves

A supply curve may shift for a number of reasons. Greater quantities of a commodity may be supplied at any price because:

1. the technology used to produce the commodity improves,
2. new sources of supply are discovered, as in the case of minerals when new deposits are discovered,
3. the weather or environmental conditions may be favourable to production, as may be the case for agricultural crops,
4. the prices of alternative products that can be produced falls,
5. its costs of production decline owing to a fall in the market prices (costs) of resources employed in its production,
6. the *relative* cost of producing the commodity under consideration falls so that it becomes relatively more profitable to produce it, and for other reasons.

Smaller quantities of a commodity are supplied under the opposite conditions.
   The effect of an increase or decrease in supply caused by a shift in the supply curve is illustrated in Figure 5.7. A change in conditions of supply that increase supply shifts the supply curve to the right, and change that decreases supply shifts the supply curve to the left. Thus, taking the example of oysters illustrated in Figure 5.6, the supply curve from SS to S_2S_2 indicates an increase in supply of oysters at any price of oysters, and a shift from SS to S_1S_1 represents a reduction in supply at any price. For instance, at a price of $1.00 per bottle, the shift of the supply curve to the right from SS to S_2S_2 implies that 15,000 bottles of oysters are supplied per day, whereas previously only 10,000 bottles per day were supplied. The supply of oysters may increase, for example, because improved methods are discovered of increasing the spawning rate of oysters. A shift of the supply curve to the left from SS to S_1S_1 indicates that at $1.00 per bottle 5000 bottles of oysters are supplied daily, whereas previously 10,000 bottles were supplied. A fall in supply may occur, for instance, if water pollution destroys some oyster beds.

Variations in Market Equilibrium Prices and Traded Quantities

Shifts in the supply-and-demand curves are liable to change market equilibrium prices and traded quantities. Normally, but not invariably, a rise in demand (a shift to the right in the demand curve) raises the equilibrium price and quantity

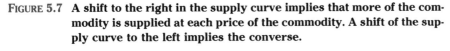

FIGURE 5.7 **A shift to the right in the supply curve implies that more of the commodity is supplied at each price of the commodity. A shift of the supply curve to the left implies the converse.**

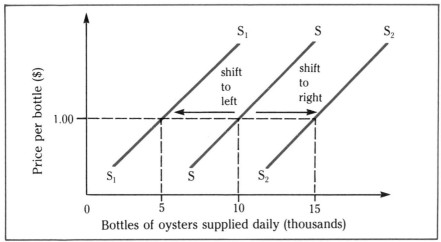

traded of the commodity under consideration, *if* supply conditions remain unchanged. Normally, an increase in supply (a shift of the supply curve to the
right) lowers the equilibrium price of the commodity and raises the equilibrium
quantity traded, *if* demand conditions remain unaltered. Shifts of these curves
in the opposite direction normally have the opposite effects.

These changes in market equilibrium values reflect the workings of the
price mechanism. *Equilibrium values respond to shifts in demand or in supply,
so as to reflect the preferences of buyers and the cost experienced by suppliers
of a commodity.*

Figure 5.8 illustrates the normal effects on equilibrium price and traded
quantities of a shift in the demand curve for the commodity under consideration, supply conditions unaltered. A rise in the demand for oysters from DD to
D_2D_2 raises the equilibrium price of oysters from $1.00 per bottle to $1.50 per
bottle, and the equilibrium quantity expands from 10,000 bottles daily to
15,000 bottles daily. On the other hand, a fall in the demand for oysters from
DD to D_1D_1 lowers the equilibrium price of oysters from $1.00 per bottle to 50¢
per bottle, and the equilibrium quantity from 10,000 bottles to 5000 bottles.
Equilibrium supply moves in the same direction as the change in demand.

The effect on market equilibrium of a variation in supply conditions is illustrated in Figure 5.9. An increase in supply, such as a shift of the supply curve
from SS to S_2S_2, normally reduces equilibrium price and increases equilibrium
quantity, the demand curve unchanged. In this instance, the equilibrium price
of oysters falls from $1.00 per bottle to 50¢ per bottle, and equilibrium supply
expands from 10,000 bottles daily to 15,000 bottles daily, a reduction in supply
has the opposite impact. For instance, a shift of the supply curve from SS to S_1S_1

FIGURE **5.8** **Supply conditions unchanged, a rise in the demand for a commodity
normally raises its equilibrium price and equilibrium supply. A fall
in demand has the opposite effect. This illustrates the price
mechanism at work.**

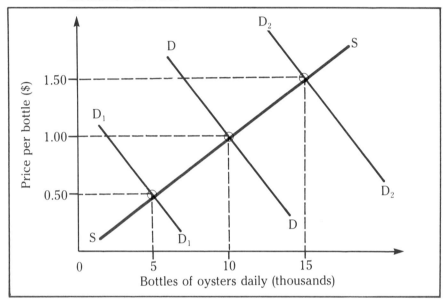

FIGURE **5.9** **Demand conditions unchanged, increased propensity to supply a
commodity normally lowers its equilibrium price and raises its
equilibrium quantity. A reduction in the propensity to supply has the
opposite effect. This illustrates the price mechanism at work.**

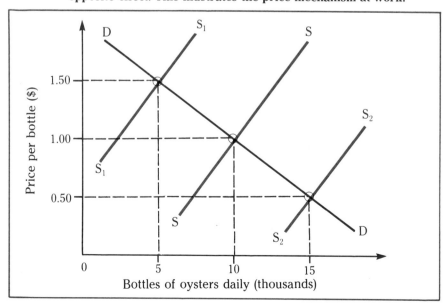

increases the equilibrium price from $1.00 per bottle to $1.50 per bottle of oysters, and equilibrium supply falls from 10,000 bottles daily to 5000 bottles. As suggested earlier, a reduction in supply could occur because of pollution of waterways where oysters are commercially cultivated.

The above discussion considered the consequence of a shift in the demand curve and in the supply curve for a product, assuming that both curves do not vary. If both curves shift, the effect on market equilibrium varies depending on whether both curves shift in the same direction, and on their relative shifts. For instance, if an increase in the demand for a product (shift to the right of the demand curve for it) is accompanied by an even greater rise in supply (shift to the right of the supply curve), the level of the equilibrium price of the product falls. But if the relative leftward shifts of the curves are reversed, the equilibrium price of the product rises.

The above discussion is also based on the assumption that the supply-and-demand curves for a commodity are normal. This implies that the demand curve for a commodity is downward sloping, indicating that as the price of a commodity is lowered, other things being equal, the quantity demanded of it rises, and that its supply curve is upward sloping. When supply-and-demand curves are not of normal slope, our earlier conclusions require modification.

Application of the Analysis of Shifts in Supply and Demand

The above analysis has many applications. For example, it can be used to help explain why the prices of agricultural products have fallen (in real terms) relative to the prices of manufactured goods. Because of this trend, individuals have drifted away from agriculture, and there has been a population shift from the country to the city.

Trends in Agricultural Prices

The demand for agricultural products has risen as population and incomes have increased, but not as fast as the increase in supply resulting from improvements in farming methods. Because the demand curve for agricultural products appears to decline steeply, indicating that the quantity demand of agricultural products does not vary much in response to price variations, supply need only expand at a slightly greater rate than demand for equilibrium price to fall significantly. This is illustrated in Figure 5.10. A shift in the demand curve for agricultural products from DD to D_1D_1 accompanied by a shift in the supply curve for agricultural products from SS to S_1S_1 is shown. As a result of this variation, the equilibrium price for agricultural products declines from P to P_1.

It may be noted that the steep slope of the supply curve and the steep slope of the demand curve for agricultural products help to explain why the prices of unregulated agricultural products tend to fluctuate considerably. Given the

FIGURE 5.10   **Decline in agricultural prices owing to supply increasing at a faster
rate than demand**

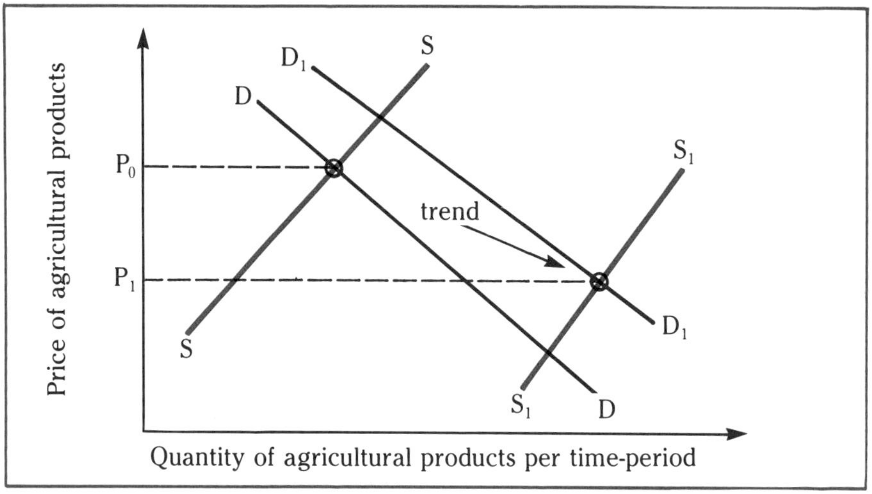

Quantity of agricultural products per time-period

steep slope of the demand curve, small variations in supply (shifts of the supply
curve) caused by variations in weather conditions are liable to result in
considerable fluctuations in the equilibrium prices of such products.

Influences of Labour Unions and Professional Associations on Wages

To take another example, consider attempts by labour unions such as the Canadian Union of Public Employees, or by professional bodies such as the Canadian
Medical Assocation, to raise or maintain incomes in their occupations. Apart
from the possibility of obtaining above-equilibrium wages by bargaining and
using threats of strikes and so on, or of obtaining such wages through concilia-
tion and arbitration, trade unions or professional bodies may influence the
salaries of their members through shifts in the supply-and-demand curves for
the services of their members. For instance, supplies may be reduced by requir-
ing longer training than is strictly necessary, or by imposing strict residency
requirements. It is sometimes claimed that these means are used by the medical
profession to maintain doctors' incomes. Their effect is to keep the supply
curve of medical services farther to the left than would otherwise be the case,
so tending to maintain the equilibrium price of medical services.

   Again, a trade union or professional organization may try to influence the
demand for the services of its members. It may try to raise this demand curve
in an attempt to raise the wages or salaries of its members. It may do this:

1. by advertising the *final* product produced by the labour, and so raise the
   derived demand for labour,

2. by slowing down or accelerating, as appropriate, the installation of equipment to be used in conjunction with labour, and

3. by increasing the range of jobs in which the members of the trade union or association can be engaged, that is, by altering "demarcation" boundaries.

It is rare for a union to adopt strategy 1. mentioned above; but instances of this have been recorded. In case 2., the appropriate strategy may depend on whether new machinery displaces labour or increases the demand for labour.

A situation is illustrated in Figure 5.11 in which a labour union raises the demand for the services of its members and lowers the supply of such services. Let us say that the union is a welders' union. The effect of the welders' union operating on both the supply and demand fronts is to raise the equilibrium wage rate for welders from $400.00 per week to $600.00. The number of employed welders rises from 100,000 to 120,000.

This result may also occur when the supplier of a service is also the agent for the consumer. It is sometimes suggested that medical doctors can create their own demand as they prescribe the required treatment. This permits them to shift the demand curve. This principle may also apply to dentists and motor mechanics. For these cases, the position of the demand curve may depend

FIGURE 5.11   **A labour union may increase wages in an occupation by increasing the demand for labour in the occupation and by reducing the supply of labour to the occupation.**

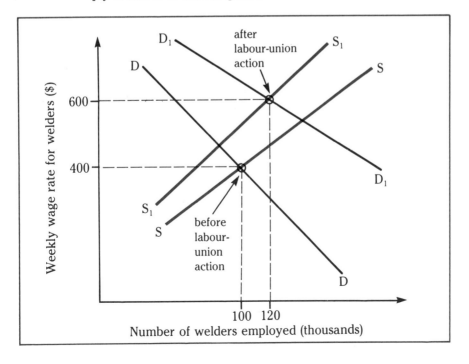

upon the information supplied to the consumer. Although labour unions or professional bodies can be successful in raising the incomes of their members, they do on occasion benefit at the expense of the rest of the community.

Subsidies for Production

The previous analysis can be used to examine the effect on market equilibrium of subsidizing the production of a product. The effect of a subsidy on production is to increase the supply of the subsidized product. Take oil as an example, and suppose that producers of oil are paid a subsidy of $4.00 for each barrel produced. If the supply curve of oil before the subsidy is introduced is as indicated by SS in Figure 5.12, the supply curve after the subsidy is introduced is as indicated by S_1S_1. The latter curve is lower than the former curve by an amount equivalent to the subsidy, $4.00. The same amount of oil is supplied at a market price after subsidy as would be supplied at a market price $4.00 higher than in the absence of the subsidy. In both instances, producers receive the same amount for each barrel of oil provided. For example, after the subsidy, 100,000,000 barrels of oil are supplied daily at a market price of $20.00 per barrel. The market price plus the subsidy amounts to $24.00. In the absence of a subsidy, 100,000,000 barrels are supplied at a market price of $24.00 per barrel. In both instances producers receive the same amount for each barrel of oil produced.

The effect on equilibrium prices and traded quantities of a subsidy on the production of a product depends on the slopes of the supply-and-demand curves for the product. In the example given in Figure 5.12, the downward slope of the demand curve equals the upward slope of the supply curve, and the equilibrium price falls by an amount equal to half the subsidy on each barrel of oil. Both buyers and sellers of oil gain from the subsidy. Buyers have a lower price, and sellers receive a higher effective price. If the demand curve is relatively flat, the fall in equilibrium price is smaller. The steeper the demand curve, other things equal, the greater is the fall in the equilibrium price of a product when its production is subsidized. Also, the steeper the supply curve, other things being equal, the smaller is the fall in equilibrium price of a product when its production is subsidized. A steeply sloped supply curve indicates that supply responds little to an increase in the price of the product being considered. Thus, its production also expands little in response to a subsidy, and the subsidy may not significantly lower the equilibrium price of the product.

Suppose that before the imposition of a sales tax the supply of liqueurs is as shown by SS, and that the demand curve is as shown by DD in Figure 5.13. After the imposition of a sales tax of $10/L, the supply curve for liqueurs shifts up to S_2S_2. As illustrated, the equilibrium price of liqueurs rises and the equilibrium supply falls. The steeper the demand curve, other things being equal, the greater the rise in equilibrium price as a result of the imposition of a sales tax. In addition, the flatter the supply curve, other things being equal, the

FIGURE 5.12   **The introduction of a subsidy on a product increases the supply of the product and normally lowers its equilibrium price.**

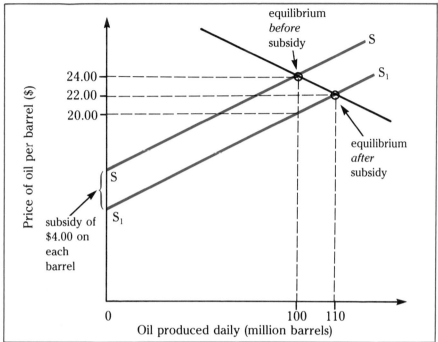

FIGURE 5.13   **A sales tax has the reverse effect of a subsidy, and normally raises the equilibrium price of the taxed product and lowers its equilibrium supply.**

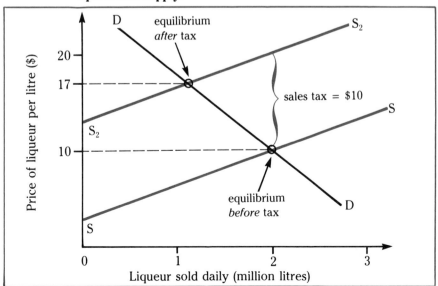

greater the rise in equilibrium price of the product. When the demand curve for
a product is very steep, the imposition of a sales tax causes the price of the product to rise by the whole, or almost the whole, amount of the sales tax, and
does not result in a very large fall in demand. A tax on a product of this nature
is likely to be very productive of revenue for the government. It is suggested
that this is one of the reasons why excise and sales taxes are commonly levied
by governments on liqueurs, tobacco, and tobacco products.

Elasticities of Demand

Own Price Elasticity of Demand

Elasticities measure the proportionate change in one variable relative to a proportionate change in another related variable. They find a number of applications in economics. For instance, the elasticity of the quantity demanded of a
commodity in relation to variations in its own price, sometimes called the *own
price elasticity of demand* for the commodity *e*, is equal to

$$e = \frac{\textit{percentage change in the quantity demanded of the commodity}}{\textit{percentage change in the price of the commodity}}$$

For example, suppose that the price of eggs is increased by 1 percent and
that, other things unchanged, the quantity demanded of eggs falls by 0.5 percent. Disregarding the negative sign,

$$e = \frac{0.5}{1} = 0.5$$

As the own price elasticity, *e*, is less than 1, the price elasticity of demand for
eggs in relation to their price is said to be inelastic.

It is worthwhile distinguishing between cases in which the elasticity of
demand is said to be *elastic*, of *unitary elasticity*, or *inelastic*. When the elasticity coefficient, *e*, is greater than unity (elastic), the proportionate change in
quantity demanded exceeds the proportionate change in the commodity's
price; when *e* equals unity, the proportionate change of quantity demanded
and the proportionate change in price are equal; and when the elasticity coefficient is less than unity (inelastic), the proportionate variation in the quantity
demanded of a commodity is less than the proportionate change in its price.
These relationships are summarized in Table 5.2.

Total Revenue and Elasticity of Demand

The elasticity of demand for a product and total revenue are related to one
another. (*Total revenue* is the total sum of money received from the sale of a
product, and equals the quantity of the product sold times the price of the product.) A small proportionate rise in the price of the product lowers total

TABLE 5.2 **Relationships between elasticities of demand, variations in the price of the product, and variations in the quantity demanded of the product, and changes of total revenue**

Value of Elasticity Coefficient	Nature of Elasticity	Proportionate Change in Quantity Demanded in Relation to a Proportionate Increase in the Product's Price	Change in Total Revenue for an Increase in the Price of the Product
e > 1	Elastic	Former exceeds latter	Declines
e = 1	Unitary	Former equals latter	Unchanged
e < 1	Inelastic	Former less than latter	Increases

revenue when the demand for the product is elastic, raises total revenue when demand is inelastic, and leaves total revenue unchanged when demand is of unitary elasticity. Conversely, when a small proportionate rise in the price of the product, other things unchanged, lowers the total revenue received from its sale, the demand for the product is elastic; when such a change leaves total revenue unchanged, the demand for the product is of unitary elasticity; and when total revenue rises as a result of a small proportionate rise in the price of a product, the demand for the product is inelastic. Thus, *variations in total revenue can be used as a method by which to determine the elasticity of demand for a product.*

The relationship between the elasticity of demand for a product and total revenue can be applied in a number of ways. For instance, a company that is considering raising the price of its product is able to predict whether this will increase or lower its total receipts if it knows the elasticity of demand for its product. For example, a car manufacturer may be considering raising the price of its cars. It is estimated that the price elasticity of demand for its cars is 0.8, and therefore, being less than unity, is inelastic. Consequently, a small rise in the price of the company's cars will raise its revenue. Again, suppose that an agriculture board is considering whether to lower the selling price of wheat, and is aiming to raise the revenue, or receipts, of wheat growers. The elasticity of demand is estimated to be $e = 1.1$. Would the receipts received by the board on behalf of wheat growers rise as a result of the lowering of price? Yes, because the demand for wheat in this case is price *elastic*. But if e happened to be 0.9 so that it is *inelastic*, the lowering in price would lower total revenue.

Slope of Demand Curve and Elasticity of Demand

It is sometimes possible to gain an *impression* of whether the demand for a product is inelastic or elastic by considering the slope of the demand curve for a product. There is a tendency for demand to be elastic when the demand curve

FIGURE 5.14   **A perfectly elastic demand curve is horizontal.**

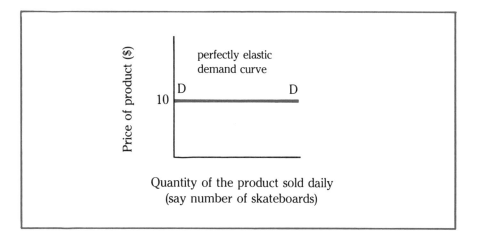

FIGURE 5.15   **A perfectly inelastic demand curve is vertical.**

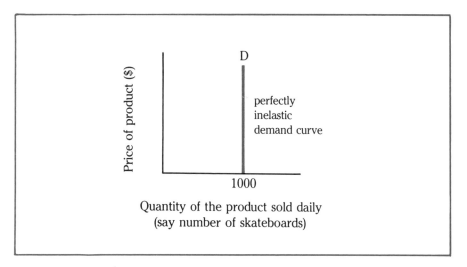

has little downward slope (tends to be horizontal), and to be inelastic when it has a steep downward slope (tends to be vertical). An example of a perfectly elastic demand curve is given in Figure 5.14, and an example of a perfectly inelastic demand curve is given in Figure 5.15.

A perfectly inelastic demand curve is also most unusual. It implies that the same amount of the product is purchased no matter what is the price of the product. At a high enough price, the demand for any product must eventually fall because, the incomes of individuals being given, they are insufficient to main-

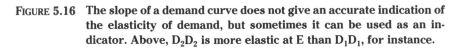

FIGURE 5.16   The slope of a demand curve does not give an accurate indication of the elasticity of demand, but sometimes it can be used as an indicator. Above, D_2D_2 is more elastic at E than D_1D_1, for instance.

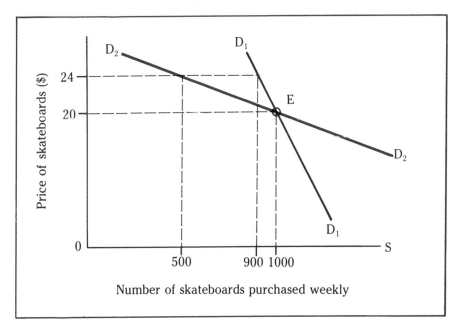

tain their volume of purchases once prices reach very high levels. Nevertheless, the demand for necessities such as food has been shown to be relatively inelastic.

Although the slope of a demand curve can be related to its elasticity (this is clear in the extreme examples given in figures 5.14 and 5.15), the *relationship is not an exact one*. When we compare two products, and their price relative to the quantity demanded of them is the same, the product with the steepest demand-curve exhibits the greatest inelasticity at that point. Thus, in Figure 5.16, the demand curve D_1D_1 for skateboards indicates a more inelastic demand for skateboards than D_2D_2 when the price of skateboards is $20.00 each. In the former instance, there is a smaller percentage decline in skateboard sales for a 1 percent rise in the price than in the latter. In the former instance, a 20-percent rise in the price of skateboards leads to a 10-percent fall in the volume of sales of skateboards, whereas in the latter it leads to a 50-percent fall in the number of skateboards sold.

As a rule, although not invariably, the elasticity of a demand curve varies for different points on the demand curve, that is, for different prices of the product. If the demand curve, for instance, is a downward sloping straight line, a curve of the same slope throughout its elasticity varies along the curve. This underlines the point that *the slope of demand curve does not measure its elasticity.* It can be shown that when the demand curve for a product is a downward sloping straight line, demand for the product is inelastic at low prices, and is elastic at high prices. At low prices, an increase in the price of the product raises the total revenue received from sales of the product, and at high prices, an increase in the price of the product lowers total revenue.

Factors Influencing the Elasticity of Demand for a Product

Several factors affect the price elasticity of demand for a product. The greater the number of *close substitutes* for a product, the greater is likely to be the elasticity of demand for it. For instance, in recent years man-made fibres have been developed that are to some extent substitutes for wool. These developments have increased the price elasticity of demand for wool.

A product that has a range of uses is also likely to be in relatively elastic demand. This is because substitutes are likely to exist for it in some of its uses. A product, the purchases of which absorb a small part of an individual's income, is liable to be inelastic in demand. For example, expenditure on salt or on pepper are small in relation to incomes. A rise of 50 percent in the prices of these products would have little effect on their purchase by households.

The longer the period of time for which the price change operates, the greater is likely to be the elasticity of demand. In the long period, consumers are able to search for substitutes, if the price rises, and change their habits to a greater extent than in the short term.

The demand for a product does not only depend on its price. Other factors such as incomes, and the prices of other products, also affect the demand for a product, and elasticities of their influence can be computed.

Income Elasticity of Demand

The income elasticity of demand for a product is measured by dividing the proportionate change in the demand for a product (resulting from a proportionate increase in income) by the proportionate increase in income. In terms of percentages, the income elasticity coefficient, e_y, for a product can be expressed as

$$e_y = \frac{\textit{percentage change in quantity demanded of product}}{\textit{percentage increase in income}}$$

other influences on demand being held constant. Thus, if the demand for oranges rises by 5 percent when incomes rise by 1 percent, the income elasticity coefficient for oranges is

$$5/1 = 5.$$

When $e_y > 1$, the elasticity of demand with respect to income is elastic. In Canada, the demand for recreation, travel, and electricity appear to be income elastic. When $e_y < 1$, the elasticity of demand with respect to income is inelastic. Although the quantity of food demanded rises as incomes in Canada increase, it does not rise proportionately. The demand for food as a whole is income inelastic. It is possible too for the demand for some goods to fall as incomes rise. These goods are called *inferior goods*. The demand for potatoes and the demand for bread per head of population appear to have fallen in Canada as incomes have risen.

As noted earlier, the income elasticity of demand for agricultural products is less than for manufactured products, and less than for the products and services of the tertiary sector. As a nation develops and incomes rise, this changes the structure of the economy. For instance, the relative size of the tertiary sector grows as a nation develops and incomes rise.

Cross Elasticity of Demand

The cross elasticity of demand for a product is another measure of responsiveness of demand. It measures the relative variation in demand for a product in proportion to a relative increase in the price of another product. For instance, a rise in the price of gasoline may reduce the demand for cars, and increase the demand for public transport. The relative effect on an increase in the price of one product, say Y, on that of another, say X, is measured by the cross elasticity coefficient, *c.e.*:

$$c.e. = \frac{percentage\ change\ in\ quantity\ demanded\ of\ X}{percentage\ increase\ in\ the\ price\ of\ Y}$$

If a 20-percent rise in gasoline prices leads to a 1-percent increase in the demand for public transport, other things being equal, the cross elasticity of demand for public transport in relation to gasoline prices is

$$c.e. = 1/20 = 0.05.$$

This indicates that there is some substitution of public transport for private transport when prices rise. Positive cross elasticities of demand between goods indicate that they are substitutes. For instance, one would expect a positive cross elasticity between the demand for margarine and the demand for butter. A negative cross elasticity indicates that goods are complements. Tents and camping equipment are complementary. An increase in the price of tents can be expected to reduce the demand for accessories such as sleeping bags to be used in tents. If a 10-percent increase in the price of tents reduces the demand for sleeping bags by 2 percent,

$$c.e. = 2/10 = -0.2.$$

Elasticities of Supply

Own Price Elasticity of Supply

The responsiveness of supplies to various influences on supply can be measured by means of elasticities. For instance, *the own price elasticity of supply* for a product measures the relative change in the supply of the product in proportion to a relative increase in its price, other prices remaining constant. The own price elasticity of supply coefficient, e_s, can be expressed as

$$e_s = \frac{percentage\ change\ in\ quantity\ supplied\ of\ product}{percentage\ rise\ in\ the\ price\ of\ the\ product}$$

Normally, we would expect this coefficient to be positive.

Once again it is dangerous to infer the elasticity of supply of a product from the slope of its supply curve, even though this can be done in the following extreme cases:

1. If the supply curve of a product is horizontal, the supply of the product is perfectly elastic, and vice versa. An example of a perfectly elastic supply curve is shown in Figure 5.17.
2. If the supply curve of a product is vertical, the supply of the product is perfectly inelastic. Supply is unaffected by a variation in the price of a product. An example of this is shown in Figure 5.18. Extreme cases do not, however, occur frequently.

For straight-line supply curves, it can be shown that they are elastic (elasticity greater than unity) if they intersect the positive Y axis, and inelastic (elasticity less than unity) if they intersect the positive X axis, irrespective of their slope.

FIGURE 5.17 **Example of a perfectly elastic supply curve**

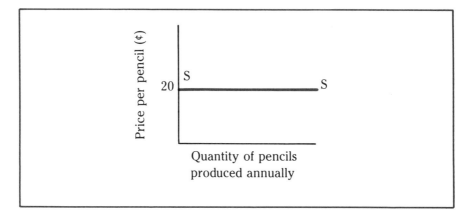

FIGURE 5.18 **Example of a perfectly inelastic supply curve**

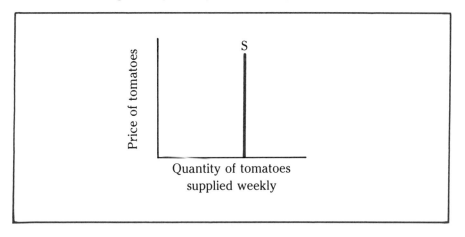

The own price elasticity of supply of a product can change for a number of reasons. It may become more elastic because new inventions make it easier to vary supply in response to price changes. The elasticity of supply is likely to be greater in the long run than in the short run because in the long run the use of more resources can be altered and new firms can easily commence production.

Cross-Price Elasticity of Supply

A corresponding concept to that of cross elasticity of demand is *cross elasticity of supply*. This measures the relative change in the supply of one product in proportion to a relative change in the price of another, other factors constant. For instance, if X represents one product and Y another, the cross elasticity of supply of X in relation to the price of Y is

$$c.e_s = \frac{\textit{percentage change in quantity supplied of } X}{\textit{percentage increase in the price of } Y}$$

Thus, if the price of Y rises by 5 percent, and the supply of X declines by 10 percent

$$c.e_s = -10/5 = -2.$$

A decline of this nature may come about because some producers find it more profitable to produce product Y rather than X once the price of Y rises, other prices remaining constant. In our economy, the supply products are interdependent, and cross elasticities of supply provide measures of the degree of this interdependence. We would expect in Canada such cross elasticities to be high between such products as wheat and coarse grains.

KEY CONCEPTS
(FOR REVIEW)

Complements
Cross-price elasticity of demand
Cross-price elasticity of supply
Elastic demand
Elasticities
Elasticities of demand
Equilibrium in a market
Equilibrium-market price
Equilibrium quantities traded
Excise tax
Income elasticity of demand
Inelastic demand
Inferior goods
Market-demand curve
Market model
Market-supply curve
Movement along demand curve
Movement along supply curve
Own price elasticity of demand
Own price elasticity of supply
Perfectly elastic demand curve

Perfectly elastic supply curve
Perfectly inelastic demand curve
Perfectly inelastic supply curve
Price mechanism
Price regulation
Production certificates
Quotas on production
Rationing
Sales tax
Shift of demand curve
Shift of demand curve to the left
Shift of demand curve to the right
Shift of supply curve
Shift of supply curve to the left
Shift of supply curve to the right
Slope of demand curve
Subsidies on production
Substitutes
Total Revenue
Unitary elasticity of demand

QUESTIONS FOR REVIEW AND DISCUSSION

1. What does the market-demand curve for a commodity indicate? List some
    of the factors that are held constant when the market-demand curve for a
    commodity (showing the quantity demanded of the commodity as a func-
    tion of its price) is constructed.
2. What is the normal relationship between the price of a commodity and
    the quantity demanded of it? Why might such a relationship exist?
3. In the example in Table 5.1, what is the effect on the quantity demanded
    of shoes of raising the price of shoes from $10.00 per pair to $60.00 per
    pair? Show how this involves a *movement along* the demand curve for
    shoes.
4. Assume that the quantities of shoes listed in the second column of Table
    5.1 are demanded at *half the price* listed in the first column. For example,
    at $5.00, 7,000,000 pairs of shoes are demanded, and at $40.00 per pair,
    no shoes are demanded. Set out the demand schedule and construct the
    corresponding demand curve.
5. What does the market-supply curve for a commodity indicate?

6. What is the normal relationship between the quantity supplied of a commodity and its price? Why may such a relationship exist?

7. In the example in Table 5.1, what is the effect on the quantity supplied of shoes of raising the price of shoes from $10.00 per pair to $60.00 per pair?

8. Assume that the quantities of shoes listed in the third column in Table 5.1 are supplied at *half the price* listed in the first column. Set out the supply schedule, and construct the corresponding supply curve.

9. "The market equilibrium price balances demand and supply." Explain.

10. "The equilibrium price of a commodity corresponds to the price at which its supply curve crosses its demand curve." Explain.

11. Are actual market prices and traded quantities always equilibrium ones?

12. Give an example of how market prices and traded quantities tend toward equilibrium ones.

13. What is the level of the equilibrium price of shoes and the equilibrium quantity of shoes traded if the demand curve is the one you constructed in answering Question 4, and the supply curve is the one you constructed in answering Question 8?

14. Explain, using a diagram, how government measures restricting the maximum price of a product to a level below the market equilibrium will result in some demands being unsatisfied at the regulated price. How may the limited supply be rationed out if price is not allowed to serve this role?

15. "Measures designed to help the needy such as the placing of ceilings on prices by the government may fail to help the needy." Explain, giving examples.

16. "The high level of youth unemployment in Canada may be attributable to some extent to the high level of the minimum wage for juniors". Discuss and explain.

17. Why is it usually necessary to introduce quotas or restrictions on the supply of a product by individual suppliers when the minimum price of the product is set in excess of its equilibrium? Discuss the advantages and disadvantages of the use of saleable certificates for specified amounts of production in the milk industry in Ontario as a means for limiting supplies.

18. List some of the factors that may cause the demand curve for a commodity (say ginger ale) to shift to the right, that is, increase at any given price of the commodity.

19. Distinguish between the reason for a movement along a demand curve and for a shift of the curve.

20. List some of the factors that may cause the supply curve of a commodity (say wheat) to shift to the right.

21. Distinguish between the reason for a movement along a supply curve and for a shift of the curve.

22. Supply conditions unchanged, what is the normal effect on the equilibrium levels of price and supply of a commodity of a rise in demand

for the commodity (shift in its demand curve to the right)? Take some product as an example (e.g., bicycles), and illustrate your answer using a diagram.

23. Demand conditions unchanged, what is the normal effect on the equilibrium levels of price and demand for a commodity of a rise in the supply of the commodity (a shift in its supply curve to the right)? Illustrate your answer by means of a diagram. Take some product (e.g., vegetable oil) as an example.

24. Why have agricultural prices tended to decline? How can supply-and-demand analysis be used to illustrate the trend?

25. "It is sometimes possible for labour unions to raise wages in their trade by shifting the demand-and-supply curves for labour in their trade." Explain.

26. Suppose that gold production is subsidized. What effect is the subsidy likely to have on the equilibrium price and supply of gold?

27. Suppose that a sales tax is imposed on video cassettes. What effect is it likely to have on the equilibrium price and supply of video cassettes?

28. Suppose that the demand for skateboards is given by

$$D = 500 - 15p,$$

and the supply is given by

$$S = 100 + 5p.$$

Determine the equilibrium price and supply for skateboards.

29. Suppose the government levies a $4.00 tax on each skateboard sold causing the supply curve to become

$$S = 100 + 5 (p-4).$$

a. Graph this supply curve and the one in Question 28, and verify that the tax has shifted the supply curve vertically by the amount of the tax.

b. Determine the equilibrium price and output. What is the price received by suppliers? Who "pays" the tax?

30. What do elasticities measure? What does the own price elasticity of demand for a commodity measure?

31. Explain the circumstances in which the own price elasticity of demand for a product is

a. elastic,
b. of unitary elasticity,
c. inelastic.

32. After conducting a market survey, a car manufacturer concludes that the own price elasticity of demand for its cars at current prices is 2. Would it be correct in believing that an increase in its prices will increase total revenue? Would this be so if the elasticity happened to be 0.5?

33. "Although the slope of a demand curve can be related to its elasticity, the relationship is not an exact one." Discuss.

34. What circumstances are likely to increase the own price elasticity demand for a product?

35. What does the income elasticity of demand for a product measure? Give examples of products

  a. for which the income elasticity of demand exceeds unity, and
  b. for which it is less than unity.

36. What does the cross elasticity of demand for a product measure? What does a positive cross elasticity between two products indicate about the substitutability of the product concerned? What does a negative cross elasticity indicate?

37. What does the own price elasticity of supply for a product measure? What does a cross elasticity of supply measure?

FURTHER READING

Auld, D.A.L., & Miller, F.C., *Principles of Public Finance: A Canadian Text*, 2nd ed., Toronto: Methuen Publications, 1982, chapters 11 & 12.

Blomqvist, A., Wonnacott, P., & Wonnacott, R., *Economics*, 1st Canadian ed. Scarborough: McGraw-Hill Ryerson Limited, 1984, chapters, 4, 19, 20, 30, & 31.

Gunderson, M., *Labour Market Economics: Theory, Evidence, and Policy in Canada.* Scarborough: McGraw-Hill Ryerson Limited, 1980.

Lipsey, R.G., Purvis, D.D., Sparks, G.R., & Steiner, P.O., *Economics*, 4th ed. New York: Harper & Row, Publishers, 1982, chapters 5, 6, 7, & 8.

Samuelson, P.A., & Scott, A.D., *Economics.* Scarborough: McGraw-Hill Ryerson Limited, 1980, chapters 4, 20, & 21.

Schmitz, A., "Supply Management in Canadian Agriculture: An Assessment of the Economic Effects." *Canadian Journal of Agricultural Economics*, v. 31 (1983), pp. 135-52.

6 Introduction to Market Structure, Welfare and Monopoly

Alternative Market Structures

Not all markets for commodities operate in the same way or with the same efficiency. For instance, a market in which there is one seller of a product is likely to operate differently from one in which there are *many* sellers of a product in competition with one another. In the latter case, competition may keep the market price of the product down.

The number of sellers of a product and the number of buyers of a product are factors helping to determine what economists describe as the *structure* of the market. The extent to which production is concentrated in the hands of one or a few producers may be another material factor to consider in describing the structure of a market. If most of the production of a product is accounted for by one producer, it may be sufficiently dominant to influence the pricing and supply policies of other producers. The structure of a market and the nature of competition within it are usually related.

Let us consider some market structures and types of competition. Each market has a *buying side* and a *selling side*. The buying side for most products is competitive, and indeed would appear to approximate perfect competition. There are usually many buyers (consumers — generally households) of a product in competition with one another, and they appear on the whole to be reasonably well-informed about relevant prices.

On the selling side of the market for a product, perfect competition, or an approximation to it, is less common. In many manufacturing industries in Canada, and in several service industries, there are often only a few producers. For instance, there are few producers of refined sugar in Canada, three major car producers, and five major banks. On the other hand, there are generally a large number of producers of agricultural products. For example, there are thousands of producers of milk and of grain in Canada.

A market situation in which there are *many* suppliers of identical products competing with one another is described as a situation of **perfect competition**, or of **pure competition**. In the case of perfect competition, sellers are assumed to be extremely well informed about market prospects. This is not necessarily so for pure competition, however. Because of the large number of sellers in these market situations, each supplier is forced to take the market price of the product as given. A seller is powerless to influence the market price by withholding its supplies because they are small in relation to the total supplies. A seller will be unable to make any sales if it tries to charge more than the market price, and will be swamped with orders if it charges less than the going price. There are other market situations, however, in which sellers can influence the price of the product they are selling.

Under conditions of *monopolistic competition*, there are a large number of sellers of a product as in a perfectly competitive market, but products are differentiated to some extent. For instance, in most cities, there are a large number of restaurants each of which is slightly different in character to the other. Any one of these restaurants could raise the price of its products to some extent without losing *all* of its sales. Customers close to the restaurant and "loyal" customers may still continue to patronize a restaurant that raises its prices. But its sales may fall substantially for any significant rise in its prices because the dinners from other restaurants are likely to be close substitutes. The market power of an individual restaurant, and most retailers of goods, is limited. The demand curves for their products slope downward, but are relatively flat.

Oligopoly refers to the market situation in which there are comparatively few sellers of a given product. Each seller realizes that the other sellers have a significant impact upon the operation of the market. Any firm that considers changing its market strategy (for example, changing the price of its product) must also consider the possible responses made by other producers. If Ford Motor Company considers lowering the price of compact cars in order to stimulate Ford sales, it must consider the possibility that other car producers such as Chrysler and Volkswagen may follow with similar price reductions in order to maintain their own sales. If the Bank of Nova Scotia considers raising the interest rate they charge for mortgages, it must consider the possibility that other banks such as the Toronto-Dominion Bank and the Royal Bank may not. In this instance, the Bank of Nova Scotia could lose customers to the other banks. Given the uncertain nature of possible reactions, firms in oligopolistic industries may tend to "stick" to a conventional price or may follow the "lead" of one of the firms in altering prices. The firm that sets the trend for prices is referred to as the *price leader* for that market.

Monopoly refers to a market situation where there is only one seller of a product. In Canada, telegraph communications are a monopoly of CNCP. Provincial government liquor stores have a monopoly in the retail of liquor and imported wine in many provinces. A monopolist generally has market power, power to raise or lower the price of its product. The extent of its market power depends upon whether suitable substitutes for its product are readily available. It also depends on how easy it is for other producers to enter the industry. The threat of entry by other producers can limit a monopolist's market power.

As a monopolist is the sole producer or seller in a given market, the market demand curve is the demand curve facing the monopolist. With a downward sloping demand curve, the monopolist is able to control the product's price by controlling the supply of the product made available to the market. As the monopolist reduces the available supply to the market, price rises as a result of a movement leftward along the demand curve. Such reductions in supply may permit the monopolist to increase profits more than if there were competitors that could also supply the product. Thus, when production is in the hands of a monopolist, price will tend to be higher and production lower than is possible and socially desirable.

Perfect Competition, Monopoly, and Scarcity

Perfect Competition and Scarcity

The market demand curve for a product shows the prices that buyers of a product are willing to pay for various quantities of it. It also shows the *additional value* that buyers or consumers place on additional quantities of the product. Under conditions of perfect competition, the supply curve of a product indicates the additional costs of producing an extra unit of the product. As long as the value placed upon extra production of a product by buyers or consumers exceeds its cost of extra production, there is a social case in favour of expanding production of the product. If on the other hand, the value of additional production of a product is less than the cost of the additional production, there is a social loss involved in expanding production of the product. A social optimum is reached when the production of the product is such that the value of the last unit produced equals its cost of production. Under perfect competition, this occurs for the market equilibrium quantity of a product.

The supply curve for a firm in perfect competition is its marginal cost (MC) curve. Recall that the firm's cost curves were discussed in Chapter 4. The MC of producing a given level of output of a product, say of eighteen skateboards, is the additional costs incurred in producing the last unit — the eighteenth skateboard. A firm in perfect competition will produce at an output level for which the price of the product is equal to the marginal cost of producing that level. In Figure 6.1, the market price of skateboards is $25.00. Thus, the largest number of skateboards that the firm should supply is twenty, as the MC of producing twenty skateboards is $25.00 also. The firm will not produce more than twenty skateboards because the additional costs exceed the price the firm could receive. In Figure 6.1, the MC of twenty-one skateboards is $30.00. If the market price is only $25.00, then the firm loses $5.00 of profit by expanding production by one stakeboard. Only if the market price rises to $30.00, would the firm be willing to produce twenty-one skateboards.[1]

---

[1]This discussion presumes that market price exceeds average variable costs. If the price is below average variable costs, then even with price equal to MC the firm is failing to cover the cost of all skateboards produced. In this case, the firm should stop production altogether.

FIGURE **6.1 Firms in perfect competition produce a level of output for which price equals marginal cost.**

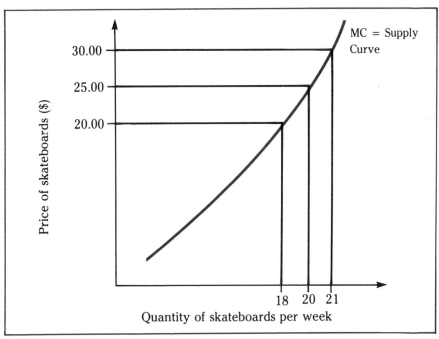

Suppose that the average cost of producing twenty skateboards is $22.00. Then the firm makes $60.00 profit on the total production. Although perfectly competitive firms may earn such profits for a while (in the short-run), these profits will ultimately be reduced to zero (in the long-run). The profits being earned in the industry will attract new firms and the market supply expands from S to S'; that is, the market-supply curve shifts outward. As supply increases, the price of the product will fall as the economy moves downward along the market-demand curve.

In terms of Figure 6.2, price would fall from $25.00 to $22.00 per skateboard, and the number of skateboards purchased would increase from 2000 to 3000. If price were to fall below $22.00, the firms would be suffering losses as the lowest average cost is $22.00. These losses would encourage some firms to close operation, and total supply would adjust back to S'. Firms enter (exit) competitive industries when profits (losses) are being earned. This entry (exit) results in market supply increasing (decreasing) and market price falling (increasing). Ultimately, the price of the product equals the minimum average cost of producing the product.[2]

[2]This average cost includes what economists call "normal profit", which is the return required by the firm to be willing to continue in operation rather than closing operations and switching to an alternative activity. The normal profits of a firm are determined by its opportunity costs.

FIGURE **6.2** **Short-run profits lead to entry of new firms, which causes a reduction in price and zero profits in the long-run for perfectly competitive industries.**

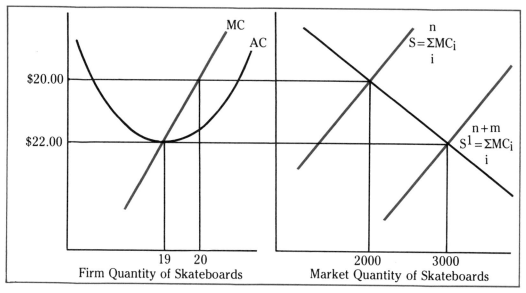

From a social point of view, this represents an efficient use of resources in this industry as the social value per unit of output (i.e., price) is just equal to the social cost of producing that unit (its average cost).

Monopoly and Scarcity

A monopolist is likely, because of the absence of competition, to create an artificial scarcity of his product. This can be illustrated by a simple example. Suppose that a single stream passes through a desert region, and that this stream is the sole source of supply of water for inhabitants in that region. Assume that the daily flow of the water in the stream is 5,000,000 L. Suppose the inhabitants draw their own water from the stream, and that their demand for water varies with the price per litre that they have to pay for the privilege of being able to draw water. The relationship between the price per litre of water and the daily demand for it might be like that set out in columns 1 and 2 of Table 6.1.

Suppose that the stream is owned by one person. He is a monopolist. What price should he charge per litre of water to maximize his profit? As the water is free, a gift of nature, he has no costs; so, the price that maximizes his total revenue will maximize his profit. Total revenue is set out in the third column of Table 6.1, and is maximized when the price of water is $1.00 per litre. The monopolist obtains a total revenue of $2 million daily when he charges this price and 2,000,000 L of water are consumed. But as the water costs nothing and is in relatively abundant supply, it can be argued that it should be a free product. When water is free, 4,000,000 L are demanded daily, a quantity less than the available daily supply. If a positive charge is made for water consumption, consumers will place a higher value on extra consumption than the extra cost of meeting this additional consumption. A case would therefore exist for reducing price and expanding water consumption.

TABLE 6.1 **An example of the relationship between the price of water and total revenue**

Price of Water Per Litre ($)	Quantity of Water Purchased Daily (Million Litres)	Total Revenue — Price × Quantity ($ million)
2.00	0	0.00
1.50	1	1.50
1.00	2	2.00
0.50	3	1.50
0.00	4	0.00

Under perfect competition, that is if different parts of the stream happen to be owned by many different individuals, water would be free or close to it. If any supplier tried to charge for access to the stream, another supplier would find it profitable to undercut him.

This case is summarized by Figure 6.3 in which DD represents the demand curve for water. The hatched area indicates the maximum revenue that can be obtained by a monopolist. As illustrated, he restricts production to obtain an "unearned" profit. This restriction in production (in comparison to the optimal level and the level under perfect competition) leads to a social loss.

The foregoing example illustrates in an easy fashion the principal results of the theory of monopoly — supply of output is reduced to the market and price is increased above the competition level. The example presumes that production is costless, however. When production costs are not zero, then the analysis is somewhat more complex.

In deciding upon the level of output to produce, the monopolist must balance marginal revenue (MR) with MC, as does a competitive producer. The MR for the monopolist, however, differs from the competitive situation. The competitive firm is a *price-taker*, and the prevailing output price is the MR earned from selling an extra unit. The monopolist is not a price-taker but rather is a *price-maker*. The monopolist determines the price by determining the level of output. As the monopolist faces a downward sloping demand curve, expanding output reduces the market price. In supplying extra output to the market, MR will be less than the prevailing price as price will decline as output expands.

When the market-demand curve for the monopolist's product is a straight

FIGURE **6.3 Illustration of the way in which a monopolist can increase scarcity by
limiting available supplies of a commodity**

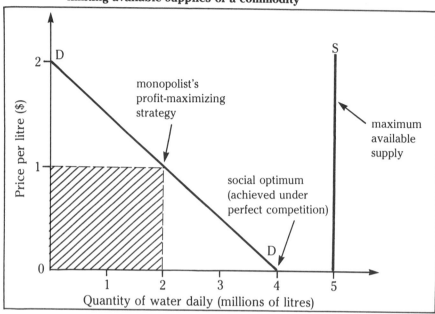

line, so is the MR curve, as shown in Figure 6.4. The demand curve and the MR
curve have a common point on the price axis, and the MR curve is twice as
steep as the demand curve. The MR curve intersects the quantity axis at half
the distance to where the demand curve intersects the quantity axis.

The MR = 0 when the price elasticity of demand is equal to unity. When
the demand curve is price elastic, then MR is positive, and when the demand
curve is price inelastic, the MR is negative. In the latter case, expanding output
reduces revenue. Clearly, a monopolist would not want to operate on the inelastic portion of the demand curve. The monopolist will operate in the elastic
portion of the demand curve in general. Where, in this portion, depends upon
the MC curve.

The monopolist will maximize profits when it produces an output for which
MR = MC, and charges a price determined by the demand curve at that output.

In Figure 6.5, MR = MC when output is 300 skateboards per month. The
market price is $25.00 and the AC is $20.00. Total profit is $5.00 × 300 =
$1500 per month.

Markets and Welfare:
Additional Factors to Consider

The above discussion indicates that a perfectly competitive market is likely to
be more desirable than a monopolized market, from the point of view of reducing scarcity. In many countries, legislation has been passed restricting the for-

FIGURE 6.4 The demand curve and the marginal revenue curve

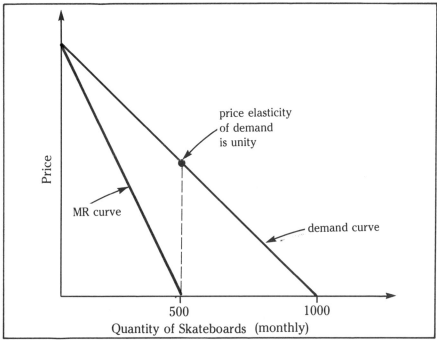

FIGURE 6.5 Maximum monopoly profits occur at MR = MC.

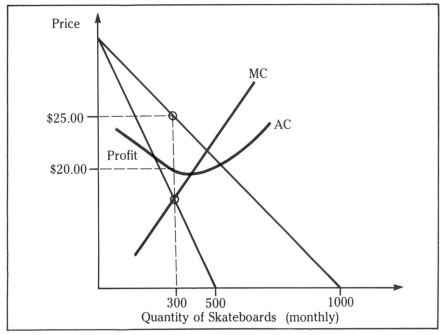

mation of monopolies, for example, legislation that prevents companies from
merging when this will result in a monopoly. The real world, however, is more
complicated than that discussed above.

Economies of Scale and Optimal Market Structure

In some circumstances, perfect competition is not a workable alternative to
monopoly. This is likely to be so when *economies of scale* are obtained, for instance, in production by a single firm expanding its size or production until it
absorbs the whole market for a product. Technical advances and the adoption
of new technology may also be faster when there is some restriction on competition. If innovations are rapidly copied, as can occur when competition is
intense, innovators and inventors may earn little for their effort and lose their
incentive to innovate and invent.

Duplication of suppliers also increases costs in other circumstances. For
instance, duplication of water, electricity, and telephone installations would
add to the cost of providing water, electricity, and communications. Consider
for instance, the extra cost of having duplicated water mains and electricity
lines in the same street.

In Canada, governments provide these services in part to guard against
possible exploitation by private monopolies. By contrast, in the United States,
many public utilities are provided by private companies. Their prices, however,
are regulated by the government to prevent overcharging.

Divergence between Private and Social Cost

In the above discussion of the efficiency of perfectly competitive markets, it is
assumed that private and social costs of production do not differ. It is assumed
that the cost to a firm of producing its product also reflects the cost to society as
a whole of producing its product. Unfortunately, this assumption is not always
satisfied. In some circumstances, production by a firm may impose a cost on the
rest of society that is not paid for by the firm. For instance, a firm may emit
pollutants into the environment without charge, and these may impose a cost
on other members of the community; for example, the emission of smoke by a
factory may mean that houses in the neighbourhood have to be cleaned and
painted more frequently, or the release of chemicals into a river may kill fish
and impose a cost by lowering the fishing catch. Effects of this kind are called
unfavourable externalities. On some occasions, a favourable externality may
occur. For instance, by keeping bees, an apiarist may benefit nearby orchards.

The effect of externalities, or of environmental spillovers, as they are sometimes called, on the efficient operation of markets can be illustrated by a simple
example. Suppose that there is a *perfectly competitive* industry producing
mechanical gadgets. Each mechanical gadget costs each firm $10.00 to pro-
duce; so, the supply curve of mechanical gadgets is the one marked S in Figure

FIGURE **6.6** **When externalities (or environmental spillovers) are present, the market equilibrium level of output of a product may not be socially optimal. In the case illustrated, the social cost of producing each unit of the product exceeds the private cost, and an excessive amount of the product is produced in an unregulated competitive market.**

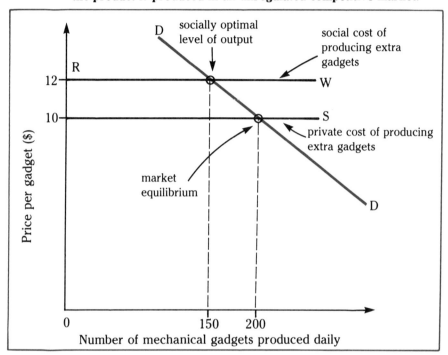

6.6. This supply curve represents the *private* costs of producing extra units or gadgets. Given the demand curve DD, market equilibrium is achieved when 200 gadgets are produced daily and sold at $10.00 each. Competition ensures that the price of gadgets falls to the private cost of producing each.

Assume that the production of each gadget, however, results in wastes that are deposited free of charge into nearby waterways, thereby reducing the edible fish population, and making these waterways less satisfactory for recreation. It is estimated that for each gadget produced, these external damages, or costs of environmental spillovers, amount to $2.00, so that the social cost of producing gadgets is $12.00 each. From a social point of view, the optimal number of gadgets to produce daily is 150. At this level of output, the social cost of extra production equals its extra value indicated by the demand curve. The level of output occurring in a free market, 200 gadgets per day, is socially excessive because at this level of output the social cost of producing an extra gadget, $12.00, exceeds its extra value of $10.00.

One way in which the socially optimal output of gadgets can be achieved is by imposing a suitable tax on their production. If the government imposes a tax

of $2.00 on each gadget produced, the after-tax cost to firms of producing
gadgets will be $12.00, and the new supply curve of gadgets will be RW (Figure
6.6). After the imposition of this tax, the market supplies 150 gadgets daily, the
socially optimal number.

In actual practice, the problem of ensuring that production and consumption decisions adequately take account of externalities, or spillovers, can be
more complex than indicated here. But the above example illustrates that
markets may not operate efficiently when spillovers are present, and that
government intervention may be necessary to ensure that private decisions are
adjusted to allow for these spillovers.

There are other circumstances in which markets do not operate as effective
providers of goods and services, some of which were outlined in Chapter 2. For
instance, it is difficult to market some commodities once they are provided
because individuals can use them without paying. Once a radio station or a
television channel provides a service, individuals may listen to or view this
without paying. It may be difficult to enforce payment in cases such as this. In
such circumstances, governments usually interfere to ensure the provision of
these commodities, and they are financed through taxes.

The general conclusion that emerges is that some government intervention
in the free operation of markets is needed to improve the way in which they
allocate resources, and provide for the wants of individuals. There is considerable room for argument about how much interference is needed and is desirable, however.

KEY CONCEPTS
(FOR REVIEW)

Economies of scale and duplication of suppliers	Perfect competition
Favourable externalities	Pollution taxes
Market structure	Private costs
Monopolistic competition	Pure competition
Monopoly	Social costs
Oligopoly	Spillovers
	Unfavourable externalities

QUESTIONS FOR REVIEW AND DISCUSSION

1. "Perfect competition is more common on the buying side of markets for
   products than on their selling side." Discuss.
2. Distinguish the following:

   a. perfect comptition,
   b. monopolistic competition,
   c. oligopoly, and
   d. monopoly.

Explain each market situation, and give examples of each.

3. Does the demand curve for a monopolist's product correspond to the market demand curve for that product? To what extent is it able to control the price of its product?

4. "Perfect competition ensures a socially optimal level of output." Discuss.

5. Suppose that the market-supply curve of a product represents the social cost of its extra production, and suppose that its market-demand curve indicates the social value of the extra production. What level of output is socially optimal?

6. Monopolists create an artificial scarcity. Why?

7. Why is scarcity of products likely to be greater when monopoly occurs than when perfect competition occurs?

8. Take the example set out in Table 6.1, and assume that, at the prices set out in the first column, *twice* the quantity of water shown in the second column is demanded. Under these conditions:

   a. What quantity of water will a monopolist supply and at what price?
   b. How much profit will the monopolist make?
   c. Compare the outcome under monopoly with that which might be expected under perfect competition.

   Draw a diagram to illustrate your answer.

9. Are there any circumstances in which it would seem to be preferable to have a monopoly rather than many producers in an industry?

10. Give some examples of favourable and of unfavourable externalities. How do such externalities cause social and private costs to diverge?

11. The private marginal cost of producing each extra tonne of caustic soda is $8.00, but the social cost is $10.00/t. Assuming perfect competition, will a socially optimal amount of caustic soda be produced? Will production be less or greater than this optimum? Illustrate your answer by means of a diagram.

12. Can a tax be used to correct the divergency between the actual and the socially optimal level of production of caustic soda (mentioned in Question 11)? What would be the appropriate amount of tax to levy on each tonne of caustic soda?

FURTHER READING

Blomqvist, A., Wonnacott, P., & Wonnacott, R., *Economics*, 1st Canadian ed. Scarborough: McGraw-Hill Ryerson Limited, 1984, chapters 22, 23, 24, 25, & 26.

Lipsey, R.G., Purvis, D.D., Sparks, G.R., & Steiner, P.O., *Economics*, 4th ed. New York: Harper & Row, Publishers, 1982, chapters 14, 15, 16, 17 & 18.

Samuelson, P.A., & Scott, A.D., *Economics*. Scarborough: McGraw-Hill Ryerson Limited, 1980, chapters 25 & 26.

7 The Circular Flow and Employment

A Simple Model of the Circular Flow

In our economy, most individuals specialize in the production or supply of one product or service, or of a limited number of goods and services, for which they receive a money income. The range and variety of commodities that they need for their own consumption is obtained by exchanging this money income. Chains, or patterns, of exchange in our economy give rise to a circular flow of income, employment, and economic activity. The level of economic activity, employment, and income depends upon how well the circular flow is maintained.

The Model

In order to illustrate the concept of circular flow, consider a simple case. Take a society in which the two main groups of decision-makers are households (consumers) and business firms. Householders (or the members of households) are the ultimate owners of resources (land, labour, and capital) in the society, and they supply these to firms in return for payments or income. Business firms in turn use these resources to produce commodities that they sell to households. The incomes of households provide the means to pay for the commodities that they buy from firms. The payments of households provide the receipts of business firms, which in turn are the means from which they purchase resources from households, and so provide them with income. A reduction of expenditure at any stage in this chain reduces income. For instance, if households do not spend all their income, the receipts of business firms fall and they do not have the means to pay out as much to households. The incomes of households therefore fall, and economic activity and employment may be reduced.

Figure 7.1 illustrates the circular flow for this simple case. The outside loop shows that households supply resources to business firms that use these to produce goods and services to supply to households. The inside loop of the figure shows that households receive money income from supplying resources to business firms; these they spend on the goods and services supplied by business firms, thus supplying the receipts of the firms and their means to pay incomes to households. *The outside loop illustrates the exchange of physical commodities and the inside loop the exchange of money, or monetary claims, that*

FIGURE 7.1 **The circular flow of real commodities and monetary claims in a simple economy**

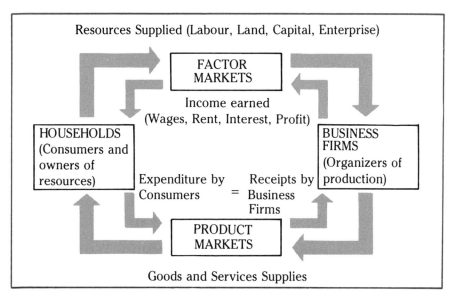

accompanies this. The upper section of the figure corresponds to markets for factors of production, and the lower sector corresponds to the market for finished products and services to be consumed.

Assumptions of the Model

This simple model is based on the assumption that there is:

1. no saving,
2. no government sector,
3. no foreign trade, and that
4. business firms only produce commodities for direct sale to consumers.

The last assumption is not a crucial one, but the others are and need to be relaxed. Attempts by consumers to save lead to leakages from the circular flow, and leakages need to be matched by expenditure elsewhere, e.g., by investment, expenditure on capital goods, if they are not to result in a reduction in economic activity. Government activity and foreign trade may result:

1. in leakages of expenditure from the circular flow, in which case they dampen economic activity, or
2. in injections of expenditure into the circular flow, in which case they lead to an expansion of economic activity.

We will consider these possibilities in the following section.

Leakages from and Injections into the Circular Flow: Savings, Investment, Taxation, Government Spending, Imports, and Exports.

A Circular Flow Model Allowing for Saving

Households, instead of spending all their income, may plan to, or may actually, save some of it. (Likewise, firms may save by not distributing all of their profits to shareholders.) Savings can be viewed as a leakage from the circular flow, and unless offset by an injection of spending, can reduce economic activity, employment, and income. For example, suppose that households are receiving an income of $100 million, and have been re-spending this on goods and services so that the receipts of firms are $100 million and the circular flow is in equilibrium at this level. Assume that households decide to save $20 million, their withdrawing this amount from the circular flow by reducing their expenditure on goods and services to $80 million. The receipts of firms now fall short of the value of their previous production, their stocks of finished goods build up, and they can be expected to reduce expenditure on resources to bring their receipts and expenditure back into line. To do this, they may reduce their employment of labour. This occurs unless there is a corresponding injection of expenditure to compensate for the attempt by households to increase their savings. The leakage from the circular flow caused by savings may be compensated for by an increase in investment, that is, *expenditure* on capital goods, but it need not be.

Decisions to save and decisions to invest are taken by different individuals in our society. Expenditure on investment is very unstable, and does not automatically come into line with planned savings. This can be a cause of considerable fluctuations in expenditure in the circular flow, and can lead to the fluctuation in employment. In the above illustration, if plans to save $20 million are offset by plans to invest $20 million, that is, to *spend* $20 million on capital goods, the gross level of economic activity is maintained at $100 million. If, however, expenditure on capital goods is only $10 million, the receipts of the business sector fall, incomes fall, and actual savings therefore also fall because of the lower incomes. Attempts to increase savings are likely to lead to a reduction in economic activity, and in actual savings, unless offset by investment spending.

In the simplified case in which households undertake all the saving in society, savings can be introduced into the circular flow diagram in the way shown in Figure 7.2. The incomes that households receive may either be spent directly on consumer goods or be saved. If incomes are saved, there is a leakage from the circular flow, unless savings are offset by investment. The dotted line between savings and investment on the bottom loop of Figure 7.2 indicates that *investment may not exactly offset planned savings.* Savers and investors tend to be different individuals. Most saving is done by households, and most investment is undertaken by business. A decision to save may not be balanced by a decision to invest, and vice versa.

An Extension of the Circular Flow Model to Allow for Government and International trade

The simplified version of the circular flow must be extended further, however, to take account of government and international trade. Leakages from and injections into the circular flow can occur because the *government* is involved in the economy. *Taxation* by the government represents a leakage from the circular flow, and *government spending* represents an injection into the circular flow. Taxation, a compulsory payment to the government, is levied on incomes (including profits), and on the sale of goods (sales taxes), for example. Taxation is levied both on households and on business firms. In Canada, taxation provides most of the revenue that the government requires to finance its expenditure. The government covers any excess of its spending beyond its receipts from taxation, and the sale of goods and services, by borrowing either from the public (by issuing government bonds for the public to purchase) or by borrowing from the Bank of Canada.

When the government increases the level of its spending on goods and services, and leaves taxation unchanged, it makes a net injection of expenditure into the circular flow, and normally this raises the level of economic activity, in-

Figure 7.2 **Savings introduce a leakage into the circular flow and unless planned savings are offset by investment spending, economic activity can be expected to decline.** *Investment spending is a volatile element in the circular flow.*

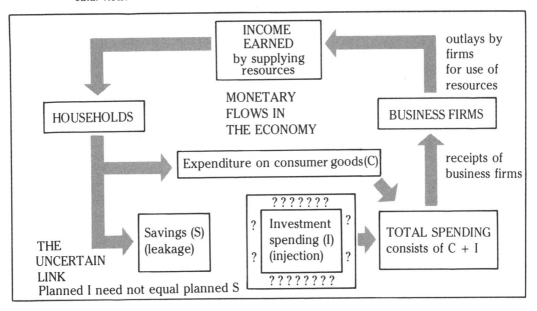

cluding employment. If it lowers its expenditure and leaves taxation unaltered, this normally reduces the level of economic activity. Taxation unaltered, the government can influence the circular flow, and the level of employment, by varying its own spending.

Similarly, if the government reduces taxation and leaves its own spending unaltered, this will reduce the leakage from the circular flow, and add to economic activity and employment. But the effect is not as direct and strong as in the case where the government increases its spending because some of the increased income resulting from a reduction in taxation can be expected to be saved. An increase in taxation, on the other hand, raises the leakage from the circular flow and tends to reduce economic activity and employment in the economy. By altering its level of taxation and the level of its spending, the government is in a position to change the level of economic activity and employment in an economy. It has policies or instruments (sometimes called *fiscal instruments*) available to it to manage the overall level of economic activity. These possibilities will be considered in more detail later.

Canada trades a significant amount of goods and services internationally; thus international trade must be taken into account because it affects the circular flow of income and expenditure in this country. Expenditure by Canadians on overseas commodities (imports) represents a leakage from the circular flow. Increased Canadian imports, other things unchanged, tend to reduce economic activity and employment in Canada, and to raise economic activity and employment abroad. Exports (purchases of Canadian commodities by overseas residents) add to the domestic circular flow.

If the total value of imports increases and the total value of exports remains unchanged, there is a *net leakage* of expenditure from the domestic economy, and domestic economic activity and employment tend to decline. For example, if exports and imports equal $2000 million per year, and imports rise by $200 million, exports unaltered, expenditure on locally produced goods declines and local incomes fall. The net effect is contractionary. On the other hand, if the reverse occurs (the total value of exports rises and the total value of imports remains unchanged) there is a *net injection of expenditure* on locally produced commodities, and local economic activity and employment tend to increase.

Measuring National Income

The methods for measuring the value of national income in the circular flow were discussed in Chapter 4. It is useful to put the discussion in perspective by observing the size and relative importance of the various components that have just been discussed. Table 7.1 presents the 1982 Canadian figures for the expenditure approach to valuing national income.

In terms of Figure 7.1, the values in Table 7.1 refer to the value of transactions in the lower half of the loop. The upper half of the loop refers to the distribution of the receipts of business firms. Table 7.2 presents the categories of income received in Canada for the year 1982.

TABLE 7.1   **1982 Gross National Expenditure (GNE) by Components**

	Value ($ millions)	Percentage of GNE
Consumption	205,952	59.0
Investment	57,081	16.4
Government	86,368	24.7
Exports	100,395	28.8
Imports	-99,150	-28.4
(Residual error of estimate)	- 1,721	- 0.5
Gross National Expenditure	348,925	100.0

SOURCE: *Economic Review*, Department of Finance, April 1983.

TABLE 7.2   **1982 Gross National Product (GNP)**

	Value ($ millions)	Percentage of GNP
Wages, Salaries, etc.	201,736	57.8
Corporation Profits	21,777	6.2
(less dividends paid to nonresidents)	- 3,356	- 1.0
Interest and miscellaneous investment income	29,704	8.5
Farm Net Income	4,646	1.3
Net Income of nonfarm unincorporated business including rents	14,031	4.0
Inventory Valuation Adjustment	- 3,784	- 1.1
Indirect Taxes less Subsidies	40,588	11.6
Capital Consumption Allowance and Miscellaneous Valuation Adjustments	41,862	12.0
Residual Error of Estimate	1,721	0.5
Gross National Product	348,925	100.0

SOURCE: *Economic Review*, Department of Finance, April 1983.

The reader will notice from tables 7.1 and 7.2 that GNE = GNP. The values in these tables are calculated at 1982 market prices. Economists refer to these as *nominal* values.

Inflation and the Measurement of National Income

Economists are frequently more interested in changes in *inflation-adjusted*, or *real*, values of commodities than in changes in nominal, or market, values. This is because inflation increases the difficulty of measuring economic performance. Under inflationary conditions, the prices of commodities rise generally and the costs of buying a representative bundle of commodities goes up. Thus, if we value commodities at their market prices, the current, or money, value of the same representative bundle of commodities rises through time if inflation occurs. Therefore, there is an illusory growth in production if we rely on GNP estimates based on current prices to indicate the level of production in an economy. Suppose that GNP is $1000 million in an economy in year 1 based upon the prices prevailing in year 1, and that the prices of all commodities rise by 10 percent in year 2 compared to those in year 1. Physical production (real output) of commodities remains unchanged, however. GNP calculated at current prices grow 10 percent between year 1 and year 2 from $1000 million to $1100 million, but there is zero growth in real production. Current figures need to be corrected to allow for the rate of inflation if one wishes to obtain an estimate of the change in real production. In terms of its purchasing power (in terms of the quantities of goods and services it can buy), $1.10 in year 2 is equivalent to $1.00 in year 1. Consequently, payments in year 1 have to be reduced by $\frac{1.00}{1.10}$ to convert them to equivalent amounts in terms of year-1 dollars. Thus, real year-2 GNP in terms of year-1 dollars is

$$\frac{100}{110} \times \$1100 \text{ million} = \$1000 \text{ million.}$$

Price indices, or deflators, are generally used to correct for price inflation in order to obtain *real* GNE (or GNP). The GNE price deflator is defined by

$$\text{GNE price deflator} = \frac{\textit{value of current outputs at current year prices}}{\textit{value of current outputs at base year prices}} \times 100.$$

The numerator of this expression is the current market value (nominal value) of goods and services. The denominator evaluates the same volume of goods and services at prices that prevailed in a particular base year. The ratio is usually multiplied by 100 for presentation.

In 1982, the GNE deflator was 272.6 with 1971 as the base year. Real GNE for 1982 can be determined by taking nominal GNE for 1982 and dividing by the GNE deflator (after moving the decimal point to the left by two places).

$$\text{Real GNE} = \frac{\textit{Nominal GNE}}{\textit{GNE deflator}/100}$$

$$= \frac{348,925}{2.726} \text{ million} \qquad = \$128,000 \text{ million, approximately.}$$

Thus, although nominal GNE is $348,925 million, real GNE in terms of 1971 prices is only $128,000 million. In 1981, nominal GNE was $331,338 million and real GNE was $134,540. Nominal GNE rose in 1982, but real GNE fell!

Another price index that is commonly used is the *Consumer Price Index*, or the CPI. The CPI is computed for a narrower range of commodities than is the GNE deflator. The CPI will be discussed in more detail in Chapter 10 when we discuss the issue of inflation more fully.

Economists are not only interested in measuring the real value of national income, but they are also interested in explaining how the value is determined. Although the circular flow provides a useful way of looking at interdependency of incomes, expenditure, and general economic activity in an economy, it is necessary to look more carefully at the relationships between these components. This can be done by using a more abstract model such as that developed by Keynes in the 1930s. His model gives one possible explanation of the relationships involved in the circular flow. Let us consider his model.

A Keynesian Model of the Factors Determining the General Level of Economic Activity

The Basic Keynesian Model

In the Keynesian model, the levels of incomes and employment in an economy depend on the level of aggregate expenditure on the commodities that it produces. *Overall, or aggregate, expenditure is the basic determinant of the level of economic activity in an economy.* This accords with our observations about the circular flow. But the Keynesian model is more specific. In it, aggregate expenditure on commodities is a function of incomes received. It is assumed that aggregate expenditure rises with gross income, but not as quickly as income. The relationship between expenditure and gross national income might be like that indicated by the line or curve marked DD in Figure 7.3. This is the *aggregate expenditure curve* for GNP, and indicates that, when GNP is $1000 million annually, it is exactly matched by the same level of expenditure, or demand. All production is sold, and the circular flow can remain in this position with GNP and GNE constant, provided that the demand relationship does not alter. This is an equilibrium position.

If GNP happens to exceed $1000 million annually, this level of national production and income cannot be maintained. If GNP is $1500 million, for example, aggregate demand amounts to $1250 million, receipts fail to cover outlays as far as business firms are concerned, and stocks of goods build up. This leads to firms curtailing production, and reducing their use of materials and employment of labour. Consequently, total GNP and gross national income fall, and continue to do so until GNE exactly matches the gross outlay incurred in producing the national product. At that point — a GNP of $1000 million in Figure 7.3 — expenditures by households and other economic agents on commodities

FIGURE 7.3 **Aggregate expenditure and supply curve. The intersection of these
curves determines the equilibrium level of GNP.**

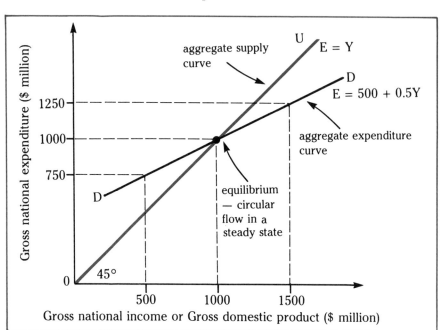

exactly return to suppliers of these commodities the costs (equals incomes to
members of society) of producing these. In the absence of a change in demand
conditions, the circular flow can be indefinitely maintained at the equilibrium
level of GNP. The equilibrium point is the one at which the 45° line, the supply
curve, equals the aggregate demand curve. The 45° line, OU in Figure 7.3, is
the supply curve on the Keynesian assumption that supply expands in proportion to effective demand for it.

If actual GNP is less than the equilibrium level of GNP, GNP expands until
the equilibrium is reached, and the size of the circular flow increases. For instance, if GNP is $500 million, and the demand curve is that shown in Figure
7.3, economic agents attempt to buy $750 million worth of commodities.
Because final commodities valued at only $500 million have been produced,
supplies are completely sold out, stocks run down, and shortages occur. Thus,
producers are stimulated to expand production, and GNP, incomes, and expenditure rise. This process continues until total expenditure is just equal to GNP,
that is, until in the case illustrated GNP equals $1000 million. Thus, the
equilibrium level of GNP, or the size of the circular flow, corresponds to the
GNP and expenditure level at which the aggregate demand curve crosses the
45° supply curve. In the simple Keynesian model, employment is proportional

to GNP (and therefore rises and falls as GNP does), therefore, the equilibrium level of employment in the economy corresponds to the equilibrium level of GNP.

The equilibrium level of GNP can also be illustrated from Table 7.3. Column 1 sets out selected values of GNP. Column 2 lists the levels of aggregate expenditure that correspond to the level of gross national income, supposing that aggregate expenditure is described by the equation

$$E = 500 + 0.5Y.$$

Column 3 specifies the level of excess demand in the economy for its supplies, and is the difference between columns 2 and 1. The equilibrium level of GNP occurs when GNP is such that excess demand is zero.

TABLE 7.3 **An example of aggregate supply and the equilibrium level of GNP in millions of dollars**

Supply: Level of GNP, Gross National Income	Aggregate Expenditure $E = 500 + 0.5Y$	Amount of Excess Demand	
250	625	375	GNP
500	750	250	rising
750	825	75	
1000	1000	0	No change
1250	1125	-125	GNP
1500	1250	-250	declining

Table 7.3 shows this is occurring, in this example, for a GNP of $1000 million. At any smaller level of gross national income, demand exceeds supply, and consequently supply expands. At any higher level of GNP, demand is less than supply, and so supply contracts.

Shifts in Aggregate Expenditure and Changes in the Equilibrium Level of GNP

A shift in the aggregate expenditure curve shifts the equilibrium level of GNP. The equilibrium level of GNP is raised by an upward shift in the aggregate expenditure curve and lowered by a downward shift in this curve. Thus, as illustrated in Figure 7.4, a shift upward in the aggregate expenditure curve from DD to D_2D_2 raises the equilibrium level of GNP from $1000 million to $1500 million. A shift downward in the aggregate expenditure curve from DD to D_1D_1 lowers the equilibrium level of GNP from $1000 million to $500 million.

FIGURE 7.4 **Shifts in the equilibrium of GNP occur as a result of shifts in the aggregate expenditure curve.**

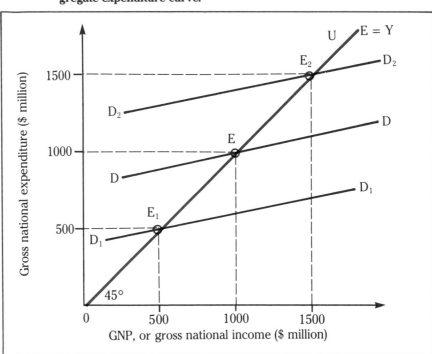

It follows from the above analysis that if the government can shift the aggregate expenditure curve, it can control the equilibrium level of GNP, employment, and economic activity, generally. Thus, if employment is too low, the government might raise aggregate expendtiture and employment by adopting appropriate policies. Keynes was of the opinion that it could do this, and later we will consider a number of possible ways.

Components of Aggregate Expenditure

Aggregate Expenditure is commonly broken down into the following components:

1. consumption expenditure by households, C,
2. private investment expenditure, I,
3. capital and current expenditure by government, G, and
4. expenditure on exports, X, less expenditure on imports, M, that is, the balance of external trade.

Symbolically, total aggregate expenditure can be viewed as

$$E = C + I + G + (X - M).$$

Aggregate expenditure = consumption expenditure + private investment expenditure + government expenditure + (expenditure on exports less expenditure on imports).

The reader will observe the similarity between the symbolic representation for aggregate expenditure E, and that for GNE presented in Chapter 4. In Chapter 4, we considered *actual* expenditures, which, when summed, produced GNE. Aggregate expenditure E is obtained by summing *planned* expenditures. If planned expenditures do not equal GNP (the value of goods and services produced) the *actual investment* expenditure will differ from *planned investment* expenditure. This difference will be *unplanned inventory changes*, and inventory changes are included as part of investment. For example, if E is less than GNP, then there will be unsold goods and services. These are added to inventories. As a result, *actual* investment is larger than *planned* by the amount of the *unplanned* inventory accumulation.

Relationships between the Components of Aggregate Expenditure (especially Consumption) and Income

The Consumption Function and the Equilibrium Level of National Income

It was assumed earlier, as illustrated in Figure 7.3, that GNE rises with gross national income, or GNP. This mainly occurs because the level of private consumption expenditure goes up as income does. The relationship between consumption and gross national income, or GNP, is described by a consumption function. The *consumption function* corresponding to the case shown in Figure 7.3 might be, *for example*:

$$C = 200 + 0.5Y$$

and is illustrated by the curve CC in Figure 7.5. This consumption function indicates that consumption expenditure rises by 50¢ for every dollar increase in national income. The *marginal propensity to consume* in this case is 0.5. The marginal propensity to consume indicates the change in consumption that occurs when national income increases by a small amount.

If a country does not engage in international trade and has no government sector, its aggregate expenditure function can be obtained by adding its private investment function to its consumption function. In the case illustrated in Figure 7.5, investment expenditure is assumed to remain constant at $300 million annually, irrespective of the level of national income, or GNP. Adding this to the consumption function, $C = 200 + 0.5Y$, yields the aggregate expenditure curve $E = C + I = 200 + 0.5Y + 300 = 500 + 0.5Y$. As discussed in relation to Figure 7.3 earlier, the equilibrium level of GNP, or gross national income, is then $1000 million annually. Economic activity in the economy as a

whole gravitates toward this equilibrium level. In a trading economy, exports
minus imports ($X - M$), as a function of national income, are added to the consumption function as a step toward constructing the aggregate expenditure
curve. In a normal economy with a government expenditure, G is added also,
along with private investment, to give the economy's aggregate expenditure
function.

The Savings-Investment Approach to Determining the Equilibrium Level of GNP

It might be observed that the determination of the equilibrium level of GNP,
national income, and national expenditure can be illustrated in yet another
way. The basic building block of this approach is the savings function. The savings function indicates the amount of savings individuals or economic agents
would like to undertake at each level of national income, or GNP. It can be
obtained by taking the difference between national income and consumption.
Table 7.4 indicates the relationship between national income, consumption,
and savings, given that the consumption function is $C = 200 + 0.5Y$ as illustrated in Figure 7.5, and assuming no taxes.

FIGURE 7.5 **Example of a consumption function, marked CC. Aggregate expenditure for goods or services in this example consists of two components: consumption demand and private investment demand.**

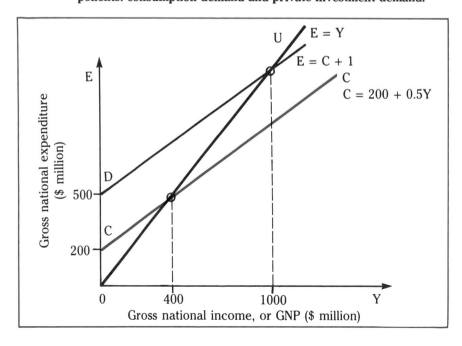

TABLE 7.4 **The relationship between national income, consumption, and savings
($ million)**

National Income Y	Consumption C = 200 + 0.5Y	Savings (S = Y - C) ∴ S = -200 + 0.5Y
0	200	-200
500	450	50
1000	700	300
1500	950	550
2000	1200	800

The savings function corresponding to a consumption function is found by taking the difference between national income, Y, and aggregate consumption, C. Where S represents savings, $S = Y - C$. Hence if $C = 200 + 0.5Y$,

$$S = Y - 200 - 0.5Y$$
$$= -200 + 0.5Y.$$

This savings relationship has been graphed in Figure 7.6

Savings represent a basic leakage from the circular flow, and any level of national income can only be maintained at its existing level if injections (such as

FIGURE 7.6 **Savings function and the savings-investment approach to determining
the equilibrium level of national income, or GNP**

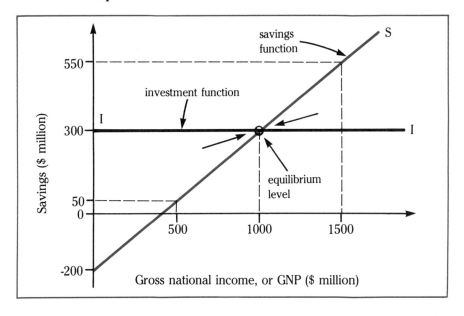

those occurring as a result of investment expenditure) counterbalance savings. In the absence of foreign trade and a government sector, private investment expenditure provides an injection that helps to counterbalance savings. Indeed, in this case, national income changes until savings and investment are brought into balance.

Take the example above in Figure 7.6. Investment in this case is $300 million annually, irrespective of the level of income. The savings function is as shown. When gross national income exceeds $1000 million, it falls until equilibrium is established. For example, when gross national income is $1500 million annually, individuals wish to save $550 million, which is $250 million more than is being invested. Hence, there is some net leakage from the circular flow — not all income is returned as expenditure — and gross national income, or GNP, therefore declines until savings and investment are brought into equality. In the above example, gross national income declines until it equals the equilibrium level of $1000 million. On the other hand, if gross national income is less than its equilibrium level of $1000 million, national income rises. At income levels less than $1000 million, investment expenditure exceeds savings, and there is a net injection of expenditure into the circular flow. For instance, if gross national income is $500 million, investment expenditure, $300 million, exceeds savings, $50 million, by $250 million. This net injection of expenditure has an expansionary impact on economic activity.

Exports and imports, and government expenditure and taxation, can also be allowed for in the above exposition. They may be taken into account in Figure 7.6 by adding the functions, or relationships, for these components to the private investment function. The equilibrium of national income and expenditure is then established at the point, or income, where the curve showing the sum of the net injections $I + G + X$ is equal to the leakage shown by the savings plus taxes plus imports curve.

The Multiplier and the Effect on Economic Activity of an Alteration in Aggregate Expenditure

Multiplier Based on Marginal Propensity to Consume

A permanent change (a rise or a fall) in aggregate expenditure by any amount generally changes the equilibrium level of gross national income, or GNP, by *a greater* amount. A shift in aggregate expenditure has a multiple effect on the equilibrium level of economic activity. The extent of this multiple effect is measured by a *multiplier*, the nature of which will be discussed shortly.

The multiplying effect of a permanent change in aggregate expenditure can be seen from the example illustrated in Figure 7.7. When the aggregate expenditure curve is D_1D_1, the equilibrium level of GNP is $1000 million. The aggregate expenditure curve in this case is described by the equation $E = 500 + 0.5Y$. If the aggregate expenditure for GNP rises by $500 million annually, the aggregate expenditure curve in Figure 7.7 rises from D_1D_1 to D_2D_2.

The new expenditure curve is described by the equation $E = 1000 + 0.5Y$, and the equilibrium level of GNP becomes $2000 million. Hence, the rise in aggregate expenditure by $500 million gives rise to a $1000 million rise in the equilibrium level of GNP. This is a multiple effect of two; the multiplier is two in this instance.

FIGURE 7.7 **A rise in aggregate expenditure for GNP has a multiplying effect on the equilibrium level of gross national income and GNP.**
In the case below, a rise of $500 million in aggregate expenditure leads to a $1000 million rise in the equilibrium level of GNP and gross national income.

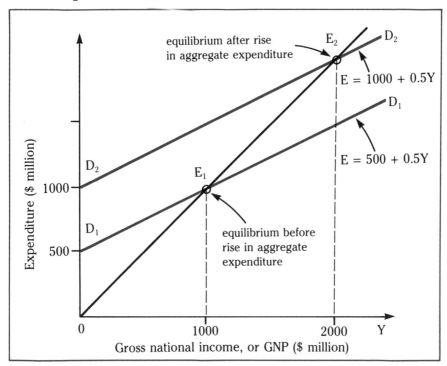

Expenditure leads to a $1000 million rise in the equilibrium level of GNP and gross national income.

If we suppose that aggregate expenditure for consumers' goods (the consumption function) is the only component of aggregate expenditure to vary with gross national income, this multiplier, k, can be calculated by using the following formula. The multiplier,

$$k = \frac{1}{1 - c}$$

where c is the marginal propensity to consume, as indicated by the slope of the consumption function. Assume that, as in the case illustrated in Figure 7.5 the consumption function is of the form $C = 200 + 0.5Y$ so that the marginal propensity to consume, c, is 0.5. The multiplier is then

$$k = \frac{1}{1 - c}$$

$$= \frac{1}{1 - 0.5}$$

$$= \frac{1}{0.5}$$

$$= 2.$$

If all components of aggregate expenditure except consumption are independent of GNP, the impact of an increase in aggregate expenditure on the equilibrium level of GNP can be found by multiplying the increase by k. An increase in aggregate expenditure of $500 million annually increases the equilibrium of GNP by *$500 million* $\times k = $500 \times 2 = $1000 million$. This accords with the result illustrated in Figure 7.7.

Suppose that the $500 million increase occurs because firms desire more investment goods. When they spend $500 million for these goods, this creates $500 million additional income for the factors of production involved. The persons receiving this income will spend half of the increased income on additional consumption. This creates a second-round increase in spending of $250 million. But this creates additional income of $250 million for those employed in the consumption producing sector. Half of this will be spent creating a further $125 million. At this stage, the initial expansion of $500 million has increased total income by $(500 + 250 + 125)$ million, or $875 million. The process continues until the ultimate increase is $1000 million. This chain reaction is called the *multiplier effect*.

Multiplier Based on Marginal Propensity to Save

As observed earlier, the amount individuals wish to save is the difference between their income and the amount they wish to spend on consumption in the absence of taxes. Because of this, the multiplier in the above case can also be expressed as

$$k = \frac{1}{1 - c}$$

or,

$$k = \frac{1}{s}$$

where s is the marginal propensity to save. In the above instance, $c = s = 0.5$. But consider the example in which the marginal propensity to consume is 0.6.

The marginal propensity to save is then $s = 1 - 0.6 = 0.4$. In this instance,

$$k = \frac{1}{1-c}$$

$$= \frac{1}{1-0.6}$$

$$= \frac{1}{0.4}$$

$$= 2.5$$

using the marginal propensity to consume to calculate it, or

$$k = \frac{1}{s}$$

$$= \frac{1}{0.4}$$

$$= 2.5$$

using the marginal propensity to save as the denominator in the calculation. One might observe that the multiplier is higher in this case than in the last one. This is because the marginal propensity to consume is higher, or the marginal propensity to save is lower, in the latter case. When this occurs, the *leakage* from the circular flow as a result of savings is smaller, and therefore any injection of expenditure is able to sustain a higher level of national income.

Import and Taxation Leakages and the Multiplier

The above multiplier applies if the only component of aggregate expenditure, which varies with GNP, or gross national income, is consumption. But in a trading economy, imports may rise with national income, and in a normal economy, taxation receipts are liable to rise with national income. These are all leakages that can be allowed for in the multiplier. Where m represents the marginal propensity to import (additional imports as a result of a small rise in national income), and t represents the marginal tax rate (the additional tax receipts received as a result of a small increase in national income), the multiplier is

$$k = \frac{1}{s+m+r}.$$

Notice that the size of the multiplier is reduced as a result of the leakages of income taxes and imports. As income rises, so does the amount of taxes owed to the government; hence, the amount available to spend on consumption is less than if taxes were zero or did not increase with income. Similarly, if, when income rises, Canadians buy more foreign-produced cars rather than Canadian-produced ones, less income is created for Canadian car producers, and hence they have less to spend than if all cars purchased were Canadian produced. These points are shown in the following numerical example.

When taxes depend upon income, there is a difference between the marginal propensity to consume out of national income and the marginal propensity to consume out of *disposable income*. Disposable income Y_d is income minus taxes, T; that is

$$Y_d = Y - T.$$

Suppose we hypothesize that consumption expenditure depends upon Y_d. For example, assume the consumption function is

$$C = 200 + 3/4\ Y_d.$$

The marginal propensity to consume out of disposable income in this example is 3/4. Suppose the marginal tax rate and average tax rate are constant and equal to 1/3. Then $T = 1/3\ Y$ is the tax function, and $Y_d = 2/3\ Y$ from the definition of disposable income. Using this result in the above consumption function yields

$$C = 200 + 3/4\ (2/3\ Y)$$

or

$$C = 200 + 1/2\ Y.$$

Thus, the marginal propensity to consume out of national income is 1/2.

In general, if the marginal propensity to consume out of disposable income is b, and the marginal tax rate is t, then the marginal propensity to consume out of national income, c, is given by

$$c = b\ (1 - t).$$

The reader can verify that this formula works for the above example.

Saving is the difference between disposable income and consumption

$$S = Y_d - C.$$

Using the previous example, the saving function can be written as

$$S = \ \ 2/3\ Y - (200 + 1/2\ Y)$$

or

$$S = -200 + 1/6\ Y.$$

The marginal propensity to save out of national income, s, is 1/6. In general, s is determined by the following equations

$$s = 1 - c - t$$

or

$$s = 1 - b(1 - t) - t$$

or

$$s = (1 - t)(1 - b).$$

Using the above expression for s, the following equivalent forms of the multiplier can be derived:

$$k = \frac{1}{1 - c + m}$$

or

$$k = \frac{1}{1 - b(1 - t) + m}.$$

The value of the multiplier for the above example, and assuming $m = 0.1$ is

$$k = \frac{1}{0.6}$$
$$= 1.67.$$

The leakages from the circular flow are so great that the multiplier is quite small. In these circumstances, a rise in aggregate expenditure has a small impact on the equilibrium level of GNP. After taking account of a tax and/or import leakage, a rise in aggregate expenditure by $500 million in the above circumstances only raises the equilibrium level of GNP by $835 million. An increase to save, s, the marginal propensity to import, m, or the marginal tax rate, t, other things unchanged, tends to reduce the multiplier because these imply an increased leakage from the circular flow.

Changes in Canadian Expenditure and the Multiplier

In 1982, the Canadian economy was in the midst of the worst recession since the Great Depression of the 1930s. Various components of Canadian GNE had fallen to produce the recession. Consumer spending was lower as consumers worried about the impact of possible unemployment on their own financial position. It is ironic that these actions may actually worsen the situation. As people eat out less, and make their own repairs in order to increase savings, they take income away from those people who earn their living by providing these services. By postponing the decision to purchase refrigerators and other appliances, automobiles and new houses, consumers reduce the demand facing the producers of these goods. As a result, these producers of goods and services are forced to lay off workers. These producers also will have a reduced demand for raw materials such as steel, copper, nickel, and energy. Thus, these sectors are hit, and so on it goes. This is the multiplier at work. This multiplier decrease in income induced by the attempt to increase savings is sometimes called the *paradox of thrift* — in the end, savings in the aggregate are not increased — in fact, they may actually fall. The paradox of thrift may be illustrated by an upward shift in the savings curve in Figure 7.6.

Drops in investment expenditure (including new construction) result in a drop in the investment schedule in Figure 7.6, and will lead to multiplier decreases in income following a chain of events similar to that listed above.

The Government and the Circular Flow

The Canadian government, like governments in most present-day economies, is able to and does influence the general level of current economic activity in this country. It has both a direct and indirect influence on the level of aggregate expenditure. By influencing the level of aggregate expenditures in the economy, the government is able, within limits, to vary the levels of employment, and gross national income, or GNP, within the country.

Direct expenditures by the government on goods and services, G, adds to aggregate expenditure, and may offset decreases by consumers — business or foreign purchasers of Canadian goods. This direct expenditure by government may be for the purchase of defence equipment, roads, hospitals, and so on. An increase in government expenditure (with taxation and other components of aggregate expenditure held constant) has a multiplier effect on GNP. If the multiplier, k, equals 3, and the government increases its annual expenditure by $100 million, then the equilibrium level of GNP rises by $300 million. In order to pay for these expenditures with no change in tax revenue, the government must either spend from its deposits with the Bank of Canada, borrow from the Bank of Canada, or borrow from the general public. The effects of these financing options are important, and will be discussed in subsequent chapters.

On the other hand, taxation receipts lower the level of aggregate expenditure indirectly by reducing the disposable incomes of households. Taxes act as a leakage from the circular flow. If tax rates are increased and other components of aggregate expenditure are unaltered, the equilibrium level of GNP falls. An increase in the tax rate reduces the marginal propensity to consume, and hence flattens the aggregate expenditure curve in Figure 7.3. A reduction in tax rates normally has the opposite effect.

The annual budget of the federal government is important from a number of points of view. In Canada, the budget has been considered by Parliament in the autumn in recent years. The government may, however, bring in a budget at other times if it feels that this is necessary. Apart from a budget's direct effect on the size of the circular flow, a government may announce in the budget taxation or subsidy charges that provide incentives for private consumption or private investment. For example, if the government wishes to stimulate private investment, it may allow companies to deduct an extra amount from their taxable income when they have undertaken new investment.

Some entries in the budget concern only the transfer of income from one section of the community to another section. For instance, the payment of pensions to the aged and invalids involves a transfer of income from those with taxable incomes to the aged and invalids. The government itself is not involved in the purchase of goods and services. Such transfers, however, can affect the general level of economic activity. For instance, if the aged and invalids have a higher marginal propensity to consume from their income than those on taxable incomes, the transfer will tend to expand economic activity.

The measures that the government can take through its budget to influence the level of economic activity are sometimes described as *fiscal measures*. We will discuss these further in a later chapter.

The Keynesian analysis of economic activity indicates that the government is in a position (by fiscal and monetary means) to influence the level of aggregate demand in the economy, and the level of GNP and employment. But it does not have unlimited power to change economic activity. In recent years, for example, the government has not succeeded in maintaining full employment *and* keeping the rate of inflation at socially acceptable levels. As a result, consideration has been given to 1. *supply-side* policies designed to stimulate the growth of production by creating incentives to increase work effort and investment, and 2. policies for restraining the growth in the supply of money, as ways to moderate inflation.

KEY CONCEPTS
(FOR REVIEW)

Aggregate demand curve	Investment
Aggregate expenditure	Leakages from circular flow
Aggregate supply curve	Marginal propensity to consume
Budget	Marginal propensity to import
Circular flow	Monetary flows in the economy
Consumption function	Monetary policy or measures
Expenditure on consumer goods	Multiplier
Fiscal instruments or measures	Savings
Foreign trade	Total spending
Government expenditure	Transfer payments
Government outlays	Value of exports
Injections into the circular flow	Value of imports

QUESTIONS FOR REVIEW AND DISCUSSION

1. Illustrate the concept of the circular flow and explain the flow. In doing so, distinguish between the flow of physical commodities and the flow of money or monetary claims.
2. What factors need to be allowed for in the simple circular flow model (illustrated in Figure 7.1) to make it more realistic?
3. "Savings can be viewed as a leakage from the circular flow, and, unless offset by an injection of spending, can reduce economic activity, employment, and income." Explain.
4. Why is the relationship between planned savings and investment important in influencing the level of employment in the economy?
5. What influence does government spending and taxation have on the level of employment and economic activity in an economy? Explain this in terms of leakages from, and injections into, the circular flow.
6. What influence does international trade have on the circular flow? In par-

ticular, how does international trade affect the level of economic activity
and employment?

7. Suppose that government spending rises by $2000 million annually, but
the amount received from taxation remains unchanged. What would the
effect be on economoic activity?

8. What happens to economic activity if the value of exports rises by $1000
million, and the value of imports increases by $500 million?

9. Why is the aggregate expenditure curve important?

10. Why does the aggregate expenditure curve in the Keynesian model slope
upward?

11. Explain why the *equilibrium* level of gross national income corresponds
to the point at which the aggregate expenditure curve crosses the 45° aggregate supply curve. (See Figure 7.3.)

12. Why does the aggregate expenditure curve cross the 45° line from
above? (See Figure 7.3.)

13. Let E represent aggregate expenditure in millions of dollars, and Y indicate gross national income in millions of dollars. Assume that aggregate
expenditure can be represented by the equation $E = 250 + 0.5Y$. Draw
the aggregate expenditure curve. Determine the equilibrium level of
gross national income.

14. Given the expenditure curve mentioned in Question 13, why is it impossible for equilibrium to occur when gross national income is $250 million
or $750 million?

15. Show by means of a diagram the way in which shifts in the aggregate
expenditure curve change the equilibrium level of GNP.

16. List the components of aggregate expenditure. Divide the components
into leakages and injections.

17. List changes in components of aggregate expenditure that may shift the
aggregate expenditure curve upward. What is the implication for the
level of GNP of an upward shift in the aggregate expenditure curve?

18. What does a consumption function indicate? What does the marginal propensity to consume indicate?

19. "The consumption function can be used as a building block for the aggregate expenditure function." Explain.

20. How is the savings function related to the consumption function?

21. Assume that the aggregate consumption function (in millions of dollars) is
$C = 100 + 0.5Y$. What is the corresponding savings function? Suppose
that the only injection into the circular flow (apart from consumption expenditure) is private investment of $400 million per year. Determine the
equilibrium level of GNP. Illustrate the equilibrium by drawing a similar
diagram to Figure 7.6.

22. Suppose the consumption function is $C = 500 + 4/5 Y_d$, and the marginal
tax rate = average tax rate is 1/4. What is the marginal propensity to
consume out of national income?

23. What is the savings function for the example in Question 22?
24. If the marginal propensity to import is zero, what is the value of the multiplier in Question 22? Suppose that the marginal propensity to import is 0.2. What is the value of the multiplier now? Explain the difference in values.
25. Suppose that consumption expenditure is the only component of expenditure that varies with gross national income. What is the multiplier, if the marginal propensity to consume is:

   a . 0.8,
   b . 0.75,
   c . 0.25,
   d . 0?

   In these four circumstances, what would be the ultimate effect of a rise in government spending of $100 million annually (other components of aggregate expenditure unchanged)?
26. Suppose that the marginal propensity to save is one-third. What is the multiplier in this case?
27. How does:

   a . the marginal propensity to import commodities, and
   b . the marginal tax rate affect the multiplier?

28. What fiscal means can the Canadian government use to influence the level of economic activity?
29. What are transfer payments? Why do transfer payments need to be distinguished from direct expenditure by the government on goods and services when one is considering the impact of government outlays on expenditure?
30. Can the government influence the level of national spending by other than fiscal means?

FURTHER READING

Auld, D.A.L., & Miller, F.C., *Principles of Public Finance: A Canadian Text*, 2nd ed. Toronto: Methuen Publications, 1982, chapters 5 & 15.

Blomqvist, A., Wonnacott, P., & Wonnacott, R., *Economics*, 1st Canadian ed. Scarborough: McGraw-Hill Ryerson Limited, 1984, chapters 7, 8, & 9.

Lipsey, R.G., Purvis, D.D., Sparks, G.R., & Steiner, P.O., *Economics*, 4th ed. New York: Harper & Row, Publishers, 1982, chapters 29, 30, 31, 32, 33, & 34.

MacEachen, A.J., "The Budget Process," Department of Finance, April, 1982.

8 The Financial Sector and Macroeconomic Activity

The Nature and Functions of Money

Functions and Forms of Money

The economic operations of modern societies are facilitated by the presence of the sophisticated financial system and financial sector. Money in advanced forms is the backbone of the financial system.

In early times, most commodities were exchanged by barter; but in Europe, this means of exchange was rapidly replaced by the use of precious metals as an intermediate for effecting exchange and as a store of value. Coins, containing specified amounts of precious metal such as gold or silver, were minted by the sovereign, and widely used to effect exchange. The next development was the use of notes, given by goldsmiths, for example. A client could deposit gold with a goldsmith for safekeeping and obtain a voucher or note specifying the amount of the deposit. A transaction could then be made by exchanging one of these notes. A buyer could transfer one of these notes giving rights to a specified amount of gold to a seller, who could claim the amount of gold, but who likely as not would not do so, rather exchanging the note later to make other purchases. Although notes were originally backed in value by precious metals, this system was modified.

It became apparent to goldsmiths (early bankers) that most depositors of precious metals would not as a rule wish to withdraw their deposits all at once. Bankers, or goldsmiths, could therefore issue notes or promises to supply gold or precious metals in exchange for notes beyond the amount actually deposited with them. Notes thus became only partly backed by the precious metals into which they were convertible.

Book entries rather than notes and coins are now used to facilitate transactions. The use of chequing (bank) accounts is widespread; through these, exchanges may be effected by mere book entries. For instance, a cheque drawn by a buyer in settlement of a sale may be deposited by the seller in his or her account in the same bank. The bank debits the buyer's bank account and credits the seller's bank account to record the exchange. The use of credit cards, such as *Visa* and *Mastercard*, represents a further extension of the monetary system.

Money (or monetary unit) in our society:

1. is a medium of exchange,
2. makes it easy to compute the relative prices of commodities,
3. provides a unit of account,
4. provides a standard of measure for deferred payments, and
5. provides a means of storing value or wealth.

The utility of money in many of these roles depends on its retaining a relatively stable value. If, as a result of inflation, money rapidly falls in value, and especially if the extent of that fall is uncertain, money becomes less useful as a unit of an account, as a means for repayment of debts over a period of time, and as a store of value or wealth.

1. Money as a medium of exchange provides a means of facilitating the exchange of goods. Suppose that we have economics books to sell and wish to buy fish. It would be most inconvenient to have to barter these for fish. the sellers of fish may not want such books. If they take them, they may not know what they can obtain in exchange for them, and may find it difficult to find students wishing to exchange something of value in return for the economics books. On the other hand, if we offer them money, the exchange is facilitated and the above problems disappear.

2. Money provides an easy means of relating the prices or costs of commodities because the prices of *all* are expressed in dollars and cents. If prices were expressed in terms of how much of the commodities can be exchanged for other commodities, it would be confusing. For instance, if we are told the following: 2 jars of peanut butter exchange for 3 jars of jam; 1 kg of sausages exchange for 1.5 jars of peanut butter, and so on. Incidentally, this implies that 2.25 jars of jam exchange for 1 kg of sausages. It is easy to see that this would be confusing, and would be especially so if thousands of commodities were involved, as would be the case in our economy.

3. When we say that money provides a unit of account, we mean that it provides a standard in which to record transactions or an economic position. For instance, our incomes are expressed in terms of money, and the profit-and-loss accounts of businesses are expressed in dollars and cents.

4. When we say that money provides a standard for deferred payments, we mean that debts are to be paid or loans repaid in this unit of account. Credit-card debts are paid in dollars, and so are mortgages on houses.

5. Money provides a means of storing wealth, although it is less effective in this role under inflationary conditions. Many people hold money balances in savings accounts as a method of storing their wealth, however.

The Demand for and Supply of Money

Money is one way of storing ones wealth, but it is not the only way. People may instead make financial investments or purchase financial securities such as bonds that will earn income. Why would an individual want to hold money rather than income-earning assets? Money is demanded by individuals and firms for a number of reasons. Stocks or reserves of money are needed to finance transactions because cash receipts do not always match the need for payments to be made in cash. Furthermore, the flow of receipts and payments is to some extent uncertain, and stocks of money are required by individuals and firms to reduce their risk of a possible liquidity crisis. As national output grows, the volume of money needed to finance transactions and allow for normal business risk grows. Thus, the demand for money, in general, increases as GNP rises.

Money also plays a role in speculation concerning financial investments. For simplicity, let us consider the decision concerning whether an individual wishes to hold money or purchase bonds. If a person owns bonds, he or she earns income as a result. The income earned is called the interest payment. The rate of return on the investment, or the interest rate, is basically the interest payment divided by the price of the bond. That is, the interest rate, r, is defined by

$$r = interest\ rate\ or\ yield = \frac{interest\ payment}{price\ of\ bond}.$$

If a bond promises to pay the owner $10 per year and it sells for $100, then the rate of return, or interest rate, is $r = \$10/\$100 = 0.10$ or 10 percent.

Suppose that all other bonds available in the market yield a rate of return of 20 percent, what would happen to the price of the bond that promises to pay $10? Its market price must fall from $100 to $50 in order to be competitive with the rest of the bonds. Nobody would want to pay $100 for this bond in order to receive the promised $10 when there are alternative financial investments that would pay $20 on a $100 purchase. If, on the other hand, interest rates on other bonds were 5 percent, then the price of the bond paying $10 per year would rise to $200 as a result of competitive bidding. This simple example illustrates the general result that *bond prices and interest rates are inversely related.*

When it is felt that interest rates are high and hence likely to fall causing bond prices to rise, then investors will want to hold their wealth in bonds rather than money in order to benefit from the capital gain owing to the appreciation of the price of bonds. They will be able to sell their bonds at a higher price, i.e., for more money! When it is believed that interest rates are low and likely to rise causing bond prices to fall, then investors will want to hold their wealth in money.

This discussion suggests that the demand for money is inversely related to the rate of interest as shown in Figure 8.1.

FIGURE 8.1 **The demand for money and the interest rate**

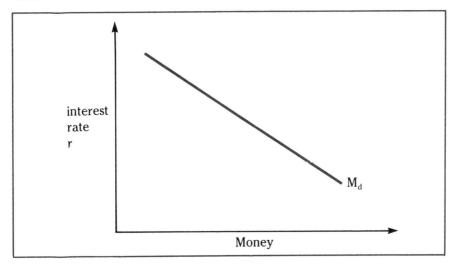

The supply of money in Canada is to a considerable extent regulated by the Bank of Canada. The Bank has a number of means available to it to reduce or increase the money supply. The policies of the Bank of Canada in principle are the ultimate responsibility of the Canadian government.

Money and Macroeconomic Activity

Change in the Money Supply and Changes in National Income

Changes in the volume of money in the Canadian economy will have an impact upon macroeconomic variables such as gross national income and prices. In this section, let us consider how changes in the volume of money will affect the level of GNP.

In short, changes in the money supply will cause a change in GNP by causing changes in the level of aggregate expenditure. But how does this happen? Consider the following simplified story in which the demand for money depends only upon the rate of interest paid on bonds, and the money supply is under the complete control of the Bank of Canada. Suppose the Bank of Canada decreases the money supply from MS^1 to MS^2 as in Figure 8.2.

The people in the economy find that at the interest r_1 they want to hold more money than currently exists. People in attempting to obtain more money, sell their bonds. This increases the number of bonds being offered for sale in the bond market, however, and hence puts downward pressure on the price of bonds. If bond prices fall then interest rates rise. The increase in interest rates reduces the public's demand for money, and when the rate of interest has risen

FIGURE 8.2 **Changes in the money supply and interest-rate changes**

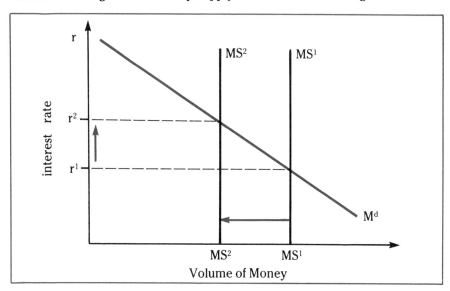

to *r²*, the money market will again be in equilibrium. Increases in the money supply will have the opposite effects.

We have seen that changes in the money supply will cause changes in interest rates that are opposite in direction to the change in the money supply. How does this affect aggregate expenditure? The rate of interest is the cost of borrowing money in order to finance expenditure, and we would expect that when the cost of borrowing increases people would be more reluctant to finance expenditures by borrowing. Thus, aggregate expenditure is inversely related to the rate of interest. What components of aggregate expenditure are likely to be related to the rate of interest? Investment expenditures by firms in new buildings or new equipment may be financed by borrowing if the firms do not have their own funds. Suppose that they do have their own funds — does this mean they can ignore the cost of borrowing? No, because the interest rate is also the payment for lending. As interest rates rise, some firms will find it more profitable to lend their money to others rather than expand their own activities. So investment expenditures are inversely related to the rate of interest. Expenditures on durable goods by consumers may also be inversely related to the rate of interest. Items such as automobiles, refrigerators, and stoves fall into this category.

The above analysis shows that changes in the money supply will change the rate of interest, which in turn causes a change in aggregate expenditure, which in turn causes a change in the level of GNP, as shown in Chapter 7. In general, we expect the change in GNP to be in the same direction as the change in the money supply. Decreases in the money supply will increase interest rates, decrease aggregate expenditures, and decrease GNP. Increases in the money supply will have the opposite effect.

Money and the Level of Prices

The preceding discussion presumes that it is possible to increase the volume of goods and services as a result of increased planned expenditures. This may not be possible if the economy is already operating at capacity. A rapid increase in the quantity of money, when not matched by a corresponding increase in the available volumes of goods and services, is liable to result in general increases in prices. A rapid increase in the quantity of money can cause or add to inflation, although this is not the only possible cause of inflation of prices. When the growth in the money supply outstrips the growth in the supply of goods, a situation is said to exist in which there is too much money chasing too few goods. In this situation, the general level of prices tends to rise. Indeed, the crude *quantity theory of money* predicts that a given percentage change in the money supply will result in the same percentage increase in prices when output is at capacity levels.

A more complete model of the macroeconomy is discussed in the Appendix to this chapter. That model will allow for price changes and income changes as well as the extreme cases discussed in this section. A more complete treatment of inflation and unemployment is contained in Chapter 10.

An Overview of the Canadian Financial System

Measuring the Canadian Money Supply

The basic monetary units in Canada (coins and notes making up the currency) have several desirable properties. The monetary unit is divisible and the currency is portable, durable, easily recognized, and widely accepted. The amount of money available is relatively scarce — at least, sufficiently scarce to retain its value. It is desirable that objects used for money have these properties.

Most of Canada's money supply is held in bank deposits. Only about 40 percent, given one definition of money (and only about 6 percent by another) is held by the public in notes and coins (see Table 8.1). Economists consider that the money supply consists of notes and coins held by the public plus bank balances that can be converted rapidly into currency. Economists differ in their views about how *liquid* (readily convertible into currency) a bank balance has to be before it should be regarded as part of the money supply. Some regard only demand deposits with the chartered banks as part of the money supply, whereas others regard all deposits with the chartered banks as part of the supply. Four common measures of the Canadian money supply are M1, M1A, M2 and M3:

M1 = Currency in the hands of the public plus demand deposits less private
sector float.[1]
M1A = M1 plus daily interest chequable and nonpersonal notice deposits.
M2 = M1A plus other notice deposits, and personal term deposits.
M3 = M2 plus other nonpersonal fixed-term deposits, plus foreign currency
deposits of residents booked in Canada.

The supply of money in Canada in June 1983 according to these measures
is set out in Table 8.1.

TABLE **8.1** **The Supply of Money in Canada, June 1983 ($ million)**

Currency (notes plus coins)	11,512
M1 measure of the money supply	28,428
M1A measure of the money supply	35,891
M2 measure of the money supply	134,883
M3 measure of the money supply	184,449

SOURCE: Bank of Canada Review, November 1983, Table 9.

Moving from the M1A definition to the M2 definition results in the measure
increasing substantially. The M1 and M1A measures emphasize the medium of
exchange function of money, whereas the M2 and M3 measures also consider
the role of money as a store of wealth. Even though people do not have immediate access to this wealth, the knowledge that they will have access at a
specified time may affect their behaviour.

There are other assets, however, that are close substitutes for money as
defined above, and that can be regarded as "near money". These include
deposits in credit unions and caises populaire, trust and mortgage companies.

The Financial Sector

Canadian financial institutions form a bridge between those with excess money
balances, or money to lend, and those wishing to borrow money, or financial
capital. They act as financial intermediaries in the economic system. By pooling
the contributions of many depositors, financial institutions are often able to use
deposits at call, or repayable on short notice, to finance loans repayable over a
long period. Short-term savings are pooled to make long-term capital formation
possible. Such pooling also reduces the risk for an individual depositor as the
depositor is investing (in a sense) in the diversified portfolio of the institution.
Financial institutions also make a social contribution by providing knowledge

[1]Float arises when the account of one individual is credited for a cheque deposit but the
account of the person who issued the cheque has not yet been reduced.

to potential lenders and borrowers (for instance knowledge about alternative investments and sources of funds) by managing their finance, or part of it, and by facilitating, as in the case of stock exchanges, contact between those wishing to make financial exchanges.

The relative size of various financial institutions is shown in Table 8.2.

TABLE 8.2   **Assets of Selected Financial Institutions in Canada, December 1982 ($ million)**

Bank of Canada	19,423
Chartered banks	369,062
Trust and mortgage companies	76,516
Top 15 life insurance companies*	55,063
Local credit unions and caisses populaire	33,527
Sales, finance, and consumer-loan companies	12,516
Investment companies	
a. mutual funds	5,233
b. closed-end funds	662
Quebec Savings Banks	4,589

SOURCES: *Bank of Canada Review*, November 1983; *Financial Post 500*, June 1983.

The financial intermediaries may be divided into two major groups:
a. those institutions in the banking system, and
b. nonbank financial institutions.

The Canadian Banking System

The banking system consists of the chartered banks and the central bank. The central bank in Canada is the Bank of Canada, which is a Crown Corporation. The Bank of Canada is the banker to the Canadian government, and, by various means, influences the lending policies of the chartered banks. It also advises the Canadian government on monetary and financial policy. The Bank of Canada is of central importance in the Canadian financial system.

As shown in Table 8.2, the chartered banks are by far the largest group in the Canadian financial system. Chartered banks in Canada are privately owned, profit-seeking enterprises. They act as middlemen between savers and borrowers. Banks make their profits by lending at a higher rate of interest than that paid on deposits, and by charging customers for various specialized services that they provide. At the same time, it is important that banks provide depositors with maximum security. Depositors are protected by practices of the banks and by government regulations.

1. The banks follow conservative lending policies — borrowers must have a high credit-worthiness as established by the respective bank.
2. The banks are required to purchase insurance against deposit loss from the Canadian Deposit Insurance Corporation (CIDC). The CIDC guarantees deposits at the banks (and other clients of the CIDC) up to a limit of $60,000 per deposit. The CIDC is a Crown Corporation.
3. The banks are also required to maintain specified ratios of deposits as cash on hand to meet any likely run on withdrawals by depositors.

In *The Canadian Establishment*, Peter Newman suggests that the image of the Canadian financial system is one of "Careful Money", and refers to Canadian bankers as "those extraordinarily ordinary individuals who operate the safest and one of the most profitable banking systems on earth."

There are five major chartered banks as well as several smaller ones. All these banks are under the regulations of the *Bank Act*, which is a federal statute. The *Bank Act* is subject to review every ten years. The most recent revision appeared in 1980.

The five major banks are the Royal Bank of Canada, the Canadian Imperial Bank of Commerce, the Bank of Montreal, the Bank of Nova Scotia, and the Toronto-Dominion Bank. All these banks (or the banking companies that amalgamated to form them) were in existence in the 1800s. The relative sizes of these five banks is shown in Table 8.3.

TABLE 8.3   **Comparative sizes of 5 major Canadian Chartered Banks (ranked by assets as at October 1982 in $ million)**

1.	Royal Bank of Canada	88,456.0
2.	Canadian Imperial Bank of Commerce	68,436.3
3.	Bank of Montreal	62,027.0
4.	Bank of Nova Scotia	53,630.5
5.	Toronto-Dominion Bank	45,038.4

SOURCE: Financial Post 500, June 1983.

In 1982, these five banks accounted for roughly 86 percent of total bank assets. The Canadian banking system is concentrated in few hands. The workability of the system is made possible by branch banking. Each of the major chartered banking companies has branches throughout the country. In 1978, there were over 7400 branch offices in Canada. This helps to add to the stability of the system. For instance, financial difficulties or needs in one region can be countered by drawng funds from other regions.

On the other hand, the small number of major banks may tend to reduce competition between banks. The Canadian banking system is oligopolistic. In a study originally conducted for the Economic Council of Canada, George Lermer found that the 1967-73 profit rates of Canadian chartered banks were higher than average profit rates in the manufacturing sector. He also found that comparable banking services are more expensive in Canada than in the United States, which has a more competitive banking structure.

Previous to 1980, banks were required to obtain a charter by special act of Parliament in order to conduct business as a bank in Canada. The 1980 revision of the *Bank Act* allows banks to be established by obtaining letters patent — a simpler procedure. This makes entry to the Canadian banking system easier than it was previously. For example, between 1980 and June 1982, 57 foreign banks had entered into the Canadian banking system.

The nature of the business conducted by the chartered banks can be seen from the combined balance sheet for all chartered banks. This sets out their assets on the one side and on the other side their liabilities, that is, their sources of funds and therefore the individuals or groups to whom they are liable for those funds. The aggregate assets for all chartered banks as at September 1983 are set out in Table 8.4, and the aggregate liabilities are set out in Table 8.5.

Roughly 58 percent of bank assets in September 1983 were in Canadian dollars, and 42 percent in foreign currency. The bulk of the Canadian dollar assets are in the form of loans. The largest subcomponent is general loans. Mortgages are the next largest group. Roughly 12 percent of Canadian dollar assets were held as liquid assets.

The largest source of Canadian dollar funds (liabilities) is Canadian dollar deposits accounting for 81 percent of Canadian dollar funds in September 1983. Personal savings deposits accounted for 61 percent of total deposits. Demand deposits are much less significant, accounting for roughly 11 percent of total deposits. This reflects the fact that demand deposits do not earn interest for the depositor whereas savings deposits do. Roughly 44 percent of banks' source of funds is in foreign currency, which is close to the proportion of foreign currency held assets.

The Creation of Credit by Banks

As a rule, banks or financiers are able to use a new deposit to make loans, or other financial investments, and accumulate additional deposits in the banking system that are a multiple of the original deposit. This is possible because banks need only keep a fraction of the deposit as cash reserves on hand, or as a deposit at the central bank. The remaining fraction may be invested by the banks in either loans or other financial securities that earn income for the banks. A share of these loans (or payments for securities) when spent by the borrowers provide incomes, a payment for others, and at least a part of these receipts will be deposited in the banking system. These deposits allow the banks to make additional loans or investments, which in turn result in extra deposits. Thus, by a cumulative process, a new deposit in the banking system can lead to a total expansion in credit that is several times the original deposit.

Consider a simple example. Assume that there is just one bank in the bank-

TABLE 8.4   **Combined Assets of Canadian Chartered Banks as at September 30, 1983 ($ million)**

I.	Canadian liquid assets		
	1. Bank of Canada deposits and notes	5,419	
	2. Day-to-day loans	30	
	3. Treasury bills	15,047	
	4. Government of Canada direct and guaranteed bonds	2,697	
	5. Call and Short loans	1,773	
	Total liquid assets	24,967	
II.	Less liquid Canadian assets		
	1. Loans in Canadian dollars		
	a. Provinces	183	
	b. Municipalities	1,219	
	c. Canada Savings Bonds	51	
	d. General loans	111,754	
	e. Residential mortgages	31,401	
	f. Nonresidential mortgages	2,648	
	g. Leasing receivables	2,431	
	Total loans	149,686	
	2. Canadian Securities		
	a. Provincial and municipal	715	
	b. Corporate shares	4,668	
	c. Corporate, other	4,154	
	d. Corporations associated with banks	206	
	Total securities	9,742	
III.	Deposits with other banks	4,553	
IV.	Canadian dollar items in transit (net)	1,368	
V.	Customers' liability under acceptances	15,567	
VI.	All other Canadian dollar assets	5,923	
	Total Canadian dollar assets		211,806
VII.	Total foreign-currency assets	156,758	
	Total assets		368,564

SOURCE: Bank of Canada Review, November 1983, Table 7.

TABLE 8.5 **Combined Liabilities of Canadian Chartered Banks as at September 30, 1983 ($ million)**

I.	Canadian dollar deposits	
	1. Personal savings deposits	
	a. Chequable	8,438
	b. Nonchequable	52,134
	c. Fixed term	42,698
	2. Nonpersonal term and notice deposits	
	a. Notice	5,554
	b. Fixed term	39,042
	3. Gross demand deposits	
	a. Personal chequing	4,034
	b. Other	14,758
	4. Government of Canada	2,564
	Total deposits	169,222
II.	Advances from Bank of Canada	134
III.	Bankers acceptance	15,567
IV.	Liabilities of subsidiaries other than deposits	1,426
V.	Other liabilities	4,540
VI.	Minority interest in subsidiaries	104
VII.	Bank debentures issued and outstanding	2,554
VIII.	Appropriations for contingencies	
	1. Tax allowable	433
	2. Tax paid	287
IX	Shareholders' equity	
	1. Capital stock	
	a. Common	2,911
	b. Preferred	2,150
	2. Contributed surplus	1,019
	3. General reserve	25
	4. Retained earnings	7,756
X.	Total foreign-currency liabilities	160,435
	Total liabilities	368,564

Source: Bank of Canada Review, November 1983, Table 8.

ing system, and that this bank holds its assets in cash and loans. Suppose that
the legal minimum cash reserve requirement is 20 percent of its deposits.
Further, suppose the bank does not wish to hold excess cash reserves, that is,
cash in excess of the legal requirement. Now consider what happens when an
extra $100 is deposited with the bank. Because the bank wishes to remain fully
loaned up (no excess cash reserves), it will retain $20 as cash in order to satisfy
the legal requirement and make loans with the remaining $80. Individuals
receiving payment from those borrowing the $80 will deposit some of their
receipts in the bank. For simplicity, assume that they deposit all their receipts.
The deposits of the bank will then rise by $80. The bank is then able to lend 80
percent of these deposits (that is $64), and so the process will continue in the
way illustrated in Table 8.6.

TABLE 8.6   **Example of the credit-creation process assuming a cash reserve ratio
of 0.2**

Period	Chain of Deposits ($)	Chain of loans ($)
1	100	80
2	80	64
3	64	51.2
4	51.2	40.96
5	40.96	32.77
6	32.77	26.21
7	26.21	20.97
8	20.97	16.77
9	16.77	•
•	•	•
•	•	•
•	•	•
Total approached	500	400

In the long run, and under the above conditions, total deposits in the bank
increase by $500, and total loans or credit created approach $400, or four times
the initial deposit of $100. The number of times by which credit is increased in
relation to the initial deposit is 4. This is known as the *credit creation multiplier.*
It can also be called the *deposit creation multiplier* because it also equals the
ratio that *derived deposits* (that is, deposits flowing on in the chain from the
original deposit) accruing to the banks bear to the original deposit. Where R
represents the cash reserve ratio of the bank, the credit creation multiplier can
be found by subsituting the appropriate value of R into the formula

$$\frac{1-R}{R}.$$

In the above example:

$$\frac{1-R}{R} = \frac{1-0.2}{0.2}$$

$$= \frac{0.8}{0.2}$$

$$= 4.$$

The total increase in loans (and derived deposits) can be found by multiplying the initial new deposit by this multiplier. Note that this multiplier is smaller the larger is R. The total increase in deposits including the initial deposit can be found by multiplying the initial deposit by $1/R$.

Although a bank credit multiplier of greater than one is likely for the whole banking system, it is not likely to be as great as suggested above because leakages from the system are likely to occur. For instance, not all payments made from loans need be redeposited with the banks. Some may be hoarded or held in cash by recipients, or used to purchase goods overseas.

It might also be observed that the credit creation multiplier indicates the potential of the banks for increasing the quantity of money, where this is defined to include deposits with the banks. In the above example, an initial increase in the quantity of money by $100 results eventually in an increase of $500 in the quantity of money, that is an increase equal to the eventual rise in deposits. In adding or withdrawing money from the economic system, the Bank of Canada needs to take the credit creation multiplier into account. For instance, the Bank of Canada would need to take this into account if it purchased $100 worth of bonds or securities from the public, thereby adding $100 in cash to the economy.

The Bank of Canada and Monetary Policy

The Bank of Canada is the central bank in Canada. It is owned by the federal government, and:

1. is the banker for the federal government,
2. a banker to the chartered banks, which hold deposits with it, and draw upon these to settle or clear debts between them,
3. advises the government on monetary and financial policy, and may implement monetary controls, for instance, take measures to reduce the amount of lending by the chartered banks,
4. issues Bank of Canada notes, which are legal tender,
5. manages the Foreign Exchange Fund Account for the federal government on the instructions of the Minister of Finance, and

6. acts as a lender of last resort for the chartered banks, should they experience financial difficulties.

The Bank of Canada is generally charged with regulating financial conditions in a manner that will ensure high levels of employment and stable prices of goods and services, and also protect the foreign-currency value of the Canadian dollar. These three aims may very well conflict with each other as will be seen in subsequent chapters. The most important function for the Bank of Canada is to control the volume of money in Canada. In the early part of this chapter, we saw that changes in the money supply can have repercussions on the level of employment and prices. We now turn to a discussion of the tools that the Bank of Canada may use in order to influence the Canadian money supply.

The example discussed in the previous section showed that new deposits to the banking system will result in a multiple expansion in the money supply as a result of credit creation. A loss of deposits will result in a multiple contraction of the money supply. The size of the multiplier effect will depend, among other things (such as cash leakage), upon the legal required cash reserve ratio. This suggests that in principle a central bank may control the money supply by either creating or destroying deposits, or by changing the cash reserve requirements of the banking system.

Changes in the Cash Reserve Ratio

Although a change in the legal cash reserve ratio would have a powerful effect on the money supply, the Bank of Canada has never used this as a tool of discretionary monetary policy. From 1954 to 1967, the Bank of Canada had the right to change the required ratio between 8 and 12 percent, but chose not to exercise this right: the reserve ratio remained at 8 percent of total deposits during that period. The right to discretionary changes in the reserve requirement was withdrawn in the 1967 *Bank Act* revision. At that time, the reserve requirement was split with the banks being required to hold 12 percent of demand deposits as reserves, and 4 percent of savings and notice deposits. The 1980 *Bank Act* revisions specified a gradual reduction in these reserve requirements that will result in 10 percent on demand deposits, 2 percent on notice deposits less than $500 million, and 3 percent on notice deposits over $500 million. The rate for demand deposits was reduced 1/4 percent every six months commencing March 1981. The rate on notice deposits was reduced by 1/8 percent every six months commencing March 1981.

Secondary Reserve Requirement

In the 1967 revision of the *Bank Act*, the Bank of Canada was given the right to require the banks to hold an additional proportion of their assets in highly liquid form. These liquid assets include excess cash, day-to-day loans, and government Treasury bills. These reserves are called secondary reserves. The Bank of Canada can vary the secondary-reserve requirement between zero and 12 percent of deposits. The historical pattern of the secondary-reserve requirement is given in Table 8.7.

FIGURE 8.3 Time profile of the required reserve ratio

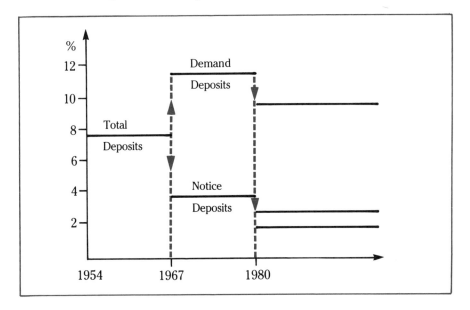

TABLE 8.7 History of the secondary-reserve requirement

Date of Change		Rate Set (%)
1968	March	6.0
	April	7.0
1969	June	8.0
1970	July	9.0
1971	December	8.5
1972	January	8.0
1974	December	7.0
1975	January	6.0
	March	5.5
1977	February	5.0
1981	December	4.0

SOURCE: Bank of Canada Review, March 1983, p. 5156.

Open Market Operations

The Bank of Canada can affect the size of deposits in the banking system by purchasing or selling government securities in financial markets. These types of transactions are called *open market operations*. If the Bank of Canada purchases a security from the public, it makes payment by issuing a cheque drawn upon itself. The person who sells the security cashes the cheque and places the proceeds (or some fraction thereof) in a deposit. This is a new deposit (called a primary deposit) for the banking system, and leads to a multiple expansion of deposits in the fashion shown in the previous section. Open market transactions not only affect the size of the money supply, but they may affect interest rates directly. If the Bank of Canada wishes to purchase large quantities of securities, this may result in bond prices rising as a result of demand pressure, and hence interest rates fall.

The reverse happens if the Bank of Canada sells a security to the public. The individuals pay the Bank of Canada with cheques drawn on their own deposits. Their deposits will be lower by the value of securities purchased. This will cause a multiple contraction of deposits. The sale of securities by the Bank of Canada will also tend to push up interest rates, as the increased supply of securities will tend to depress bond prices.

Transfer of Government of Canada Deposits

If the Bank of Canada wants to affect credit conditions without the direct effects on interest rates associated with open market operations, it can choose to transfer the federal government's deposits between itself and the chartered banks. If the Bank of Canada wishes to increase the money supply, it can decide to allocate more of the government's account to the government's deposits with the chartered banks. If a decrease in the money supply is desired, the Bank of Canada can choose to hold more of the account with itself, and hence withdraw funds from deposits held with the chartered banks. The Bank of Canada is able to do this in its capacity as the banker to the federal government.

The Bank Rate

The Bank of Canada is the lender of last resort for the chartered banks. The *bank rate* is the interest rate charged by the Bank of Canada for short-term advances to the chartered banks. As Canadian chartered banks seldom borrow from the Bank of Canada, the main function of the bank rate is to signal the changes in interest rates and credit conditions that the Bank of Canada believes to be appropriate. Since March 1980, the bank rate has been set a 1/4 percentage point above the interest rate established for 91-day Treasury bills at the weekly Thursday auction. The bank rate is thus a floating rate that the Bank of Canada influences through participation in the weekly auction as well as the secondary market.[2] Between June 1962 and March 1980, the bank rate was specified directly by the Bank of Canada, and was changed only at its discretion.

Moral Suasion

Moral suasion is the term used for discussions held between the Bank of Canada and the chartered banks whereby the Bank of Canada attempts to achieve special arrangements or agreements concerning the financial system.

Nonbanking Financial Institutions

Important nonbanking financial institutions include trust and mortgage companies, life insurance companies, credit unions and caisses populaire, sales-finance and consumer-loan companies, investment companies, and Quebec Savings Bank. Although it is difficult to measure the contribution of these institutions to the functioning of the financial capital market, Table 8.2 gives some indication of their relative sizes. It can be seen that their combined assets are less than those of the chartered banks.

Because many of their services are similar to those offered by the chartered banks, institutions such as trust and mortgage companies, credit unions and caisses populaire, and the Quebec Savings Bank are frequently referred to as "near banks".

Trust and mortgage loan companies combined have the largest amount of assets held by nonbanking financial institutions. Life insurance companies, and credit unions and caisses populaire are also fairly large groups within the nonbanking financial sector.

Trust and Mortgage Loan companies obtain the bulk of their funds from term deposits, guaranteed investment certificates, and debentures. In June 1983, this source accounted for 63 percent of their funds. At the same time, 68 percent of their funds were tied up in mortgage loans and sales agreements. A more detailed breakdown of combined assets and liabilities is presented for June 1983 in Table 8.8. Mortgage loan companies are regulated by provincial legislation or the federal *Loan Companies Act*, whereas trust companies are regulated by provincial legislation, or the federal *Trust Companies Act*. Deposits held with trust and mortgage loan companies are insured with the Canada Deposit Insurance Corporation (or the Quebec Deposit Insurance Board).

---

[2]The auction here refers to the first-round sales of Treasury bills. The secondary market refers to retrading once the security has been offered and purchased, and thus enters, potentially, the secondary market. In this way, the Bank of Canada can influence the rate by trading (or not) in either market, as they are substitute investments. (That is, investors can buy a newly issued Treasury bill or a recently issued one. Operating in one market has a direct impact on the other.)

TABLE 8.8 **Balance Sheet for Trust and Mortgage Loan Companies, June 1983**
($ million)

A.	Assets		
	1.	Cash and demand deposits	747
	2.	Government of Canada Treasury bills	2,477
	3.	Provincial and Municipal Treasury bills and short-term notes	842
	4.	Term and notice deposits	1,928
	5.	Short-term paper	2,929
	6.	Canadian bonds	7,458
	7.	Mortgage loans and sales agreements	57,747
	8.	Personal loans	2,068
	9.	Collateral loans	108
	10.	Canadian preferred and common shares	2,547
	11.	Foreign securities	22
	12.	Investment in affiliated companies	1,466
	13.	Other assets	4,569
		Total assets	84,908
B.	Liabilities		
	1.	Savings deposits	
		a. Chequable	2,986
		b. Nonchequable	8,761
	2.	Term deposits, guaranteed investment certificates, and debentures	53,458
	3.	Bank loans	2,571
	4.	Accounts payable	3,168
	5.	Owing parent and affiliated Canadian companies	1,100
	6.	Debentures issued under Trust-Indenture	987
	7.	Promissory notes	6,772
	8.	Other liabilities	789
	9.	Shareholders' equity	4,315
		Total liabilities	84,908

SOURCE: *Bank of Canada Review,* November 1983, Table 40.

The balance sheet for *credit unions* and *caisses populaire* for June 1983 is presented in Table 8.9. The main source of funds is deposits, which accounted for 87 percent in June 1983. Forty-five percent of their funds are invested in mortgages. Slightly less than one-quarter is in the form of loans of which 71 percent are personal loans.

The Montréal City and District Savings Bank has been the only institution

TABLE 8.9 **Aggregate Balance Sheet for Local Credit Unions and Caisses Populaire, March 1983 ($ million)**

A.	Assets		
	1.	Cash on hand	435
	2.	Demand deposits	3,528
	3.	Term deposits	3,837
	4.	Government of Canada securities	153
	5.	Provincial securities	98
	6.	Municipal securities	209
	7.	Shares in central credit unions	263
	8.	Cash Loans	
		a. Personal	5,847
		b. Other	2,380
	9.	Mortgages	15,586
	10.	Other assets	2,258
		Total	34,595
B.	Liabilities		
	1.	Loans payable	795
	2.	Deposits	29,990
	3.	Other liabilities	1,045
	4.	Members' equity	2,765
		Total	34,595

SOURCE: *Bank of Canada Review,* November 1983, Table 39.

since 1969 to operate as a *Quebec Savings Bank.* Virtually all of its funds are obtained from deposits held with it. More than half of its assets are held in mortgages.

In addition to private financial intermediaries, there are also government financial institutions. These include the Province of Ontario Savings Office, the Federal Business Development Bank, the Farm Credit Corporation Canada, the Canada Mortgage Housing Corporation, and the Export Development Corporation. The relative size of these financial enterprises is shown in Table 8.10.

Although the *stock exchange* and stock brokers (agents of buyers and sellers of stocks or shares in companies) are not financial institutions in the sense of principally borrowing and advancing money in their own right, they play a not insignificant role in the functioning of the capital market. The stock exchange facilitates the marketability of the shares, debentures, and notes of companies listed on the stock exchange. Stock brokers also arrange for the floating of new public companies on the stock exchange, that is, the raising of capital for new companies by inviting subscriptions from the public, and they, or associated underwriters, may guarantee or underwrite the company for the

amount of capital it seeks. In the event of a shortfall in subscriptions, the under-
writer makes up the difference between the amount sought and the amount
subscribed. The stock exchange and stock brokers thus play an important role
in assisting companies raise capital, and the marketability of the securities of
companies listed on the stock exchange is a factor encouraging members of the
public to subscribe capital to such companies.

TABLE 8.10   **Assets of Selected Government Financial Enterprises, 1982
($ million)**

1.	Canada Mortgage and Housing Corporation (Dec.)	10,700
2.	Export Development Corporation (Dec.)	5,282
3.	Farm Credit Corporation Canada (Mar.)	3,853
4.	Province of Alberta Treasury Branches (Mar.)	2,730
5.	Federal Business Development Bank (Mar.)	1,958
6.	Province of Ontario Savings Office (Mar.)	699

SOURCE: The Financial Post 500, June 1983.

FIGURE 8.4   **The Toronto Stock Exchange: facilitating the marketing of shares of
companies**
Courtesy The Toronto Stock Exchange

As can be seen, the financial system, and the assets of financial institutions involved in the system, is large and diversified. A financial system of the type that has evolved is essential to the efficient operation of our market economy, which is so dependent on the use of money. Variations in financial activity can be affected by changes in the quantity of money and other factors under the control of the Bank of Canada. Such variations can change employment, production, and also prices. The Bank of Canada, however, cannot perfectly control the system.

Appendix to Chapter 8

The Determination of National Income and the Price Level: The Aggregate Demand and Aggregate Supply Model

The discussion of the determination of national income in Chapter 7, and in the text of the present chapter, treated the price level as being constant. The current chapter did discuss the possible implications that changes in the money supply would have on the price level if the level of national income were constant at potential output. The purpose of this Appendix is to present a framework that will allow for variations in both prices and national income as well as allowing for the special extreme cases where only one of the two items responds. The framework to be discussed is called the Aggregate Demand and Aggregate Supply (AD-AS) model. In this model, the level of aggregate demand (AD) for commodities and the aggregate supply (AS) of commodities are assumed to depend upon the prevailing price level.

AD is assumed to be inversely related to the prevailing price level as shown in Figure 8.5, whereas AS is assumed to have the shape shown in Figure 8.6.

FIGURE 8.5 **The Aggregate Demand Curve**

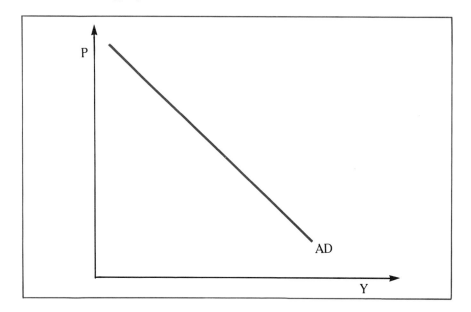

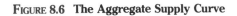

FIGURE 8.6 **The Aggregate Supply Curve**

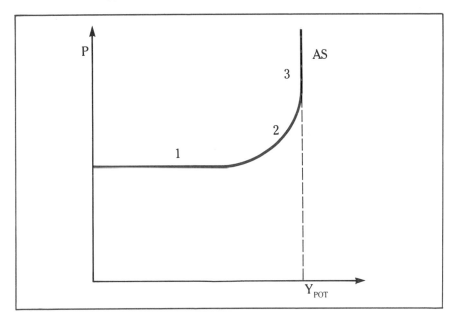

Why is AD inversely related to P? A simple answer will suffice for the present discussion. Price changes, other things being equal, will cause changes in interest rates. Why? This occurs because a price increase, for example, will mean that people need more money to finance expenditures. With no change in the supply of money, this increased demand for money will put upward pressure on interest rates. This can be shown by shifting the demand for money curve upward in Figure 8.2. An alternative but equivalent way to express this is to say that an increase in P decreases the "real value" of a given "nominal" money supply. Interpreting the money demand and supply in Figure 8.2 as being in real terms, this means that the real money supply shifts leftward and pushes up interest rates. With higher interest rates, aggregate expenditure will be lower. This inverse relationship between aggregate expenditure and the price level is called the aggregate demand curve. The position of the AD curve is determined by the components in the aggregate expenditure relationship, the nominal money supply, and the factors determining the position of the demand for money curves.

The AS curve has three essential sections: 1. a relatively flat section, 2. an upward sloping section, and 3. a relatively vertical section. In the relatively flat section of the curve, variations in output take place without much response in prices. In this section, we can suppose that there is substantial unemployment so that firms may expand output without raising factors costs such as wage rates very much, and hence prices do not have to change very much. In section

2, resources require higher rates of compensation as firms compete for the use
of their services. As wage rates and other factor costs rise, firms require higher
prices. In section 3, the economy is at the potential level of GNP, denoted Y_{POT},
where all resources are fully utilized. In this section, if firms attempt to expand,
they can do so only by attracting factors of production away from other firms.
As a result, factor costs rise, but the resources are merely redistributed with no
real change in the actual volume of production in the economy. Because factor
costs are higher, the price level must rise. This relationship between GNP produced and the price level is called the aggregate supply curve. The position of
the AS curve is determined in the producing sector.

In order to determine the level of production and the price level, combine
the AD and AS diagrams into one, as in Figure 8.7.

FIGURE 8.7 **Possible Equilibrium Positions**

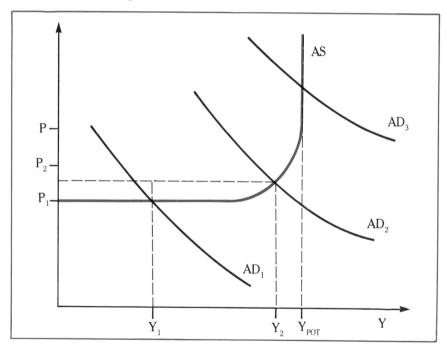

Figure 8.7 represents three possible AD curves with one AS curve. The
intersection of an AD curve with the AS curve determines the equilibrium level
of national income and the general price level. If the relevant AD curve is AD_1,
then the equilibrium is (Y_1, P_1). Small changes in AD around AD_1 will produce
mainly changes in Y with relatively little response in P. If the relevant AD curve
is AD_2, then small changes in AD will produce a mixture of income and price
changes. If AD_3 is the AD curve, then small changes in AD will result mainly (or

entirely) in price changes with national income constant at Y_{POT}. Changes in AD may be the result of changes in policy variables such as government expenditures or taxes, or the money supply. Changes in AD may also occur as a result of changes in the planned expenditures (at given interest rates and income levels) by other purchasers such as consumers, domestic firms or foreigners. Upward (downward) shifts in the aggregate expenditure (AE) curve correspond to rightward (leftward) shifts in the aggregate demand curve (AD).

KEY CONCEPTS
(FOR REVIEW)

Aggregate Demand Curve
Aggregate Supply Curve
Assets
Bank of Canada
Bank Rate
Banking System
Canada Deposit Insurance
   Corporation
Cash Reserve Ratio
Cash Reserves
Chartered Banks
Credit Unions and caisses populaire
Currency
Demand Deposits
Deposit Creation
Excess Reserves

Financial Intermediaries
Interest Rates
Lender of Last Resort
Liquidity
Money
M1, M1A, M2, M3
Moral Suasion
Near Banks
Near Money
Open Market Operations
Quebec Savings Bank
Required Cash Reserve Ratio
Savings Deposits
Secondary Reserve Requirement
Trust and Mortgage Loan
   Companies

QUESTIONS FOR REVIEW AND DISCUSSION

1. How did paper money come into existence?
2. Are Canadian notes convertible into gold or other precious metals? Why are they acceptable?
3. What functions does money (or monetary units) perform?
4. What properties is it desirable for monetary units (notes and coins) to have?
5. Where is most of Canada's money supply held?
6. Distinguish between M_1, M_2, and M_3 as measures of the volume of money.
7. What factors influence the demand for money?
8. What factors or institutions help to determine the supply of money in Canada?
9. What is the quantity theory of money?
10. Is there any evidence that price levels tend to rise with the quantity of money?

11. What are the main functions performed by financial institutions?
12. Outline the general structure of the Canadian banking system.
13. What are the most important nonbanking financial institutions in Canada? How do they compare in size?
14. What objectives do banks pursue, and how are they limited by security considerations in following their main objectives?
15. List the five major Canadian chartered banks. How do they compare in size?
16. "The Canadian banking system is concentrated in few hands, and the workability of the system is made possible by branch banking." Discuss.
17. What are the main purposes and functions of the chartered banks?
18. What are the main sources of funds for the chartered banks? What are the main forms in which the chartered banks hold or utilize their funds?
19. What is the Bank of Canada, and what are its main functions?
20. What are cash reserves? Excess cash reserves?
21. What is the required cash reserve ratio?
22. "A new deposit in the banking system can lead to a total expansion in bank credit and deposits that is several times the original deposit." Explain.
23. Assume that the cash reserve ratio in the banking system is 0.1 and that no leakages occur. Trace through the chain of deposits and loans flowing from an initial new deposit of $100.00. In the long run, how much credit or derived deposits will be created? (You may also wish to carry out this exercise assuming a cash reserve ratio of 0.25.)
24. What is the credit creation multiplier? What types of leakages are likely to reduce the size of this multiplier?
25. What tools does the Bank of Canada have available to influence the size of the money supply?
26. How do variations in the supply of money affect economic conditions in Canada?

FURTHER READING

Binhammer, H.H., *Money, Banking, and the Canadian Financial System*, 4th ed. Toronto: Methuen Publications, 1982.

Blomqvist, A., Wonnacott, P., & Wonnacott, R., *Economics*, 1st Canadian ed. Scarborough: McGraw-Hill Ryerson Limited, 1984, chapters 7, 8, & 9.

Lermer, G., "The Performance of Canadian Banking." *Canadian Journal of Economics* (November 1980), pp. 578-93.

Lipsey, R.G., Purvis, D.D., Sparks, G.R., & Steiner, P.O., *Economics*, 4th ed. New York: Harper & Row, Publishers, 1982, chapters 35, 37, & 38.

Neave, E.H., *Canada's Financial System*. Rexdale: John Wiley & Sons Canada Limited, 1981.

International Economic Relations   **9**

Canada's International Trade and Balance of Payments

International trade provides a means of reducing scarcity throughout the world, and a way of better utilizing the world's limited resources. It enables resources from different parts of the world to be drawn upon and shared.

   International trade is important to the well-being of Canadians. In 1982, for instance, the value of Canadian exports accounted for 29 percent of Canadian GNE. The value of Canada's imports was almost 28 percent of GNE at market prices. Between 1971 and 1981, the value of Canada's exports increased by

FIGURE 9.1 **Canadian goods for sale in Japan. International trade is important to the welfare of Canadians and to our trading partners.**

   COURTESY Canada Packers Inc.

462.5 percent, and the value of imports increased by 506.5 percent. Most of the
increase in exports and imports, however, is owing to increases in prices. Over
these ten years, the prices of exports and imports roughly tripled. The volume
of exports increased only 50 percent, whereas the volume of imports increased
71 percent. In constant 1971 dollars, exports in 1981 accounted for 24 percent
of GNE, and imports for 27 percent.

Composition of Canada's Exports

Exports account for a large share of the output of primary industry in Canada.
Slightly more than half of Canada's exports arise from exports of primary, or
resource, products. About 27 percent of Canada's exports comprised of metals
and minerals in 1981, and another 28 percent from forest, farm, and fish products. Other manufactured goods accounted for 40 percent. As shown in Table
9.1 and in Figure 9.2, the share of exports accounted for by metals and
minerals has fallen since 1975, whereas the proportion contributed by
chemicals and fertilizers, and other manufactured goods, has risen.

TABLE 9.1 **Commodity Classification of Domestic Exports ($ million)**

	1975	1981
Farm and fish products	4,248	9,830
Forest products	5,094	12,855
Metals and minerals	10,005	21,831
Chemicals and fertilizers	1,053	4,617
Other manufactured goods	12,148	32,071
	32,548	81,204

SOURCE: Bank of Canada Review, November 1982, Table 74.

Canada's Trading Partners

Canada's major trading partner is the United States, which accounts for over
two-thirds of Canada's international merchandise trade. In the period between
1971 and 1981, Japan displaced the United Kingdom as Canada's second largest
single country trading partner. The U.K. occupied third place as a trading partner in 1981. The details of Canadian trade by area are shown in tables 9.2 and
9.3.

The share of Canadian exports destined for the U.K. has fallen from 7.8 percent in 1971 to 4.0 in 1981. The share of exports destined for Japan rose from
4.7 to 5.4 percent. The European Economic Community accounts for a larger
share of exports than Japan or the U.K.

FIGURE 9.2 **Commodity Classification of Canada's Exports in 1975 and 1981**

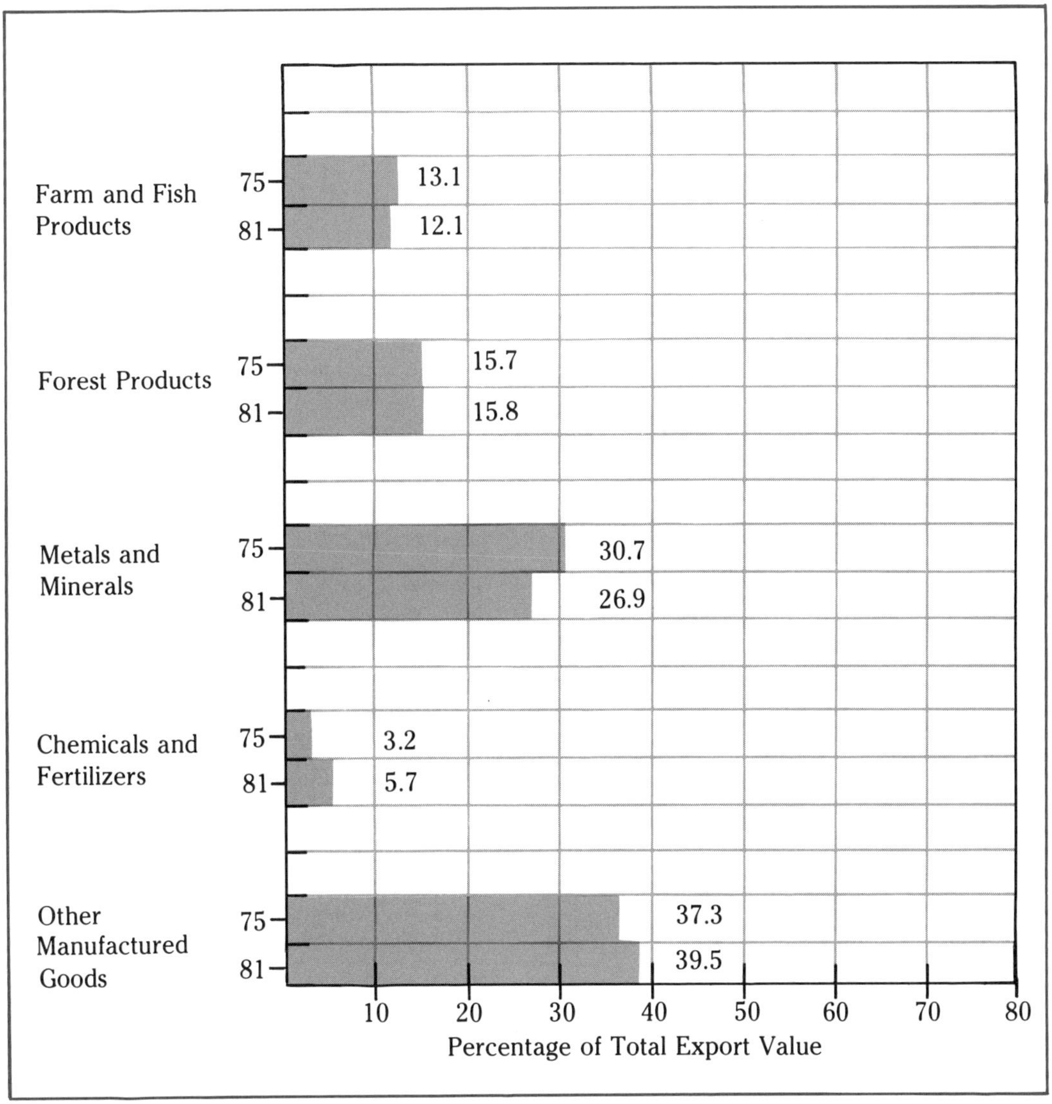

SOURCE: *Bank of Canada Review*, November 1982, Table 74.

The share of imports from the United Kingdom declined from 5.4 percent in 1971 to 3.0 in 1981. The "Other America" category did not rate a mention as a source in 1971, but in 1981, 6.4 percent of imports came from this group. Much of this may be explained by the substantial increase in oil prices in 1973-74. The price of oil quadrupled in these two years, substantially increasing the value of imported oil from Venezuela.

TABLE **9.2** **Destination of Canadian Merchandise Exports***

	1971 ($ million)	(%)	1981 ($ million)	(%)
United States	12,025	67.5	55,378	66.2
Japan	831	4.7	4,522	5.4
United Kingdom	1,395	7.8	3,347	4.0
Other EEC	1,109	6.2	5,628	6.7
Other OECD Europe	445	2.5	1,723	2.1
Other America	-	-	4,226	5.0
All Other Countries	2,013	11.3	8,854	10.6
Total	17,818	100.0	83,678	100.0

*Figures include exports of foreign products

SOURCE: *Bank of Canada Review*, November 1982, Table 72.

TABLE **9.3** **Origin of Canadian Merchandise Imports**

	1971 ($ Million)	(%)	1981 ($ Million)	(%)
United States	10,951	70.1	54,350	68.7
Japan	803	5.1	4,038	5.1
United Kingdom	837	5.4	2,337	3.0
Other America	-	-	5,093	6.4
Other EEC	935	6.0	4,117	5.2
Other OECD Europe	423	2.7	1,862	2.4
All Other Countries	1,668	10.7	7,292	9.2
	15,617	100.0	79,129	100.0

SOURCE: *Bank of Canada Review*, November 1982, Table 72.

As the United States is a major supplier of commodities for Canada and also a major purchaser of Canadian goods, it is not surprising that the health of the Canadian economy is heavily dependent upon the health of that in the United States.

International Receipts and Payments on Current Account

The total value of a country's exports of goods less the total value of its import of goods is referred to as its balance of trade. When the value of a country's exports exceeds its imports, the balance of trade is sometimes said to be favourable, and when the opposite is the case, it is said to be unfavourable. The value of Canada's exports and the value of its imports between 1971 and 1981 are graphed in Figure 9.3. Throughout most of these years, Canada had a favourable balance of trade. Only in 1975 was the balance unfavourable. This may be attributed to the world recession that occured following the oil-price increases in 1973-74. The trade surplus has increased since 1976.

FIGURE **9.3 The total value of Canadian Merchandise Exports and Imports 1971-81**

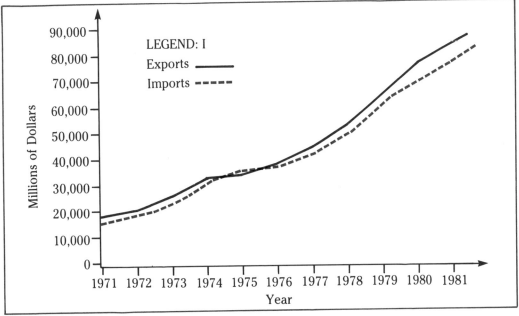

SOURCE: *Bank of Canada Review*, November 1982

The balance of trade only takes account of *goods* exchanged internationally, that is, *visible* items, and not services exchanged internationally, that is, *invisible* items. Payments for services include transport charges for shipping, payments for international travel, royalties paid on use of inventions, and profits or interests on investments, as well as transfers such as inheritances and remittances. Canada runs a large and increasing deficit on invisible trade. This is largely owing to investment income paid abroad far exceeding that received from abroad because of the large foreign investment in Canada. Canada also has a deficit on the international travel account.

The total receipts for exports of visible and invisible items less payments for imports of visible and invisible items is the *balance* of a country's international transactions *on current account*. The balance on current account is also equal to the balance of trade plus the balance of international transactions in invisible items. This is graphed for Canada in Figure 9.4. Because of the large

Canadian deficit on invisibles, there were only two years (1971 & 1973) between 1971 and 1981 in which Canada had a favourable balance on current account, even though the balance of trade was favourable in all years except 1975.

FIGURE 9.4 **Canada's balance of trade and balance on current account 1971-81**

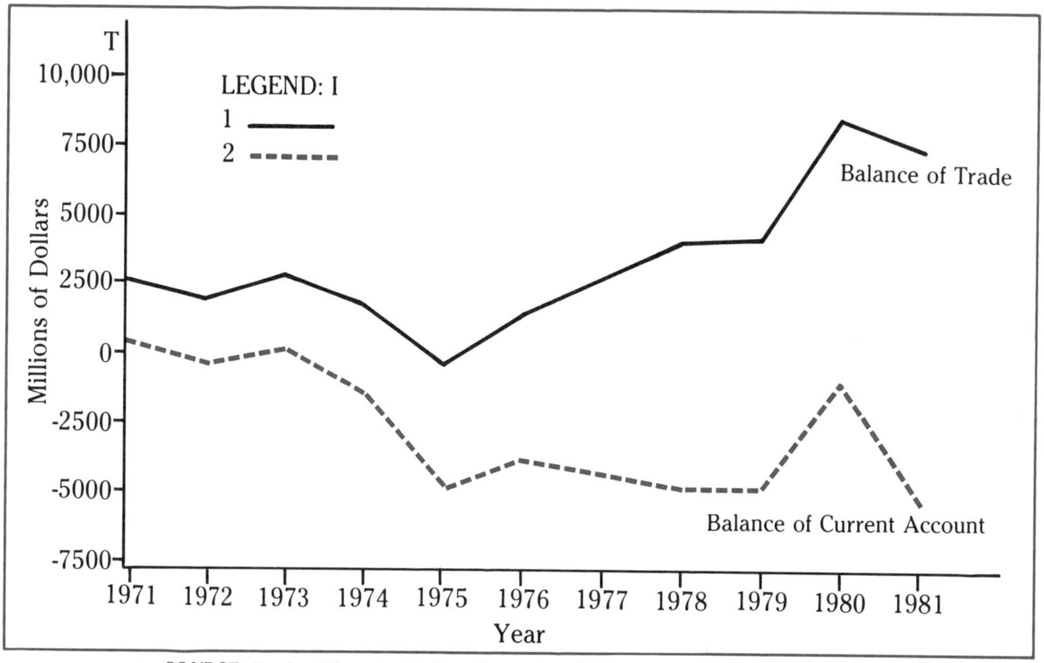

SOURCE: *Bank of Canada Review*, November 1982.

When a country runs a deficit on current account, that is when its payments to foreigners for goods and services exceeds the amount received from them, its net payments are financed from sources other than current receipts. The deficit on current account may be financed from net capital inflows from abroad or by drawing on reserves of foreign currency held by the Bank of Canada.

International Capital Flows

International capital flows refer to the flow of funds between countries for investment, speculation or other purposes, other than in return of goods and services currently exchanged. Capital inflows to Canada occur when foreign companies transfer funds from say the U.S.A., Japan or Germany for investment in business operations in Canada, or when a citizen of the U.S.A. purchases bonds or minority share holdings of companies listed with the Toronto Stock Exchange. The first-mentioned transfer is for *direct investment*, the second is for *portfolio investment*. Foreign currencies may also be converted into Canadian dollars and held for speculative reasons, for example, if it is believed that the value of the Canadian dollar will rise in relation to other currencies. When this occurs, a greater quantity of foreign currency than was initially paid can be obtained for each Canadian dollar. On the other hand, if it is believed that the value of the Canadian dollar will decline in relation to other currencies, that is, *depreciate* rather than *appreciate*, then Canadians will want to convert Canadian dollars into foreign currency in order to be able to purchase more Canadian dollars in the future.

Borrowing abroad by Canadian governments, say from the sale of its bonds in Germany or the U.S.A., also results in a capital inflow. Funds from a net capital inflow are available to meet any deficit on current account. If the net capital inflow in any year is more than sufficient to meet any deficit on current account, the surplus of foreign currency is added to the reserves of such currencies held by the Bank of Canada. If net capital inflows do not cover any deficit on current account, these reserves are drawn on to meet the deficiency.

Figure 9.5 shows that Canada has had a positive net capital inflow for each year in the 1971-81 period. Figure 9.6 indicates those years between 1971 and 1981 when Canada added to its reserves of foreign currencies (international reserves), and those years in which it was forced to reduce its reserves. When a country's total receipts of foreign currencies exceed its total payments of foreign currencies, the country is said to have a favourable *balance of payments*, or a *surplus*, in the balance of payments. When the opposite is the case, the country is said to have an unfavourable balance of payments, or a *deficit* in the balance of payments.

FIGURE 9.5 **Net capital inflow to Canada 1971-81**

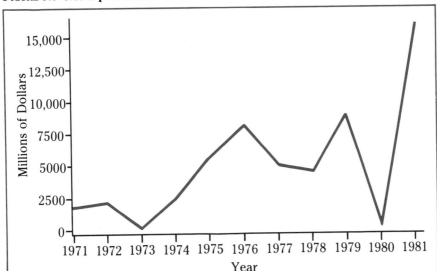

SOURCE: Bank of Canada Review, November 1982.

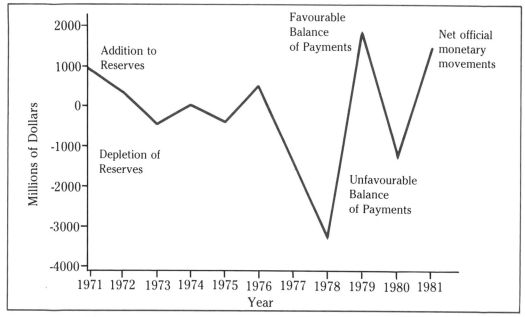

FIGURE **9.6** **Canada's net official monetary reserve movements 1971-81**

SOURCE: *Bank of Canada Review*, November 1982.

A surplus in the balance of payments adds to international reserves, and a deficit is met by drawing on these reserves. For instance, the surpluses in the Canadian balance of payments in 1971, 1972, 1974, 1976, 1979, and 1981 added to international reserves. Deficits in 1973, 1975, 1977, 1978, and 1980 resulted in declining international reserves in those years.

Summary of the Relationship between Main Components of the Balance of Payments

To recapitulate: a nation's balance of trade is equal to the value of its exports of visible items less its imports of visibles. Additional international transactions are taken into account to obtain its balance on current account. A nation's balance on current account is equal to its balance of trade plus its balance of exports of invisible items less its imports of invisibles. A nation's balance of payments is equal to its balance on current account plus net capital inflows to the country; that is, capital inflows less capital outflows. A surplus in the balance of payments adds to international reserves (reserves of foreign currencies); a deficit must be met by drawing on international reserves.

These relationships are presented in tabular form in Table 9.4, and an arithmetic example is provided. In this example, an unfavourable balance on current account of $1000 million is more than offset by a favourable balance on capital account of $1500 million, so that the balance of payments shows a surplus of $500 million. This surplus will add to international reserves.

TABLE 9.4 **Hypothetical relationships between the main components of the balance of payments**

Nature of Account	Receipts from Overseas	Payments Overseas	Balance of Account
VISIBLES (Goods, e.g., wool, petroleum, coal)	Exports of ($10,000 million)	- Imports of ($9000 million)	= BALANCE OF TRADE ($1000 million)
INVISIBLES* (Services, e.g., freight, tourist expenditure)	Services sold overseas ($2000 million)	- Services purchased overseas ($4000 million)	= BALANCE OF INVISIBLES (-$2000 million)
			BALANCE ON CURRENT ACCOUNT (-$1000 million)
CAPITAL	Inflows ($3000 million)	- Outflows ($1500 million)	= BALANCE ON CAPITAL ACCOUNT ($1500 million)
			BALANCE OF PAYMENTS ($500 million)

*Noncommercial transactions are not distinguished from invisibles in this example.

Foreign Exchange

In order to finance international transactions, it is necessary to convert one currency into another. The Canadian dollar is generally acceptable as a means of payment within Canada, but it is not generally acceptable as a means of payment in the U.S.A. (except in some border towns perhaps), Japan, Britain or Germany. Each country has its own monetary unit. Firms must pay for factor services in the monetary unit of their own country. A Canadian labourer would not normally want to be paid in Japanese yen each week; he or she wants Canadian dollars that can be used to finance his or her own transactions for food and clothing, and so on.

People wanting to convert currencies form the *foreign exchange market.*
Foreign currencies collectively are referred to as *foreign exchange.* The
domestic price of foreign exchange is called the *foreign exchange rate.* Foreign
exchange rates are equalized, in the absence of government controls to the
contrary, across geographic market locations by a process called *arbitrage.*
Suppose that the British pound costs $2.00 Canadian in New York, but is worth
$2.50 Canadian in London, England. Individuals who notice the price difference
would contract to purchase British pounds in New York and simultaneously
contract to sell in London. With large numbers of people doing this, the New
York price will be bid up and the London price will be bid down as a result of
the increased supply of pounds being exchanged for Canadian dollars. The two
prices will eventually be equalized (except for transactions costs).

Figure 9.7 presents the foreign exchange rates as published by the Toronto
newspaper, *The Globe and Mail.* This table gives the name of the basic currency unit for each country and the Canadian dollar price for one unit of the
currency for immediate delivery (the *spot* rate of exchange). For the U.S.A.,
Britain, and West Germany the prices for delivery in the future are also given.
These prices (known as the *forward* rates) are the prices *currently* agreed upon
for *future* delivery.

The forward rate may be higher or lower than the spot rate, depending
upon whether foreign interest rates are lower or higher than Canadian interest
rates. To see this result, consider an example in which the spot rate is the same
as the forward rate for British pounds. Suppose that the British interest rates
are 20 percent but that Canadian interest rates are 10 percent. Individuals with
money to invest can earn a higher return in Britain. As the spot and forward
rates are equal, the individual can buy pounds in the spot market for investment in Britain and simultaneously offer to sell British pounds in the future at
the forward rate to avoid any worries of a *depreciation* in the British pound.
The profit earned by this type of transaction would attract a number of participants. Their action will bid up the price of spot pounds but lower the forward
rate for pounds. This process of *interest arbitrage* will continue until the
discrepancy between the spot and forward rates just offsets the interest differential to be earned. Higher foreign interest rates lead to a *discount* on the
forward foreign exchange rate, that is, the forward rate is lower than the spot
rate. Lower foreign interest rates lead to the reverse, a *premium* on the forward rate.

Determination of Foreign Exchange Rates

The foreign exchange rate may be determined by government decree, by
market forces of supply and demand, or by a combination of market forces and
government intervention.

Under the Bretton Woods agreement that governed international
monetary matters between 1945 and 1973, countries were supposed to have

FIGURE 9.7 **Foreign exchange rates published in a newspaper.**

Courtesy Bank of Nova Scotia

FOREIGN EXCHANGE

Mid market rates in Canadian funds, June 4, 1985. Prepared by the Bank of Montreal Treasury Group.

Country	Currency	Noon	Previous Noon	Country	Currency	Noon	Previous Noon
United States	Dollar	1.3685	1.3658	Italy	Lira	0.000704	0.000703
1 month forward		1.3708	1.3683	Jamaica	Dollar	0.2534	0.2529
2 months forward		1.3729	1.3705	Japan	Yen	0.005493	0.005495
3 months forward		1.3748	1.3723	Jordan	Dinar	3.4085	3.2911
6 months forward		1.3793	1.3772	Lebanon	Pound	0.0855	0.0854
12 months forward		1.3865	1.3840	Luxembourg	Franc	0.02226	0.02235
Britain	Pound	1.7462	1.7680	Malaysia	Ringgit	0.5556	0.5559
1 month forward		1.7417	1.7643	Mexico	Peso	0.00495	0.00480
2 months forward		1.7382	1.7605	Netherlands	Guilder	0.3974	0.3976
3 months forward		1.7343	1.7567	New Zealand	Dollar	0.6156	0.6173
6 months forward		1.7254	1.7484	Norway	Krone	0.1560	0.1555
12 months forward		1.7157	1.7383	Pakistan	Rupee	0.08549	0.08532
Algeria	Dinar	0.2668	0.2672	Poland	Zloty	0.01007	0.01005
Antigua, Grenada				Portugal	Escudo	0.00788	0.00783
and St. Lucia	E.C.Dollar	0.5078	0.5068	Romania	Leu	0.3014	0.3008
Argentina	Peso	0.00224	0.00227	Saudi Arabia	Riyal	0.3791	0.3783
Australia	Dollar	0.9057	0.9089	Singapore	Dollar	0.6178	0.6183
Austria	Schilling	0.06278	0.06366	South Africa	Rand	0.6884	0.6863
Bahamas	Dollar	1.3685	1.3658	Spain	Peseta	0.00790	0.00792
Barbados	Dollar	0.6808	0.6795	Sudan	Pound	0.5474	0.5463
Belgium	Franc	0.02226	0.02235	Sweden	Krona	0.1546	0.1543
Bermuda	Dollar	1.3685	1.3658	Switzerland	Franc	0.5326	0.5336
Brazil	Cruzeiro	0.00025	0.00025	Taiwan	Dollar	0.0344	0.0343
Bulgaria	Lev	1.3077	1.3051	Trinidad, Tobago	Dollar	0.5714	0.5703
Chile	Peso	0.0089	0.0089	USSR	Rouble	1.6041	1.6042
China	Renminbi	0.4812	0.4803	Venezuela	Bolivar	0.10609	0.10506
Cyprus	Pound	2.2162	2.2190	West Germany	Mark	0.4481	0.4490
Czechoslovakia	Koruna	0.1969	0.1965	1 month forward		0.4496	0.4506
Denmark	Krone	0.1251	0.1246	3 months forward		0.4526	0.4533
East Germany	Mark	0.4481	0.4490	Yugoslavia	Dinar	0.00500	0.00499
Egypt	Pound	1.8269	1.8233	Zambia	Kwacha	0.5919	0.5993
Finland	Markka	0.2159	0.2159				
France	Franc	0.1470	0.1473				
Greece	Drachma	0.01019	0.01019				
Hong Kong	Dollar	0.1761	0.1758				
Hungary	Forint	0.02680	0.02675				
Iceland	Krona	0.03279	0.03288				
India	Rupee	0.11027	0.11041				
Ireland	Punt	1.4054	1.4068				
Israel	Shekel	0.00128	0.00128				

The U.S. dollar closed at $1.3705 in terms of Canadian dollars, up $0.0010 from yesterday. The pound sterling closed at $1.7307, down $0.0261.

In New York, the Canadian dollar closed down $0.0005 at $0.7297 in terms of U.S. funds. The pound sterling was down $0.0200 to $1.2628.

The ECU exchange rate for the Canadian dollar was $1.0059.

declared *par values* for their currencies in terms of either gold or U.S. dollars. Exchange rates were to be allowed to fluctuate only within a narrow range of the par value. Between 1950 and 1962, Canada ignored the rules of the Bretton Woods system and let its exchange rate be determined by market forces. In the early years, there was minimal intervention. From 1962 to 1970, Canada rejoined the Bretton Woods system and had a fixed exchange rate. In May 1970, the Canadian dollar was again allowed to float, but with government intervention. The Bretton Woods system collapsed in March 1973, and today most industrial countries have managed exchange-rate systems. That is, the rate is determined by a combination of market forces and government intervention with no declared par value.

In order to further understand the determination of the exchange rate, consider the following diagram in which the demand-and-supply curves for foreign exchange (U.S. dollars) are those in the absence of government intervention.

FIGURE 9.8 **Determination of the exchange rate**

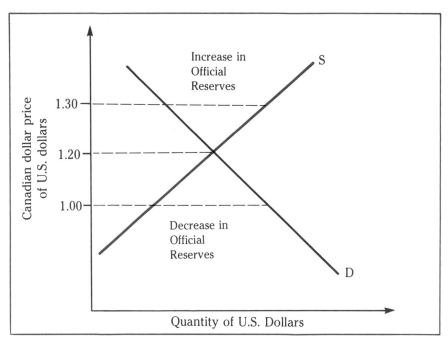

The demand for U.S. dollars is derived from the desires of Canadians to import U.S. produced goods and of Canadians who wish to make financial investment in the U.S. The supply of U.S. dollars is derived from exports of Canadian produced goods to the U.S. and from the desires of Americans to invest in Canada.

In the illustration, the equilibrium exchange rate is $1.20 Canadian for $1.00 U.S., and in a perfectly free market this would be the prevailing exchange rate. If the government were to declare a value different from the equilibrium rate, or at least attempt to influence the rate away from the equilibrium rate, it must intervene to either buy or supply U.S. dollars. Suppose that the government desires the exchange rate to be $1.00. At this exchange rate, the demand for U.S. dollars exceeds the supply of U.S. dollars. This excess demand must be supplied by the Bank of Canada from the Exchange Fund. This results in a decrease in official reserves. Excess demand for foreign exchange corresponds to a deficit in the Balance of Payments. On the other hand, if the government desires to maintain the price of U.S. dollars at $1.30 Canadian then there is excess supply of U.S. dollars. In this case, the Bank of Canada must purchase the excess U.S. dollars, which results in an increase in official reserves. Excess supply of foreign exchange corresponds to a Balance of Payments surplus.

The Foreign Sector and Macroeconomic Policy

The exchange rate and the foreign exchange market add an extra dimension to the analysis of macroeconomic policy that can be quite complicated. The discussion in this section is largely illustrative.

Suppose that the government desires to increase the level of GNP and hence increases the money supply. The analysis of Chapter 8 showed that the increased money supply would depress interest rates in Canada. This has an impact in the foreign exchange market causing the demand for U.S. dollars to shift rightward as U.S. investments are now more attractive. What happens to the exchange rate? If the rate is purely floating in response to market pressures, then the price of U.S. dollars rises — the Canadian dollar *depreciates*. This makes imports to Canada more expensive and Canadian exports cheaper in foreign markets. Thus, there is additional stimulus to the Canadian economy owing to the increase in net exports.

If, on the other hand, the exchange rate is fixed, then the increased demand for U.S. dollars generates excess demand for U.S. dollars. The Bank of Canada must supply the required U.S. dollars. This tends to decrease the Canadian money supply as the Bank of Canada takes Canadian dollars from Canadians, however, and gives them U.S. dollars in return, which are then presented to U.S. exporters. This tends to offset the original expansionary monetary policy. Monetary policy is more effective under floating exchange rates than under managed or fixed exchange rate systems.

Gains from International Trade and Interdependence through Trade

Trade between countries can have a number of economic advantages for the nations concerned. International trade can reduce scarcity or make commodities more plentiful in nations undertaking trade. This is because international trade:

1. enables advantage to be taken of differences in the comparative relative cost of producing different commodities in different countries,
2. enables the exploitation of economies of scale in production and specialization,
3. helps cater for variations in tastes between nations relative to their resources,
4. provides a means of taking advantage of differences in knowledge or technical know-how between nations, and
5. enables a wider pool of supplies to be drawn on, thus making supply less irregular in certain circumstances.

Let us briefly consider each of these possible advantages of international trade.

Theory of Comparative Advantage, Specialization, and Trade

The fact that a country can improve its welfare through international trade was discussed briefly in Chapter 1. International trade allows a nation to consume at a point beyond its own production possibility frontier by being able to exchange commodities with another nation at prices that are different from those that would prevail domestically in the absence of trade, and by specializing production in their export-oriented industries.

For the purpose of illustration, consider a simple example in which two countries, say Canada and Japan, produce two commodities, say manufactured goods and agricultural products. Suppose that in Canada, in the absence of trade the *relative price* of agricultural products is 1/2. That is, in Canada one (appropriately defined) unit of agricultural goods costs 1/2 of what 1 unit of manufactured goods costs. Suppose that in Japan the relative price of agricultural products is 2. That is, in Japan agricultural products are twice as expensive per unit as manufactured goods — or alternatively, manufactured goods in Japan are one-half as expensive as agricultural products.

In the absence of trade, Canadian consumers would have to forego the equivalent of 2 units of agricultural products to acquire 1 unit of manufactured goods. In Japan, consumers would have to give up 2 units of manufactured goods to obtain 1 unit of agricultural produce. Suppose that the two countries sign a trade agreement whereby they agree to exchange agricultural products for manufactured products on a one for one basis — that is the relative price of agricultural products is 1 with international trade. Now if Canadian consumers forego 2 units of agricultural produce they can obtain 2 units of manufactured goods from Japan, and Japanese consumers receive 2 units of agricultural produce for their 2 units of foregone manufacturing goods. Consumers in both countries are able to obtain more commodities because of international exchange.

Countries will import those goods that are less expensive in international markets than they would be in their own market in the absence of trade, and export those that are relatively more expensive in world markets. Domestic buyers will purchase foreign-produced goods only if they are at least as inexpensive as domestic goods, and domestic producers will sell to foreign markets only if they are paid at least as much as domestic consumers would pay in the absence of trading opportunity.

Why would pretrade relative prices differ between countries? Writing in the nineteenth century, the economist David Ricardo suggested that relative prices are determined by relative labour productivities in the two countries. In the example above, Ricardo would argue that Canadian labour is twice as productive in agriculture than it is in manufacturing. If both industries pay the same wages, then production costs in manufacturing will be twice as high as in agriculture. If prices are competitively determined, then prices in manufacturing must be twice as high in manufacturing in order to produce manufactured goods. Ricardo would suggest that Japanese labour is twice as productive in manufacturing. Ricardo's explanation is known as the *labour theory of value*.

To illustrate the above principles, consider the following hypothetical example. Suppose that in Canada it takes eight hours of labour to produce one suit jacket, and four hours of labour to collect one tonne of agricultural produce. In Japan, suppose that the numbers are reversed. This information is summarized as follows.

	Labour effort required to produce one unit	
	Suit Jackets	Agricultural Produce
Canada	8 hrs.	4 hrs.
Japan	4 hrs.	8 hrs.

Suppose that labour is the only paid factor of production and earns the same wage in either industry in a given country. (If labour is not free to migrate between countries, then the wages in the two countries may differ.) Let us assume that labour in Canada earns $10 per hour. The wage cost of one suit jacket is $80 whereas the cost of one tonne of agricultural produce is $40. If the industries are competitive, then the price of jackets will be $80 each and the price of agricultural produce will be $40 per tonne. Notice that the relative price of agricultural produce is $40/$80 = 1/2, which is the ratio of labour requirements. Similar arguments would show that for any wage rate in Japan, the relative price of agricultural produce is two.

In Canada, in order to produce one extra jacket at home requires eight hours of extra labour. This means a sacrifice of two tonnes of agricultural produce, if domestic labour is withdrawn from the agricultural sector. If Japan will trade one jacket in return for one tonne of agricultural produce, however, then Canada is better off. A similar argument shows that Japan is also better off.

Some economists believe that the theory of Swedish economists Eli Heckscher and Bertil Ohlin explains the differences in relative prices between countries. They suggest that (under appropriate conditions) relative prices will be determined by relative supplies of important factors of production. According to the Heckscher-Ohlin theory, countries will have a relatively lower price for that commodity that is a heavy user of the factor of production that is relatively abundant in that country. Suppose that agriculture is a heavy user of land whereas manufacturing is a heavy user of labour. Canada is abundantly supplied with land compared to Japan, and Japan is abundantly supplied with labour compared to Canada. Thus, Canada should be able to produce agricultural products relatively more cheaply than Japan, and Japan should be able to produce manufacturing goods more cheaply than Canada. Prosperity in the two countries will be increased if they specialize in those products that are heavy users of their abundant factors, and then export these goods in return for the commodities which are heavy users of their scarce resources.

Decreasing Costs and International Specialization in Production

When economies of scale or increasing returns to production occur, international specialization in production is likely to increase world supplies of commodities without using more resources, even if there is no difference in comparative advantage in production between the countries. This is another reason why international trade can be beneficial. There are substantial economies of scale to be achieved in the production of many manufactured goods. The advantages of specialization and trade when decreasing costs occur can be seen from the example illustrated in Figure 9.9. The curve ABC is a country's production possibility frontier for producing cars and household appliances. Because this frontier bulges toward the origin of the figure, it indicates that as production of any one of these commodities is increased extra production of the commodity expanding in production can be obtained by sacrificing smaller and smaller quantities of production of the other commodity. Assume that two countries, say Germany and Japan, have the same frontier, and that each produces at point B before trade. Each produces 0.5 million cars annually and 0.5 million household appliances.

FIGURE 9.9 **Production frontier showing decreasing costs (in terms of the alternative foregone) of producing cars and household appliances. International trade and specialization is likely to be beneficial in these circumstances.**

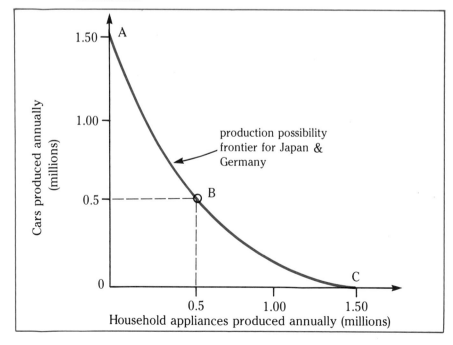

Trade opens up the possibility of specialization. Japan or Germany could specialize in car production and the other in the manufacture of household appliances, and trade these commodities. For instance, Germany might specialize in car production producing 1.5 million units annually, and Japan in the manufacture of household appliances manufacturing 1.5 million units annually. Each could exchange half of its total production, and consequently each would enjoy an additional quarter of a million cars and a quarter of a million household appliances compared to their pretrade position. Both countries gain as a result of trade and international specialization in production.

Means for Controlling Imports

There are a number of ways available to governments to limit the import of commodities. These include tariffs on the import of particular types of commodites, and quotas limiting the amount imported of particular commodities. Tariffs on imports are taxes imposed on imported goods. Canada makes widespread use of tariffs and considerable use of quotas to restrict the import of selected commodities.

Effect of a Tariff on Imports

The effects of tariffs can be illustrated by using simple supply-and-demand analysis. Consider the import of cotton vests for instance, and suppose that the market for cotton vests is perfectly competitive. In Figure 9.10, the curve marked S_HS_H indicates the supply of cotton vests by Canadian producers at various prices, and D_HD_H represents the demand of Canadian consumers for cotton vests at various prices. In the absence of international trade, the equilibrium price of vests is $20.00, and 2 million vests are produced and traded annually.

Assume that any amount of vests can be imported from abroad at a cost of $10.00 each. The supply of cotton vests from abroad in the absence of trade restrictions is the perfectly elastic line marked S_FS_F in Figure 9.10. Under conditions of free trade, the price of cotton vests in Canada will be $10.00. Canadian producers will not be able to charge more because of competitive imports from abroad. At a price of $10.00 per vest, Canadian producers supply 1 million vests annually and 2 million are imported to meet the total purchases of 3 million by Canadians.

Now consider the effect of introducing a tariff, or a tax, of $5.00 per imported vest. This tariff raises the cost of importing a vest from $10.00 to $15.00. In Figure 9.10, the after-tariff supply curve of imported vests therefore becomes the horizontal broken line marked MM. The price of vests in Canada rises to $15.00. At this price, Canadian producers find it profitable to increase their production to 1.5 million vests per year. The total demand for vests contracts because of the higher price (from 3 million vests per year to 2.5 million) and

FIGURE 9.10 **The effect of a tariff. In the case illustrated, a tariff of $5.00 on cotton vests increases the Canadian price of vests, raises local production, and lowers imports.**

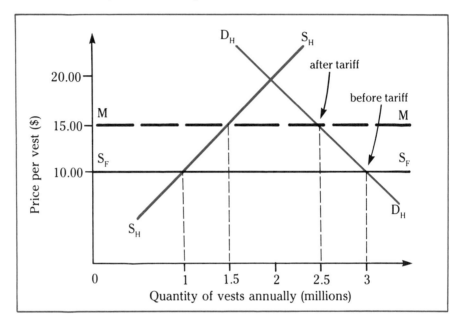

imports go down from 2 million per year to 1 million. The effect of the tariff is normally to encourage Canadian production, reduce imports, and lower consumption of the commodity in question. Canadian producers of a protected product tend to gain and Canadian consumers to lose as a result of tariff protection. Incidentally, the government obtains revenue from the imposition of a tariff. In the above example, the tariff would yield the government $5 million per year, that is, $5.00 times the number of vests imported.

The tariff discussed above is what is called a *nominal* tariff. The nominal tariff for a commodity may not be a good measure of the protection given to Canadian producers. It is important to consider the tariff structure on intermediate goods and other barriers to trade such as quotas.

Tariff Structure

A domestic industry is interested in the change in *value added* owing to tariff protection. The industry value added will depend not only upon the nominal tariff on the final product of the industry, but also on the nominal tariffs on imported intermediate goods used in their production processes.

By way of illustration, consider a simple numerical example. Suppose that the free-trade price of cotton vests is $10.00, as in the above example, and that the free-trade price of cotton used in the vest is $5.00. With free trade, the value added in the textile industry is $5.00. Suppose that a $5.00 nominal tariff is levied upon imported vests, but cotton is still subject to free trade. As in the above example, the price of vests rises to $15.00. The nominal tariff rate on vests is 50 percent. The value added in the domestic textile industry rises to $10.00 — a 100 percent increase. The percentage change in value added is called the *effective tariff rate*. In this example, the effective tariff rate is 100 percent whereas the nominal tariff is only 50 percent.

If a nominal tariff of 50 percent is also levied on cotton, then the price of cotton rises to $7.50. Value added for domestic producers is now $7.50 ($15.00 − $7.50). This is 50 percent higher than the free-trade value added. The effective rate of protection is equal to the nominal rate of tariff protection. If the nominal tariff on intermediate goods is higher than the nominal tariff on the final good, then the effective tariff rate on the final good is lower than the nominal rate. If the nominal tariffs on the intermediate goods are sufficiently high relative to the nominal tariff on the final good, then it is possible to obtain negative rates of effective protection — domestic producers actually suffer from the tariff structure owing to a reduction in value added.

In 1970, the nominal tariff on textiles was 17 percent; however, in a study for the Economic Council of Canada, professors Bruce Wilkinson and Ken Norrie determined that the effective rate of protection was 23.67 percent. For the leather industry, the nominal tariff was 19.23 percent, whereas the effective rate was 33.78 percent. In the rubber industry, the nominal tariff was 14.36 percent, but the effective rate was marginally lower at 13.17 percent. For fishing and trapping, the nominal tariff was a very low 0.61 percent, and the effective rate was *negative* 2.59 percent.

Effect of a Quota on Imports

A quota on imports can be used to obtain a similar effect to that of a tariff. In the above example, consider the effect of imposing a quota, or limit, of 1 million imported vests per year. When the domestic price of vests equals or exceeds $10.00, the full quota of vests is imported and the supply of *imports* is completely elastic. The supply to the Canadian market of vests is then the supply of Canadian producers plus the import quota. This supply curve is indicated in Figure 9.11 by the line marked $S_H + Q$, which is made up of the domestic supply, $S_H S_H$ and the import quota.

In the absence of import restrictions, the same market conditions prevail as discussed earlier — the price of vests is $10.00, 1 million are produced locally, and 2 million are imported. The effect of the quota is to raise the equilibrium prices of vests to $15.00, and to reduce the quantity traded in Canada to 2.5 million annually. These quantities correspond to the intersection point of the supply curve, $S_H + Q$, and the demand curve $D_H D_H$.

After the introduction of the quota, 1.5 million vests are produced locally

FIGURE 9.11   **The effect of an import quota. In the case illustrated, an import
quota of 1 million vests annually raises the domestic price of vests
by $5.00, and leads to an increase in domestic production.**

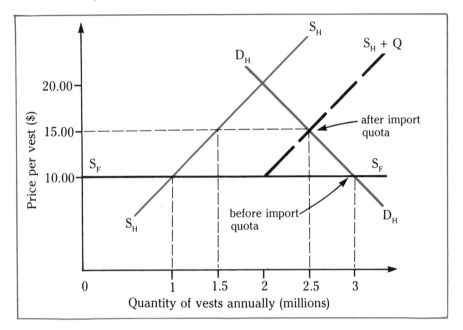

(an increase in production of 0.5 million), and 1 million vests are imported (a fall
of 0.5 million in imports). Thus, the quota has the same impact on prices, production, and imports as the tariff. An appropriate import quota can normally be
imposed that will have the same impact on prices, production, and imports as a
particular level of tariff. But the government will not raise revenue from a
quota, unless it sells the right to import, or at the same time as imposing a quota
also levies an import tax. The demand for quotas by importers may well exceed
their availability, and their allocation is therefore open to administrative abuse.

Although quotas have some drawbacks as means of restricting imports,
from the point of view of local producers, they have the advantage of providing
certainty about the levels of imports. The effect of a tariff on imports is often
uncertain because the appropriate supply-and-demand relationships are not
always known, and they may vary unpredictably. This is probably one of the
reasons why import quotas have been increasingly used in Canada in recent
years to limit imports, for instance, the import of clothing and footwear. The
main aim of such quotas is to reduce imports and bolster the demand for Canadian production, thereby maintaining employment in the industries concerned.

Another quantitative restriction is the Voluntary Export Restraint (VER)
Agreement. Under a VER agreement, the exporting nation agrees to limit the

quantity of goods exported to the signing import country voluntarily. Canada has used VER agreements to protect the textile industry since the 1950s.

The use of quantitative restrictions on imported goods is generally contrary to the rules of the General Agreement on Tariffs and Trade (GATT), except as a temporary measure when the domestic industry is faced with serious injury. The use of VER agreements in the textile trade was legitimized by GATT with the Long-Term Arrangement Regarding International Trade in Cotton Textiles signed in 1962. This agreement was replaced in 1974 by the Multifibre Arrangement, which covers a wider range of products than did the Long-Term Arrangement.

It is possible to compute the tariff-equivalent of a quota, that is, the tariff that would have the same restriction and price effects that the quota has. For example, the nominal tariff on cotton yarn and cloth production in 1970 was 15.48 percent. According to Wilkinson and Norrie, the tariff equivalent of the quota for this sector was 25.81 percent. The total tariff and nontariff protection then was the equivalent of a single tariff of 41.29 percent!

Bodies Reviewing Trade Protection in Canada

The main bodies in Canada that review applications from Canadian producers for protection against imports are the Tariff Board, the Textile and Clothing Board, and the Anti-Dumping Tribunal. The Tariff Board is concerned with any matters related to imported goods that may be subject to, or exempt from, duties. The Textile and Clothing Board receives complaints concerning possible injury to domestic producers of textile and clothing goods. Its recommendations are made to the Minister of Industry, Trade, and Commerce. The Anti-Dumping Tribunal investigates similar complaints for other industries as well as cases concerning the sale of foreign-produced goods at a price lower than normal (dumping). The Tribunal reports to the Minister of Finance. The Textile and Clothing Board and the Anti-Dumping Tribunal may recommend quantitative restrictions if it is believed that serious injury has occurred.

Canadian export producers are able to obtain financial services to assist them in international markets from the Export Development Corporation (EDC). The EDC does not subsidize exporters directly, but does provide loans, etc.

Trade Agreements and Aid-Canadian Trade Agreements

Canada has entered into a number of trade agreements some of which are aimed at reducing barriers (such as tariffs and quotas) to international trade between a number of countries (multilateral trade agreements). Other agreements (bilateral trade agreements) are aimed at reducing trade barriers between Canada and individual countries entering into the agreement with it.

The most important multilateral agreement is the General Agreement on Tariffs and Trade (GATT). GATT has become the international body that is concerned with matters of international trade between countries. GATT specifies certain trading principles such as 1. countries should not employ quantitative restrictions (except for temporary Balance of Payments problems) but rather should use tariffs, and 2. countries should not employ discriminatory trade restrictions against different supply countries. GATT also provides a forum for the settlement or hearing of trade disputes between trading partners. The Agreement is aimed at reducing tariffs and barriers to the free exchange of goods between nations. It sets up a framework for negotiation of an all-round reduction in tariffs and trade barriers by parties to GATT.

Since GATT came into force on January 1, 1948, there have been a number of series (rounds) of multilateral trade negotiations. The seventh round commenced in 1973 in Tokyo with 92 countries participating. Apart from considering further general reductions in trade barriers, participants considered the problem of dislocation of domestic industries from imports, and gave special consideration to the difficulties of developing countries. The Tokyo Round of discussions concluded in 1979.

Although GATT has been successful in reducing tariff rates, there has been an offsetting increase in a variety of nontariff barriers to international trade. Canada has a British preferential tariff structure that applies to goods imported from British Commonwealth countries, except Hong Kong. Canada also has a general preferential tariff that applies to manufactured and semi-manufactured goods (except textiles) imported from a number of developing countries.

Free Trade with the U.S.A.

The U.S.A. is our closest and largest trading partner. Economists frequently suggest that Canada and the U.S.A. should engage in free trade. Professor Ronald Wonnacott has estimated that Canadian and U.S.A. tariffs had a total cost of 8.2 percent of GNP in 1974. Free trade between Canada and the U.S.A. could increase Canadian real incomes by 5 to 10 percent.

Not all sectors or regions of Canada will gain from free trade. Resource based industries such as mining, smelting, and forest products are likely to gain, whereas manufacturing industries such as food processing, textile and clothing, household appliances, tobacco, and furniture are likely to contract. Given the regional concentration of manufacturing, it is likely that the major adjustment costs would be borne by Ontario and Quebec, whereas the West and the Maritimes would gain.

It has long been suggested that the existence of the Canadian tariff structure, which dates back to the National Tariff Policy of 1897, has promoted foreign investment in Canada, and resulted in a small-scale branch-plant economy. In fact, the attraction of foreign investment was one of the aims of the National Tariff Policy. Foreign investment, the inflow of foreign-owned capital and firms, acts as a substitute for the flow of goods that would take place in the absence of the tariff wall. It is not surprising that some of these foreign enterprises would leave and Canadian competitors disappear with free trade as it is the tariff that guaranteed their survival.

It is ironic that Canadians oppose free trade with the U.S.A. because of the fear that it will increase Canadian economic and political dependence upon that country. The tariff has led to the same result through foreign investment in Canada by American firms. In recent times, Canadians have been upset by the presence of foreign-owned enterprises, and special regulations arose to govern new foreign investments. These have been administered under the *Foreign Investment Review Act*, which was discussed briefly in Chapter 4.

A particular example of special trade arrangements between Canada and the U.S.A. is provided by the Automotive Products Agreement, known as the Auto Pact, signed in January 1965. This agreement permitted controlled free trade in automotive products between the two countries. According to Professor David Wilton, the Auto Pact (in 1971):

1. increased GNE by 5 percent compared to the non-Auto Pact level,
2. increased Canadian employment by 4 percent, and
3. decreased automobile prices by 12 percent.

Although the Auto Pact improved the Balance of Payments position during the 1965-71 period, the Canadian "motor vehicles and parts" trade balance was in a deficit position from 1975 to 1982. As Professor Wilton suggested in 1976, "For better or for worse, the Canadian economy is now even more dependent upon economic activity within the United States." This was seen very vividly during the recession of 1981-82 — particularly in the Canadian automotive industry.

KEY CONCEPTS
(FOR REVIEW)

Anti-Dumping Tribunal
Balance of Payments
Balance of Trade
Balance on Current Account
Bilateral Aid
Bilateral Trade
Commodity Composition of Exports
Comparative Advantage
Comparative Costs
Direct Investment
Dumping
Economies of Scale and Trade
Foreign Exchange
Free International Trade

GATT
Import Quotas
International Reserves
Invisible Trade
Multilateral Aid
Multilateral Trade
Portfolio Investment
Relative Prices and International
    Trade
Specialization and Trade
Tariff
Textile and Clothing Board
Voluntary Export Restraint
    (VER) Agreements

QUESTIONS FOR REVIEW AND DISCUSSION

1. How important is international trade for the well-being of Canadians? Why?
2. What proportion of value of Canadian exports is accounted for by industry sectors (farm and fish, forest products, metals and minerals, etc.) of the Canadian economy?
3. How was the direction of Canada's international trade changed in the last decade or so?
4. Which countries or regions are the main sources of Canadian imports? Which countries or regions are the main outlets for Canadian exports?
5. What is the balance of trade? Has Canada's balance of trade been in surplus or deficit in recent years?
6. What items form a part of invisible trade? Does Canada run a surplus or deficit on its invisible trade?
7. What is meant by the balance of a country's international transactions on current account? Does Canada normally have a deficit or surplus on current account? Why?
8. What items account for international capital flows?
9. What is the balance of payments? What happens to the funds from a surplus in the balance of payments? How is a deficit in the balance of payments met?
10. What are international reserves?
11. What does an *appreciation* of the Canadian dollar relative to the U.S. dollar mean? How does this affect the prices of traded commodities?
12. How is the foreign-exchange market affected by contractionary monetary policy?
13. "Monetary policy is more effective with flexible exchange rates than with fixed exchange rates." Explain.
14. How can international trade reduce scarcity?
15. "Countries can gain from international trade by specializing in the production of commodities in which they have a comparative (cost) advantage." Explain.
16. "Even if there is no difference in comparative advantage in production between countries, it may pay them to specialize in production (and then trade) *if decreasing costs occur*." Discuss.
17. What are the methods used by Canada to restrict imports?
18. What is a tariff? What effect is a tariff on the import of a product into Canada likely to have on the price of the product in Canada? What effect is the tariff likely to have on the volume of Canadian production of the product, and upon the quantity of imports of that product?
19. What is the difference between the nominal tariff and the effective tariff on a commodity? Use an example to illustrate your answer.
20. "A quota on imports may have a similar effect to a tariff." Discuss.

21. Consider the advantages and disadvantages of import quotas in comparison with tariffs as a means of restricting imports.
22. What is GATT? What does it aim to do?
23. What bodies govern trade protection in Canada?
24. Do you think that Canada should have free trade with the U.S.A.? Why or why not?

FURTHER READING

Blomqvist, A., Wonnacott, P., & Wonnacott, R., *Economics*, 1st Canadian ed. Scarborough: McGraw-Hill Ryerson Limited, 1984, chapters 13, 28, & 29.

Lipsey, R.G., Purvis, D.D., Sparks, G.R., & Steiner, P.O., *Economics*, 4th ed. New York: Harper & Row, Publishers, 1982, chapters 8, 26, 36, & 40.

Samuelson, P.A., & Scott, A.D., *Economics*. Scarborough: McGraw-Hill Ryerson Limited, 1980, chapters 33, 34, 35, & 36.

Wilkinson, B.W., "Canada-U.S. Free Trade and Some Options." *Canadian Public Policy* (October 1982), pp. 428-39.

Wilton, D.A., "An Econometric Analysis of the Canada-United States Automotive Agreement." Economic Council of Canada, 1976.

Wonnacott, R.J., "Canada's Trade Options." *Economic Council of Canada*, 1975.

10 Inflation and Unemployment

Inflation

The nature of inflation was discussed to some extent in Chapter 7 where it was pointed out that an increase in national production valued at prevailing prices need not imply an increase in the volume of commodities produced. Such an increase may come about because of a decline in the value of money, that is, because it costs more to purchase commodities. When the value of money declines because of price inflation, the same typical bundle of commodities, one that used to cost $1.00 for instance, now costs more, say $1.30.

It is usual to calculate a price index to measure the overall level of prices for commodities, and to use changes in this index as a measure of the rate of inflation. In order to calculate a price index, it is necessary to specify:

1. the *schedule of commodities* to be included in the bundle of commodities for which prices are to be taken into account,
2. the *base year*, or period, for the index; that is, the year or period for which the price index is set equal to 100, and
3. the *appropriate weightings* to be given to the prices of the different commodities.

In Chapter 7, the GNE price deflator was discussed. The GNE deflator is a price index that includes all commodities produced in the economy. Recently, the base year for the GNE deflator has been 1971. The prices in the GNE deflator are weighted by the quantities consumed in the current period. In computing this price index, one is calculating the ratio of the expenditure on this year's quantities at current prices to the expenditure on this year's quantities at prices that prevailed in the base period.

Another important price index is the Consumer Price Index (CPI). The CPI is a common indicator of inflation, and is probably more familiar to the general public than the GNE deflator. While the GNE deflator attempts comprehensive commodity coverage, the CPI is calculated for a specified "basket" of goods and services that is representative of the purchases of a particular population group. The weights chosen currently are the expenditure patterns in 1982 by all private households living in Canadian urban centres with a population of 30,000 or more.

The weights currently used in the construction of the CPI are given in Table 10.1

TABLE 10.1   **Expenditure Weights in the Canadian Consumer Price Index**

Major Components	Percentage of Expenditure
All items	100.0
Food	20.0
Housing	38.1
Clothing	8.4
Transportation	15.8
Health and Personal Care	4.0
Recreation, Reading, and Education	8.3
Tobacco and Alcohol	5.4

SOURCE: Statistics Canada, *The Consumer Price Index*, January 1985, Catalogue 62-001.

The CPI for 1971-1982 (using 1971 = 100), the percentage change in the CPI, and the value (purchasing power) of the Canadian dollar relative to 1971 are set out in Table 10.2

The CPI has continually risen during the period shown, indicating that inflation has been occuring throughout the period. Wage-and-price controls were imposed in late 1975, and administered by the Anti-Inflation Board. Inflation did drop, but it can be seen to be creeping back up after 1976. The controls ended in 1978. This inflation in prices reduced the purchasing power of the

TABLE 10.2   **CPI, % Change in CPI, and Value of Canadian Dollar since 1971**

Year	CPI	% Change in CPI	Value of Canadian dollar
1971	100.0	2.9	$1.00
1972	104.8	4.8	$0.95
1973	112.8	7.6	$0.89
1974	125.0	10.9	$0.80
1975	138.5	10.8	$0.72
1976	148.9	7.5	$0.67
1977	160.8	8.0	$0.63
1978	175.1	8.9	$0.57
1979	191.2	9.1	$0.52
1980	210.6	10.2	$0.48
1981	236.9	12.5	$0.42
1982	262.8	10.8	$0.38

SOURCE: *Economic Review*, Department of Finance, April 1983, Table 43. (The expenditure weights for the CPI in this table are those for 1978.)

Canadian dollar. The value of the dollar in terms of its purchasing power in 1982 was only worth 38 percent of its value in 1971.

The rate of change of prices as measured by the CPI is graphed in Figure 10.1, and the value of the Canadian dollar is graphed in Figure 10.2. It should be noted that suppressed inflation can exist in the sense that excess demand for commodities occurs and does not result in increased prices of these, but in waiting lists and queues.

FIGURE 10.1 **Percentage Change in CPI 1971-81**

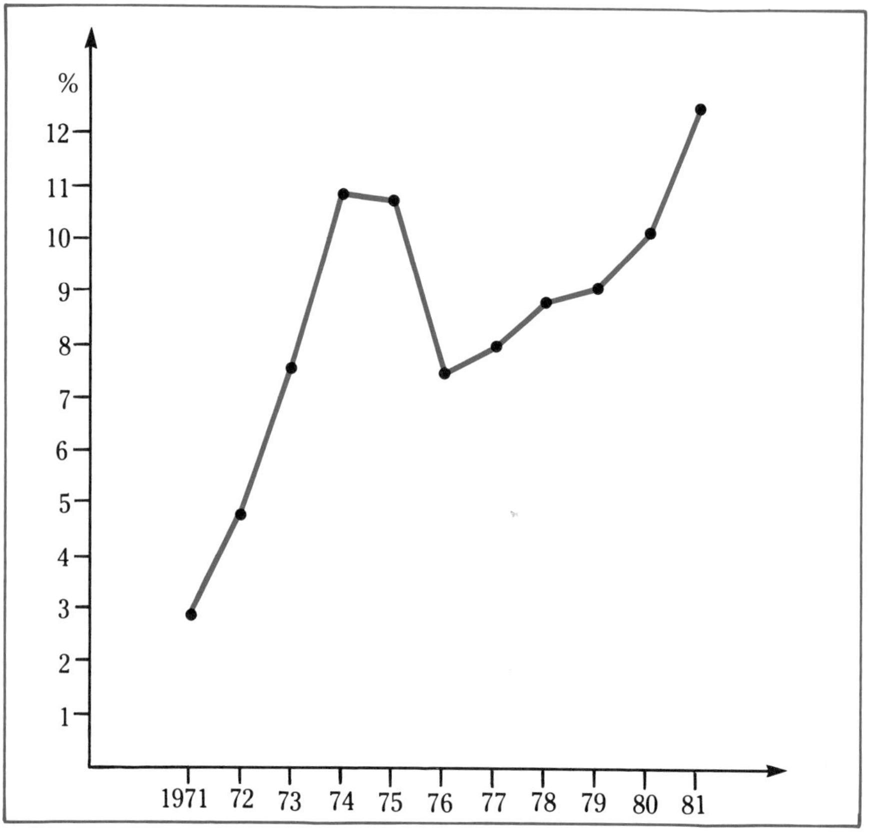

In February 1983, the CPI was converted so that in 1981 the CPI = 100. This is simply an arithmetic procedure, and can be obtained by dividing the price index (for years based on 1971 = 100) by the 1981 value for the price index (based upon the 1971 value). The 1981 CPI (with 1971 = 100) was 236.9. Dividing by 236.9 and multiplying by 100 yields a CPI of 100.

Price inflation has a number of effects. It erodes the value of money balances held by individuals and the value of liquid assets earning low interest. This can result in "a flight from money". When the rate of inflation is very

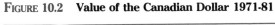

FIGURE 10.2 **Value of the Canadian Dollar 1971-81**

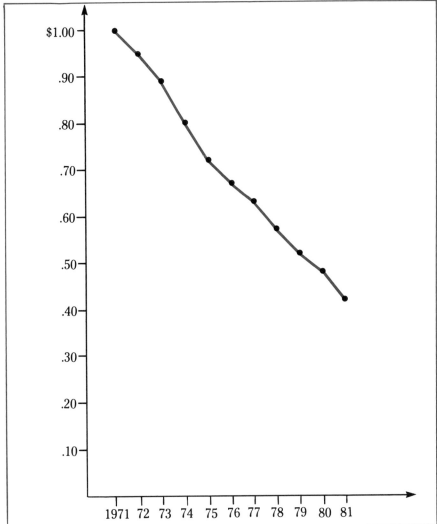

rapid, individuals refuse to hold money because it deteriorates too rapidly in value. Instead, they may hold physical commodities such as cigarettes, or request these instead of money in exchange for commodities. This is most likely to be so when *hyperinflation*, that is, an extremely high rate of inflation, occurs.

In times of inflation, individuals find that the relative advantage of holding physical assets, such as land, stamps, and gold, tends to increase in comparison to money. It is not true, however, that increased inflation is necessarily associated with a lowering in savings or a fall in holdings of cash balances. Despite the recent inflation in Canada, bank deposits have tended to rise. Infla-

tion may have encouraged prospective buyers of houses and other large assets
to save more rapidly to obtain the necessary deposit. The longer potential purchasers delay in an inflationary situation in obtaining their deposit, the higher is
likely to be the necessary deposit and the cost of the item to be purchased.

Income earners on relatively fixed money incomes suffer a reduction in
real income during periods of price inflation. Those on comparatively fixed
pensions, superannuation payments, and those earning a fixed rate of interest
on long term investments tend to be disadvantaged. The value of life assurance
policies tends to fall as these are for relatively fixed sums.

Borrowers tend to be advantaged in comparison to lenders if the rate of inflation rises, and this is not allowed for by way of higher interest payments.
Real interest payments may fail to keep pace with the rate of inflation, and the
capital sum repaid may be of much lower real value than the real value of the
sum lent at the time the loan was made. Thus, a loan of $20,000 made in June
1973 at an annual interest rate of 5 percent and repayable in June 1976 would
not have even compensated the lender for inflation, given that the inflation
rate varied from 7.5 to 10.9 percent per annum during this period. The real
value of interest paid on the loan plus the capital repaid in June 1976 would
have been less than the value of the original loan. Once inflation is anticipated,
however, this tends to be allowed for in contracts. Among other things, rates of
interest on loans tend to increase to reflect the rate of inflation. The higher interest rates in Canada in recent years is partly a result of the increased rate of
inflation.

A high and especially an uncertain rate of inflation increases social conflict
over shares in national income, and, in extreme cases, can lead to a collapse of
the monetary system. That is a situation in which money is not able to perform
its normal functions and is not accepted. A collapse in the monetary system
leads to large and unexpected losses being made by some groups in society,
such as the thrifty, and may lead to a collapse of its social framework. In a
report for the Anti-Inflation Board, P. Manga concluded that the principal losers
from the inflation of 1970-75 were the old and the poor. The principal gainers
were young, middle, and upper-middle income earners. Individuals who had
recently purchased homes and hence had a fixed nominal debt at low interest
rates, also benefited.

Unemployment

As pointed out in Chapter 1, when individuals are unemployed, the economy is
producing fewer goods and services than it could if all individuals who wanted
to work were able to find suitable jobs. There is a social-economic cost of
unemployment that may be measured in terms of foregone commodities. In addition, there may be costs associated with financial burdens placed upon family
units. These hardships may become particularly severe in cases in which the
sole income earner becomes unemployed for prolonged periods of time. These

financial burdens may lead to stress, marital disharmony, and in some cases marital separation.

How is the number of unemployed persons in Canada, reported in the newspapers, actually calculated? Although this may seem like a facile question, people are frequently surprised by the answer. We may think that it is determined by considering the number of individuals registered for unemployment benefits. Although this is one method, it is not the method used in Canada. The number of unemployed individuals in Canada is determined by statistical estimates based on the Labour Force Survey of about 56,000 Canadian households.

The survey counts as unemployed those individuals who, during the reference week used in the survey:

1. were not working, had been looking for work in the previous four weeks, and were currently availabe for work;
2. had not been looking for work but had been on layoff for less than twenty-six weeks, and were currently available for work; and
3. had not been looking for work but had a new job to start within four weeks, and were currently available for work.

The 1970s introduced Canadians to the phenomenon of *stagflation* (a situation in which high levels of unemployment are accompanied by high rates of inflation and little or no economic growth). From 1973 to 1982, the rate of inflation as measured by the CPI remained above 7.5 percent, and in several years was in the double-digit range. The growth in output in Canada from 1975 to 1980 was one of the lowest in the OECD group of countries (Organization for Economic Co-operation and Development). The overall unemployment rate has remained above 5 percent since 1970, and has been below 6 percent in only two years.

Throughout the period 1971-82, the unemployment rate for those 15-24 years of age has been consistently much higher than among members of the labour force aged 25 years or more. The unemployment rate for the younger group during this period never fell below 9 percent, and, since 1975, it has been greater than 12 percent for males and greater than 11 percent for females. During 1982, the unemployment rate for males 15-24 reached 21.2 percent. By comparison, the unemployment rate for males 25+ exceeded 5 percent in only two years: 1978 and 1982. The unemployment rate for females 25+ is consistently higher than for males 25+ by 1 to 2 percent. These patterns are shown in Figure 10.3. Notice that although the unemployment rates vary by age and sex, they all move in a similar pattern over time with the movements in the younger group's unemployment rate being more pronounced.

Another indicator of conditions in the labour market is the Help-Wanted Index (HWI), which is a measure of job vacancies. The HWI for 1971-82 is plotted in Figure 10.4. The index rises from 1971 to 1974 and then falls until 1977, after which it rises again. The U-shape in the HWI between 1974 and

FIGURE 10.3   **Unemployment Rates in Canada 1971-82**

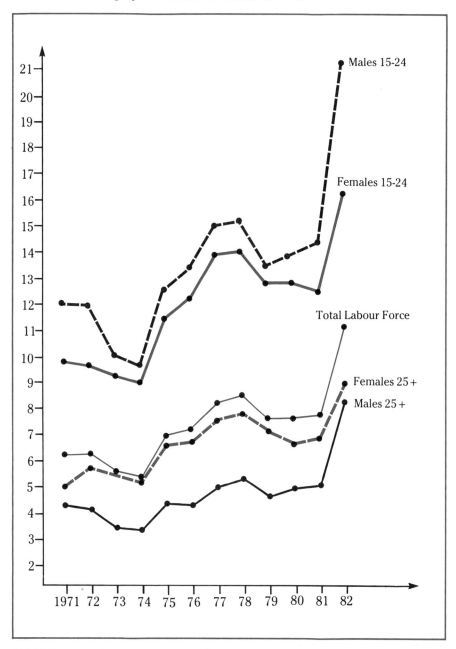

SOURCES: *Bank of Canada Review,* November 1983; *Economic Review,* Department of Finance,
1983.

FIGURE 10.4   **Help-Wanted Index 1971-82**

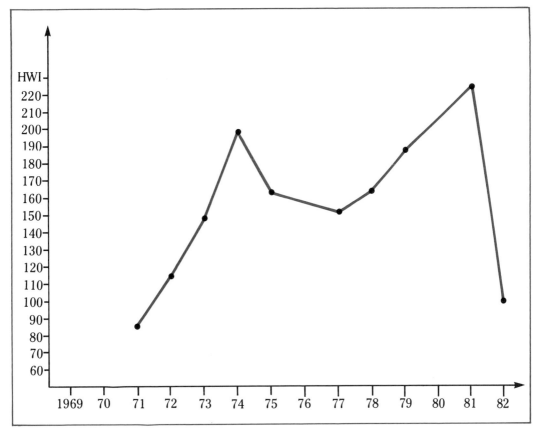

SOURCE: Based on figures from the *Economic Review*, Department of Finance, April 1983.

1981 corresponds closely to the inverted **U**-shape in the unemployment rates in Figure 10.3. The abrupt drop in the HWI between 1981 and 1982, and the corresponding abrupt increases in the unemployment rates, clearly show the impact of the recession.

Relationship Between Inflation and Unemployment

During the 1960s and early 1970s, economists believed that there was a stable relationship between the rate of inflation in an economy and the unemployment rate it experienced. This relationship is shown by the *Phillips curve*, so called in honour of the economist who first explored the relationship.

The Phillips curve suggests that the rate of inflation $\frac{\Delta P}{P}$ and the rate of unemployment are inversely related as shown in Figure 10.5.

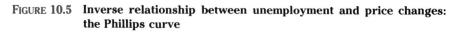

FIGURE 10.5 **Inverse relationship between unemployment and price changes:
the Phillips curve**

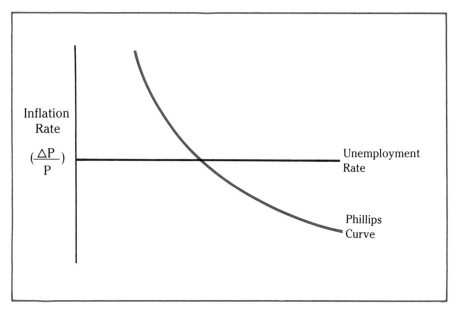

The existence of the Phillips curve led economists and policy-makers to
believe that society could make a *trade-off* between inflation and unemployment — that by accepting some inflation, they could reduce the rate of
unemployment. The relationship between unemployment and inflation in
Canada between 1961 and 1982 is shown in Figure 10.6. In the early 1960s, it
was possible to reduce the unemployment rate from just over 7 percent to
under 4 percent by accepting an increase in the rate of inflation of slightly less
than 2.5 percent.

These figures are remarkably different from those that are currently being
experienced in Canada. What has happened? As can be seen in Figure 10.6, the
Phillips-curve relationship did not remain stable over the 20-year period. By the
late 1960s, the Phillips curve starts to shift outward and upward. This movement progressed through the decade of the 1970s showing an increasingly
worse trade-off: reducing the unemployment rate from just over 8 percent in
1977 to 7.5 percent in 1980 resulted in an accompanying increase in inflation
from 8 percent to over 10 percent.

In order to explain these developments, it is necessary to consider the
underlying explanation that produces the Phillips-curve relationship between
unemployment and price inflation. The explanation relies on the link between
price inflation and wage inflation, and the link between wage inflation and
unemployment.

FIGURE 10.6 **Phillips curves in Canada 1961-82**

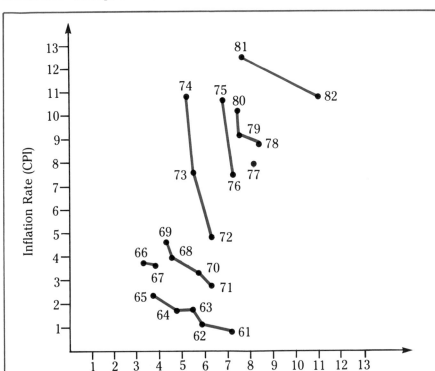

SOURCE: Based on figures from the *Economic Review*, Department of Finance, April 1983.

Reasons for Shifts in the Canadian Phillips Curve: 1961-82

The rate of change in wage rates will depend, in part, upon conditions in the labour market. If there is excess demand for labour (more jobs vacant than persons looking for work), then wage rates will tend to rise, and if there is excess supply of labour, then wage rates will decline (other things being equal). If the unemployment rate is taken as a proxy for the conditions in the labour market, then the inverse relationship between wage changes and unemployment of Figure 10.7 is obtained.

The unemployment rate U^* is the rate of unemployment that is consistent with zero excess demand in the labour market. This unemployment is generally believed to consist of frictional unemployment — workers in between jobs, or new entrants to the labour force who have not found jobs yet (but such jobs

FIGURE 10.7 **Inverse relationship between unemployment and wage changes**

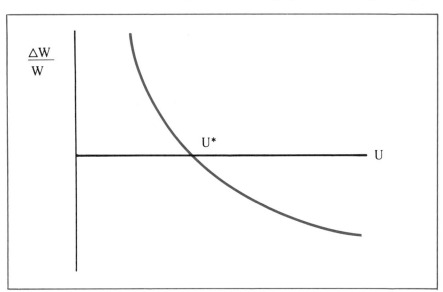

exist) — and perhaps structural unemployment — workers whose particular skills do not currently match the requirements of available jobs. If the unemployment rate is lower than U^*, then this means that there is excess demand for labour and wage rates rise. The reverse is true for unemployment rates higher than U^*.

If prices are determined by a mark-up on variable costs, then when wage costs rise these increases will be passed forward as price increases. In this fashion, it is possible to establish the Phillips curve of Figure 10.5 between price inflation and unemployment. This explanation gives rise to a given Phillips curve. It does not explain why the curve has moved around not only in Canada but in other countries. Clearly, the relationship is affected by other factors. Much effort has been devoted to explaining the shifts in the Phillips curves that have taken place in Canada since the 1960s.

One explanation that has received widespread support is that the curve can be shifted vertically as a result of the formation of inflationary expectations. If workers expect prices to rise, they will take this into account when bargaining for wage settlements. Thus, for any given state of the labour market, workers will want a settlement that incorporates the expected increase in prices so as to maintain a given change in *real* wages. The change in the nominal wage rate then reflects both the conditions in the labour market, and anticipated or expected inflation. Thus, if the expected rate of inflation, denoted π, has a value of π_1, then the relationship between $\Delta W/W$ and U in Figure 10.7 shifts vertically by π_1 as shown in Figure 10.8.

FIGURE 10.8 **Shifts in Phillips wage curve for expected inflation**

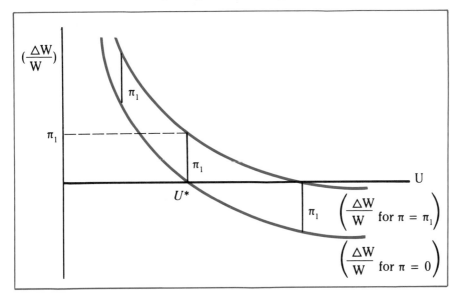

Thus, for any given rate of unemployment, the rate of wage change is higher by the expected rate of inflation. This is passed on in the form of price changes, and hence price changes will be higher by the expected rate of inflation as shown in Figure 10.9.

According to this explanation, there is a family of Phillips curves. There is one for each value of the expected rate of inflation. These may be referred to as *short-run* Phillips curves. Notice that for any expected rate of inflation, there is only one rate of unemployment for which the actual rate of inflation is equal to the expected rate of inflation. In an equilibrium situation, the expected and actual inflation rates must be equal. If the actual is higher than the expected rate of inflation, people will learn of this and revise their expectations upward, causing the Phillips curve to move further upward. Thus, in equilibrium, the unemployment rate must be U^*, suggesting that, for a stable economy the unemployment rate, although it may deviate from U^*, it will always ultimately drift back to U^* (although the approach may not be very rapid).

U^* is sometimes called the natural rate of unemployment because of its equilibrium nature. This analysis suggests that for long-time horizons there is no trade-off between inflation and unemployment. The *long-run* Phillips curve is vertical.

Empirical studies of the Canadian economy have confirmed that the expected rate of inflation is built-in to the rate of wage adjustments in accordance with the above theoretical analysis. Thus, rising inflationary expectations contribute to the shifting Phillips curves, and hence to actual inflation rates. In-

FIGURE 10.9   **Shifts in Phillips price curve for expected inflation**

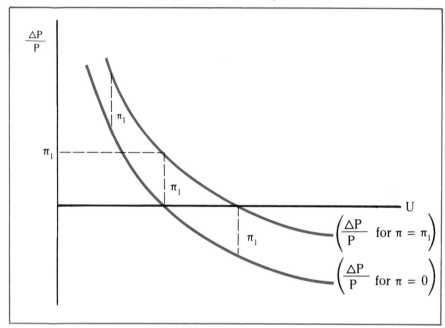

deed, one justification for the imposition of wage-and-price controls in the mid-1970s was to halt rising inflationary expectations.

Other explanations for the shifting Phillips curve have concentrated on changes in the structure of the labour market. There are two related features that are relevant. One concerns the changing composition of the labour force, and the other concerns the impact of revisions in the *Unemployment Insurance Act* of 1971. Table 10.3 shows the participation and unemployment rates by age and sex for the years 1966, 1975, and 1981.

This table shows that there has been an increase in the participation rates for those groups that have the higher unemployment rates. The lowest unemployment rate is for the male 25 + group and the participation rate for this group has decreased. These changes will lead to an increase in the overall unemployment rate. It is believed that the revisions in the *Unemployment Insurance Act* of 1971 changed the incentive structure facing the labour force by increasing benefit payments, extending payment periods, and reducing the time worked to qualify for benefits. Essentially, these changes increase the amount of income that can be earned by a short period of employment followed by a period of unemployment. This induces some individuals to enter the labour force who would not do so in the absence of unemployment benefits.

It is also suggested that the revisions may have increased search unemploy-

TABLE 10.3   **Participation and Unemployment Rates by Age and Sex**

		Participation Rate	Unemployment
Male 15-24	1966	64.1	6.3
	1975	68.8	12.6
	1981	72.5	14.3
Male 25+	1966	84.9	2.6
	1975	81.9	4.3
	1981	80.3	4.9
Female 15-24	1966	48.4	4.8
	1975	56.8	11.4
	1981	63.2	12.3
Female 25+	1966	31.2	2.7
	1975	40.0	6.5
	1981	47.9	6.7

SOURCE: Economic Review, Department of Finance, April 1983.

ment. Individuals can afford to spend more time searching for a more suitable job. More people being unemployed longer will increase the calculated unemployment rate. To the extent that the search process leads to a more compatible matching of workers and jobs, this aspect of increased unemployment (owing to search) produces social benefits.

Both the changes in the composition of the labour force and impacts of the revisions in the *Unemployment Insurance Act* of 1971 result in rightward shifts in the Phillips curve. These shifts result in an increase in the natural rate of unemployment — the long-run vertical Phillips curve shifts rightward. Empirical work for Canada suggests the demographic changes in the labour force and the revisions to the *Unemployment Insurance Act* of 1971 have both contributed to the increase in the measured unemployment rate in the 1970s.

Appendix to Chapter 10

Monetary Growth Rates, Inflation, and Unemployment

In an economy in which the potential GNP is not changing over time, the equilibrium inflation rate is determined by the rate of growth in the money supply. In order to demonstrate this, consider the macroeconomic model of Chapter 8 with a Phillips curve added. The resulting model is quite complex, as will be seen.

The model is set out geometrically in Figure 10.10. The demand for money depends only upon the rate of interest, and the nominal supply of money is under the complete control of the monetary authority. The real value of the money supply, however, depends upon the prevailing price level as well as upon the nominal money supply. The value of aggregate expenditure depends upon the level of income and the interest rate. The AE curve in Figure 10.10 is drawn for equilibrium interest rate r_0 determined in the money market.

FIGURE 10.10 **A macroeconomic model with Phillips curves**

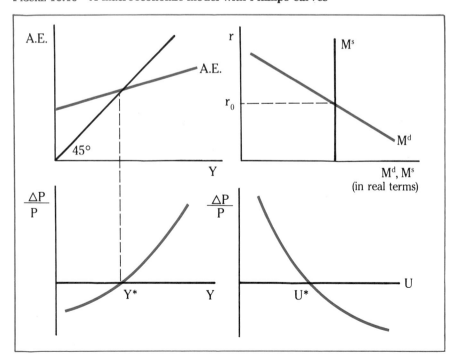

The reader will note the Phillips curve is presented as a function of GNP as well as a function of the unemployment rate. This will make the analysis more convenient. With a stable labour force, GNP will vary inversely with the unemployment rate. Hence, the short-run Phillips curve with inflation as a function of unemployment can be transformed into one with inflation as a function of GNP. Y^* is the value of GNP that corresponds to U^*. In Figure 10.10, the economy is in equilibrium with GNP at its "natural level" and zero inflation.

Suppose that the government desires to stimulate the economy by increasing government expenditures but holds the nominal money supply constant. With increased expenditures, the AE curve shifts to AE_1 in Figure 10.11, producing an equilibrium desired GNP level of Y_1. At Y_1, however, there is inflation. With prices rising, the real value of the money supply decreases (toward M_1^s) pushing up interest rates. This increase in interest rates depresses AE, and alleviates the inflationary pressure with Y, returning to Y^*.

FIGURE 10.11   **Increase in Government Expenditure leads to rising prices, which lead to a reduction in the real money supply, and hence higher interest rates. Thus, investment falls, offsetting the expansion in income.**

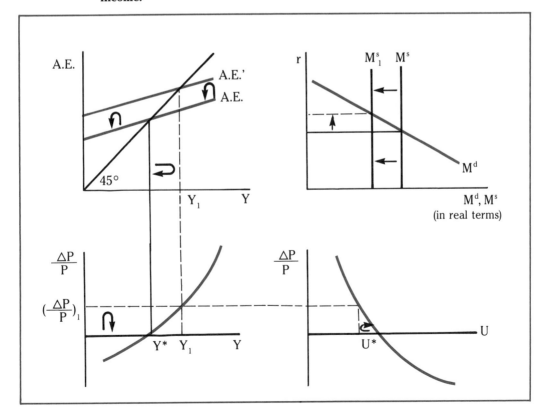

Suppose that the government authorities wish to offset the decrease in real money balances in order to hold Y above Y^* (and hence U below U^*). Thus, they increase the money supply at a rate $(\Delta P/P)_1$. This maintains a constant real money supply and holds inflation at $(\Delta P/P)_1$ for a period of time.[1] We should expect, however, that people will perceive that inflation is occuring, and hence will build this into their plans causing the Phillips curve to shift vertically by the expected inflation rate. This causes a jump in the inflation rate at Y_1. Now, prices again are rising faster than the nominal money supply, and the real supply falls ultimately reducing AE. Y falls back to Y^*, and the inflation rate is equal to the expected rate of inflation and to the rate of growth of the money supply.

Attempts to maintain Y at a level above Y^* will require further increases in the growth rate of the supply of money, and hence further increases in the rate of inflation. Inflation will *accelerate*.

The Depressing Result of Unwinding Inflation

The analysis can be used to show the economic impact of trying to reduce the rate of inflation. Suppose the money supply has been growing at 15 percent, as it was in the early 1970s, and as a result the economy has settled into an equilibrium position with unemployment at U^*, and actual and expected inflation equal to the 15-percent growth in the nominal money supply.

In order to reduce inflation, it is necessary to slow the rate of growth in the money supply. As a result, the real money supply will fall, and there will be upward pressure on interest rates. This reduces the level of aggregate expenditure, and the level of income falls causing a rise in the unemployment rate. This brings the rate of inflation down. In time, as people perceive the decreased inflation, they revise their expected inflation rates downward, and the Phillips curve moves downward. How fast this takes place depends upon how fast people revise their expectations. If expectations are sluggish, then the rate of unemployment may remain high for a long period of time.

Expectations may be sluggish if people do not believe that the monetary authorities will stick to their anti-inflation fight, but instead stimulate the economy to reduce unemployment. Monetarists suggest that the best way to unwind inflation is a gradual reduction in the growth of the money supply, which will bring inflation down slowly but avoid large increases in the rate of unemployment. They fear that rapid reductions, although they rapidly reduce inflation, will generate high unemployment, and this will cause the government

---

[1]The percentage change in the real money supply is equal to the percentage change in the nominal money supply minus the rate of inflation $\left(i.e., \frac{\Delta M^s}{M^s} - \frac{\Delta P}{P}\right)$.

to give in to public pressure to stimulate the economy. This means that inflation will not be reduced.

Some people suggest that wage-and-price controls be put in place so that inflation can be reduced without incurring the rise in unemployment. If the controls program is believed, then expectations are revised downward in accordance with the control targets. It is necessary that the money-supply growth rate be slowed as well as having controls on wages and prices. Otherwise, when the controls are lifted, the inflation rate will return to its original level equal to the growth in the money supply. Although controls may lower inflationary expectations, many economists fear that the inefficiency to resource allocation introduced offsets any benefits controls bring to moderating inflation.

Wage-and-price controls were used in Canada from late 1975 to 1978. The Anti-Inflation Board monitored prices and wages during this time period. In October 1975, the Bank of Canada announced that it would specify target ranges for the growth of M1 that would aim to gradually reduce the rate of growth in the money supply. The Bank of Canada had adopted a *monetarist philosophy* of economic management. The reliance on M1 as the appropriate target for the money supply was abandoned in late 1982.

In 1982, the federal government, and subsequently various provincial governments, imposed wage-and-price guidelines on public-sector employees and government corporations and agencies. The federal program was popularly (or unpopularly) known as the "6 and 5" program, named after the sequence of increases permitted under the scheme. This program will probably appear successful on the surface because the economy in 1982 was in the grips of the most severe recession since the Great Depression of the 1930s. This in itself would be a moderating influence on inflation as measured by the CPI.

KEY CONCEPTS
(FOR REVIEW)

Anti-Inflation Board	Price Inflation
Consumer Price Index (CPI)	Purchasing Power of the Dollar
Expected Inflation	Stagflation
Help-Wanted Index	Suppressed Inflation
Natural Unemployment Rate	Unemployment Rates
Phillips Curves	Value of Money
Price Index	Wage Inflation

QUESTIONS FOR REVIEW AND DISCUSSION

1. "In calculating a price index, it is necessary to select a schedule of commodities, a base year, and appropriate weightings." Explain.

2. What is the Consumer Price Index? What factors are taken into account in calculating it?
3. Update Table 10.2 to include 1983 and 1984.
4. "The purchasing power of the Canadian dollar is now less than half of what it was in 1971." Explain.
5. "There has been a general upward trend in prices since the early 1960s." Discuss and indicate the broad features of changes in prices in Canada since 1961.
6. What effects may price inflation have?
7. What does the short-run Phillips curve indicate?
8. How do inflationary expectations affect the Phillips curve?
9. What is the natural rate of unemployment?
10. Why do some economists believe the long-run Phillips curve is vertical? What is the significance of this?
11. What factors may have caused an increase in the natural rate of unemployment in Canada? Why? How does this affect the Phillips curve?
12. How is the rate of unemployment calculated in Canada?
13. Discuss the time pattern of unemployment in Canada between 1971 and 1981 for different age and sex groups.
14. "Ultimately, persistent inflation is a monetary phenomenon." Discuss.
15. "In order to reduce inflation, the economy will have to endure a period of high unemployment and depressed economic activity." Discuss.
16. "High interest rates are caused by inflation," "High interest rates help reduce inflation." Are these statements contradictory? Discuss each case separately.
17. How do wage-and-price controls help fight inflation while keeping unemployment relatively low?
18. What inefficiencies to resource allocation are introduced by wage-and-price controls? (Recall Chapter 5.)

FURTHER READING

Blomqvist, A., Wonnacott, P., & Wonnacott, R., *Economics*, 1st Canadian ed. Scarborough: McGraw-Hill Ryerson Limited, 1984, chapters 14, 15, & 17.

"The Challenge of Inflation and Unemployment: Has Monetarism Failed?" *Canadian Public Policy*, Supplement, April 1981.

Green, C., & Cousineau, J.-M., *"Unemployment in Canada: The Impact of Unemployment Insurance."* Economic Council of Canada, 1976.

Lipsey, R.G., Purvis, D.D., Sparks, G.R., & Steiner, P.O., *Economics*, 4th ed. New York: Harper & Row, Publishers, 1982, Chapter 39.

Samuelson, P.A., & Scott, A.D., *Economics.* Scarborough: McGraw-Hill Ryerson Limited, 1980, Chapter 19.

Wilton, D.A., & Prescott, D.M., *Macroeconomics: Theory and Policy in Canada.* Don Mills: Addison-Wesley Publishers Limited, 1982, chapters 3, 11, 12, 13, & 16.

11 Population and Economic Change

Population and Scarcity

Economists have long recognized that there is likely to be a relationship between the size of a country's population and the standard of living of its inhabitants. In relation to its available resources, a country may be underpopulated or overpopulated. As there is not common agreement about social objectives, however, there is not common agreement about what is an *optimum level of population*. In the mid-1970s, a target population of 30 million people by 2001 in Canada was mentioned in connection with Canada's immigration policy.

The Concept of an Optimal Level of Population

Sometimes, maximum income per head is suggested as a desirable goal to aim for in controlling population. Given a country's available resources and its knowledge, the relationship between the income per head of its inhabitants and its level of population might be like the one shown in Figure 11.1. Owing to the occurrence of increasing returns in production, income per head rises as the country's population at first increases. But at high levels of population (in relation to the country's resources), decreasing returns in production prevail, and income per head falls with increases in population. In the case illustrated in Figure 11.1, the level of population needed to maximize income per head is 50 million, and maximum income per year is $10,000 per head.

Changes in the Optimal Level of Population

The level of population needed to maximize income per head can alter with time, however, for instance if new technology is developed, or if available or known natural resources change. In the case illustrated in Figure 11.2, the relationship between income per head and population is shown to shift from AA' to BB'. This might be the result of the development of a new technology or a discovery of new mineral deposits. In this example, the level of population maximizing the income per head rises from 50 million to 80 million, and maximum income per head increases from $10,000 per year to $12,000 per year. This example illustrates the optimistic case of an expanding level of "optimal" population. But the opposite case is not impossible. It could occur if natural resources are seriously depleted and technological progress is slow or absent.

FIGURE 11.1   **Hypothetical relationship between income per head and the level of a country's population**

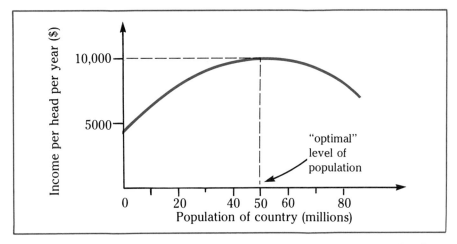

FIGURE 11.2   **The level of population required to maximize income per head may change if knowledge changes or new resources are discovered.**

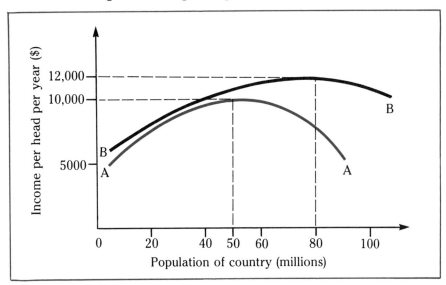

Limitations to the Concept of an Optimal Level of Population

The point of view that *the* optimal level of population is the one that maximizes income per head is open to serious questioning. Individuals value things other than their own income. Some positively like the presence of crowds or other people and would be prepared to give up some income for a more populous environment. If this sentiment prevails in society, its optimal level of population will be larger than the one that maximizes income per head. If the reverse sentiment prevails, a society will prefer a population smaller than the one that maximizes income per head.

Other considerations may also weigh in favour of a population smaller than the one that maximizes income per head. The greater the human population, the greater normally is the destruction of the natural environment, and the greater is the threat to the existence of other species of living things. The desire to preserve a balance between mankind and the natural environment may be a consideration to be taken into account in limiting human population growth. Advocates of zero population growth (ZPG) also point to the rate of depletion of nonrenewable resources such as oil and coal by human populations as an argument in support of limitations on population growth. The point is made that greater populations now use up nonrenewable resources at a faster rate, and that this will create a shortage of resources for future generations, and may impoverish them. This is not such a serious problem, however, if new technology develops continually, allowing hitherto untapped resources, such as solar power, to be used.

Just as there is an optimal size of population, there may also be an optimal *rate* of population growth. A very rapid rate of population growth creates difficulties of absorption as it takes time to build housing, urban facilities, and provide social overhead capital required for an expanding population. Rapid population growth in some less developed countries has, for instance, resulted in the growth of shanty settlements on the outskirts of cities without proper roads, water or sewerage facilities.

Changes in the level of a country's population and its age composition can have an impact on the nature of demand for commodities and upon productivity. A slow down in the rate of growth of a population because of a permanent fall in the birth rate normally results in a greater proportion of the population's being (for a number of years) in the aged group. The demand for children's wear and other children's items will tend to decline relative to the demand for items enjoyed by the aged.

Growth in Canada's Population

Canada's population level is about 24 million, and it has doubled in the last 40 years. Canada's population on decennial census dates since 1851 is shown in Figure 11.3. The graph shows that the population has been increasing over the entire period. During this period, the population increased by 10 times its original size.

The annual rate of increase of Canada's population since 1851 is shown in Figure 11.4, and is based upon figures given in Table 11.1. From Figure 11.4, it is easy to identify three decades of rapid population growth for Canada: 1851-61, 1901-11, and 1951-61. In each of these decades, the annual growth

FIGURE 11.3   **Canada's Population 1851-1981**

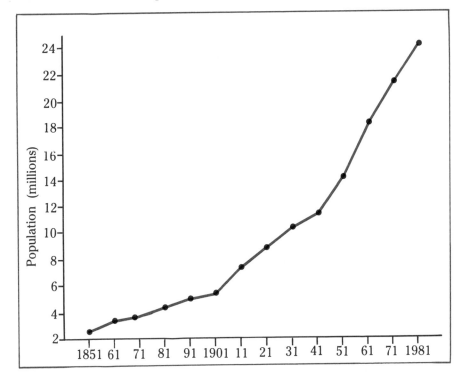

FIGURE 11.4   **Growth Rate of Canada's Population 1861-1981**

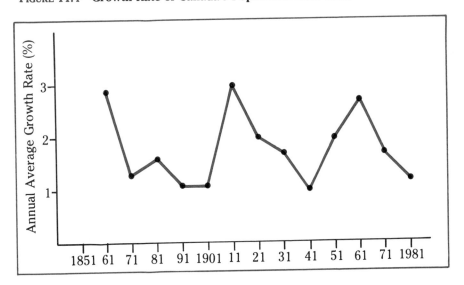

TABLE 11.1   Canada's Population and Growth 1851-1981

	1. Population Level P_t (,000)	2. Population Change ΔP_t (,000)	3. Average Annual Rate (%)	4. Natural Increase $(B_t - D_t)$ (,000)	5. Net Immigration $(I_t - E_t)$ (,000)
1851	2,436.3	-	-	-	-
1861	3,229.6	793	2.9	611	182
1871	3,689.3	460	1.3	610	-150
1881	4,324.8	636	1.6	690	-54
1891	4,833.2	508	1.1	654	-146
1901	5,371.3	538	1.1	668	-130
1911	7,206.6	1835	3.0	1025	810
1921	8,787.9	1581	2.0	1270	311
1931	10,376.8	1589	1.7	1360	230
1941	11,506.7	1130	1.0	1222	-92
1951*	14,009.4	2503	2.0	1992	166
1961	18,238.2	4229	2.7	3148	1080
1971	21,568.3	3330	1.7	2608	722
1981	24,300	2732	1.0	-	-

* includes Newfoundland

SOURCES: 1. *Canada Year Book*, 1980-81, Statistics Canada, Tables 4.1, 4.2;
2. *Globe and Mail*, p. 1, March 2, 1983.

rate was above 2.5 percent. The decade with the lowest average growth rate was 1931-41, which may reflect the influence of the Great Depression. The decades of 1891-1901 and 1971-81 also have comparatively low growth rates.

The change in total population, the natural increase, and net immigration are shown in Figure 11.5. The total change in Canada's population is attributed to natural increase for about 80 percent and net immigration for about 20 percent. Major inflows of migrants occurred in the early years of the twentieth century, and since the 1950s.

Components of Canada's Population Growth

Let us consider some of the elements underlying the two components (natural rate of increase and net immigration) of Canada's growth in population.

Rate of Natural Increase in Canada

The *birth rate*, defined as the number of births per 1000 of the population, minus the *death rate*, defined as the number of deaths per 1000, determines the

FIGURE 11.5   **Population Change, Natural Increase, Net Immigration 1861-1981**

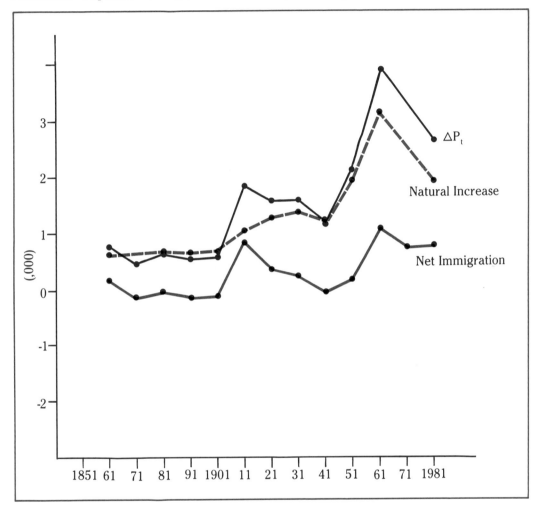

rate of natural increase of the population, that is the increase in the population per 1000 inhabitants. The birth rate, death rate, and natural rate of increase in Canada for 1921-81 are graphed in Figure 11.6. The death rate has gradually declined over the time period from 11.6 in 1921 to 7.0 in 1981.

The birth rate showed much greater variation throughout the period. In 1921, it was 29.3 per 1000 of population. It fell sharply in the 1930s owing to the Depression, rose again in the 1940s, reaching a peak in 1951 of 27.2 but remaining high during the 1950s to have a rate of 26.1 per 1000. This resurgence in the birth rate is generally referred to as the post-war "Baby Boom", and has been observed in other countries such as the U.S.A. and Australia. Since 1961,

FIGURE 11.6   **Canada's Birth Rate, Death Rate, and Rate of Natural Increase,
1921-76.**

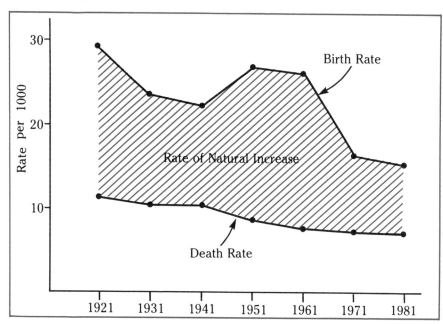

SOURCE: Foot, Table 1.5 and *Vital Statistics*, 1981 Catalogue 84-204, Table 23.

the birth rate has fallen, reaching an historic low in 1981 of 15.3 — almost a
50-percent decline since 1921. This has in recent years resulted in a drop in the
rate of increase of Canada's population.

To establish whether a population is reproducing sufficiently to replace
itself or to more than do so, we may consider either the *total fertility rate* or the
net reproduction rate. The total fertility rate refers to the number of children a
woman will have, provided that she experiences a given set of age-specific fertility rates (number of live births in a given age group). If the total fertility rate is
at least 2, then a married couple are just replacing themselves. As male mortality is higher than that of females, and as there are slightly more males born than
females, a total fertility rate of between 2.2 and 2.3 would just result in replacement of the existing married couple. A total fertility rate higher than this means
that married couples are more than replacing themselves and leads to population growth. Total fertility rates in Canada from 1921 to 1978 are given in Table
11.2 and shown in Figure 11.7.

The graph indicates that for 1921-66 the total fertility rate was above the
replacement rates, and it shows the surge in fertility that gave rise to the post-
war Baby Boom. It can be noticed that, although the fertility rate reaches its
peak in the 1950s, the increase in fertility actually started in the early 1940s,
reversing the downward trend of the 1920s and 1930s. The total fertility rate

TABLE 11.2   **Total Fertility Rates in Canada 1921-81**

1921	3.54	1956	3.86
1926	3.36	1961	3.84
1931	3.20	1966	2.81
1936	2.70	1971	2.19
1941	2.83	1976	1.83
1946	3.37	1981	1.70
1951	3.50		

SOURCES· 1. D.K. Foot, *Canada's Population Outlook* (Toronto: James Lorimer and Company Limited,
Publishers, 1982), p. 47;
2. *Vital Statistics*, 1980, 1981, Statistics Canada, Table 5.

FIGURE 11.7   **Total Fertility Rate in Canada 1921-78**

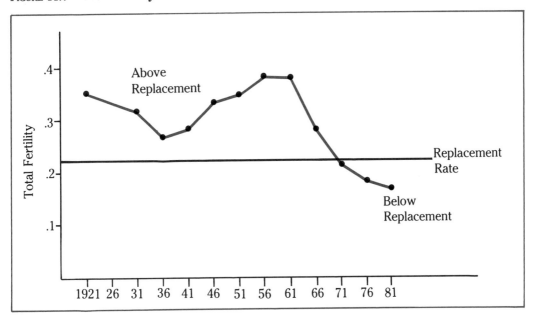

dropped during the 1960s, and, by 1971, it had dropped to or slightly below the
replacement fertility level. Throughout the 1970s, the total fertility rate remained below replacement, gradually decreasing from 2.19 in 1971 to 1.70 by 1981.
Throughout this period of the 1970s, married couples (on average) were not
replacing themselves!

The total fertility rate measures all live births, both male and female. A
more refined measure of reproductivity is given by the net reproduction rate,
which is the number of female children that a woman will bear (after adjusting
for the mortality of women over their reproductive ages). A net reproduction

TABLE 11.3   **Net Reproduction Rate for Canada 1970-73 and 1977-81**

1970	1.085	1977	0.856
1971	1.026	1978	0.837
1972	0.955	1979	0.835
1973	0.911	1980	0.828
		1981	0.810

SOURCES: 1. *1975 Demographic Yearbook*, United Nations, Department of Economics, p. 520.
Copyright, United Nations 1975. Reproduced by permission.
2. *Vital Statistics*, Statistics Canada, various issues.

rate of 1.0 indicates that on average each female will replace herself, and this implies a stationary population in the absence of migration; that is, one of zero growth in the long run. In the absence of immigration, a net reproduction rate greater than unity implies a rising population, and a rate less than unity indicates a falling population in the longer term. Table 11.3 gives the net reproduction rate in Canada for 1970-73 and 1977-81.

The figures in Table 11.1 confirm the results of Table 11.2 and Figure 11.7 that Canadian fertility levels dropped below replacement levels in the early 1970s. If this continues to be so, then, in the absence of sufficient net immigration to Canada, Canada's level of population will decline eventually.

Even if the the net reproduction rate falls to or below one, the population may continue to grow for a period of time if the composition of the population is biased toward younger age groups. Notice, for example, in Canada's case the natural increase in population in the 1970s is positive even though the total fertility-rate and net-reproduction-rate measures are below replacement levels. This is a result of the impact of the Baby Boom generation moving into the child-bearing stages. Even though on average each female is not exactly replacing herself, the fact that there has been a substantial increase in the number of child-bearing females in this age group results in an increase in population levels.

Immigration to Canada

Immigration has been the other important component of Canada's population growth. Figure 11.8 graphs net international migration between 1861 and 1981. The graph indicates that Canada's gains in population from net migration have varied considerably during this time period. Between the 1860s and the turn of the century, more people left Canada (emigrated) than came to Canada (immigrated). Net immigration was also negative during the 1930s. The first decade of this century and the 1950s are the periods for which net immigration was the largest.

The rate of net migration to Canada appears to be greatly influenced by

FIGURE 11.8 **Net Immigration 1861-1981**

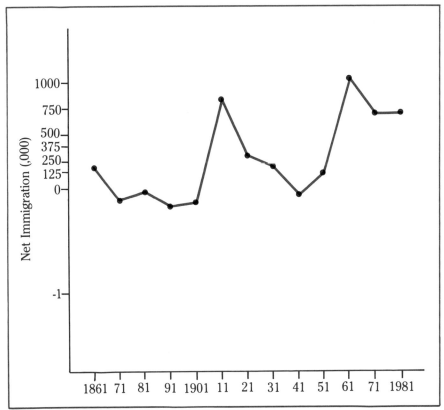

SOURCE: Based on figures from the *Canada Year Book*, 1980-81, Statistics Canada. Tables 4.1, 4.2;
and figures from the *Globe and Mail*, p. 1, March 2, 1983.

economic conditions in Canada and the rest of the world. Immigrants are reluctant to migrate to Canada when unemployment is high. Labour market conditions are a factor in the Canadian immigration program.

Immigration has been and is an important policy matter for Canadian
governments. The Canadian government is in a position to influence the
number of immigrants entering Canada. Canadian immigration policy is
governed by the *Immigration Act* of 1976, which came into force in 1978. The
objectives of immigration policy under the *Act* are:
1. family reunification,
2. nondiscrimination,
3. concern for refugees, and
4. promotion of Canada's economic, social, demographic, and cultural goals.

The *Act* is flexible. Objective 4. appears to allow the policy to be as restrictive
or as open as seems appropriate. When the *Act* was introduced, the annual
target was about 120,000 immigrants.

TABLE 11.4   Age-Sex Distribution of Canada's Population, 1980 (thousands)

Age Group	Male	%	Female	%
0-14	2,819.5	23.7	2,680.9	22.2
15-19	1,206.9	10.2	1,153.5	9.6
20-24	1,180.8	9.9	1,150.7	9.5
25-29	1,055.1	8.9	1,059.4	8.8
30-34	975.6	8.2	965.3	8.0
35-39	784.3	6.6	768.3	6.4
40-44	647.7	5.4	636.8	5.3
45-49	631.3	5.3	619.1	5.1
50-54	604.7	5.1	615.6	5.1
55-59	557.7	4.7	606.6	5.0
60-64	441.6	3.7	493.2	4.1
65-69	381.4	3.2	439.1	3.6
70-74	269.5	2.3	336.2	2.8
75-79	175.5	1.5	243.6	2.0
80-84	92.2	0.8	156.2	1.3
85-89	42.4	0.4	81.3	0.7
90+	21.0	0.2	43.4	0.4
Total	11,887.1		12,049.4	

SOURCE: Statistics Canada, *Estimates of Population by Marital Status, Age, and Sex, Canada and
Provinces*, Catalogue 91-203, Table 1.

Some Characteristics of Canada's Population

Age Distribution

The age composition of Canada's population for 1980 is indicated in Table 11.4.
Notice the bulge in the 15-19, 20-24, 25-30, and 30-34 year-old age groups.
These are the groups from the major part of the Baby Boom of the 1950s and
early-to-mid-1960s. When population is divided into females and males and
grouped by ages, we find that the histogram for females differs from that for
males. There is a greater proportion of females in the higher age groups than
males. This is because women tend to live longer than men.

The age distribution of a population can change for a number of reasons. If
the life expectancy of the population remains constant, a growing population,
that is, one with a rising birth rate, tends to have a greater proportion of young
people. The age distribution of a declining population develops the opposite
skew. As a result of a fall in the birth rate, the proportion of young people in the
population declines and the proportion of aged rises. An increase in the expectation of people to live longer (longevity) also tends to raise the proportion of

TABLE 11.5   **Age Composition of the Canadian Population**

	% Under 15	15-64	65+
1851	44.9	52.4	2.7
1861	42.5	54.5	3.0
1871	41.6	54.7	3.7
1881	38.7	57.1	4.1
1891	36.5	59.1	4.6
1901	34.4	60.6	5.0
1911	32.9	62.4	4.7
1921	34.5	60.8	4.8
1931	31.7	62.8	5.6
1941	27.8	65.5	6.7
1951	30.3	61.9	7.8
1961	34.0	58.4	7.6
1971	29.6	62.4	8.1
1981	22.5	67.8	9.7

SOURCE: D.K. Foot, *Canada's Population Outlook* (Toronto: James Lorimer, and Company Limited, Publisher, 1982), Table 1.2.

aged in the population. There has been a long-term tendency for longevity to increase because of improvements in medicine, public hygiene, and health, and this factor has worked (almost) constantly since 1851 to increase the fraction of the population over 65 years of age in Canada. Table 11.5 indicates the percentage age distribution of Canada's population since 1851, during selected years.

It is evident from Table 11.5 that the proportion of Canada's population under 15 years of age is falling, and that this process is likely to continue because of the declining birth rate. The proportion of Canada's population over 65 years is rising. An important factor contributing to the rising percentage of population over 65 years has been the increasing expectation of length of life for Canadians. These figures show that the Canadian population has been aging for a long time. In 1851, the average age (mean) was 21.7 years; in 1981 it is estimated to be 32 years. In 1851, half of the population was less than 17.2 years of age. For 1981, it is estimated that the median age is 29.6. The 1970s was a decade of particularly rapid aging of the Canadian population as the average age of the population increased by 2 years. Only in the 1930s was aging as rapid as in the 1970s.

The 1970s also saw a change in the sex ratio for Canada. Canada had previously been a male dominant society having more males than females. By the late 1970s, the number of females exceeds the number of males. This reflects the aging of the population as females live longer than males.

Life Expectancy

The expected length of life of males (at birth) in Canada rose from 60 years in
1930-32 to 71 years in 1980-82. In the same period, the expected length of life
for females (at birth) rose from 62.1 years to 78.0 years. These changes are
graphed in Figure 11.9 and presented in Table 11.6.

FIGURE 11.9   **Life Expectancy for Males and Females in Canada 1930-32 to 1975-77**

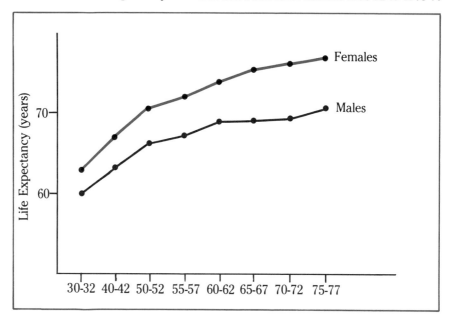

TABLE 11.6   **Life Expectancy in Canada by Sex Group (Years)**

	Male	*Female*
1930-32	60.0	62.1
1940-42	63.0	66.3
1950-52	66.3	70.8
1955-57	67.6	72.9
1960-62	68.4	74.2
1965-67	68.8	75.2
1970-72	69.3	76.4
1975-77	70.2	77.5
1980-82	71.0	78.0

SOURCES: 1. D.K. Foot, *Canada's Population Outlook*, (Toronto: James Lorimer and Company
Limited, Publisher, 1982) Table 2.6.
2. *Vital Statistics*, Statistics Canada, Catalogue 84-206.

These figures indicate:

1. that the average length of life for the Canadian population is increasing,
2. that average length of life for females is noticeably higher than that of males, and
3. that the gap between life expectancies of the two sexes is increasing over time.

Although the lengthening of expected life has benefited all age groups, there has been a remarkable reduction in infant mortality during this century. Infant mortality is measured by the number of deaths of individuals under one year of age per 1000 live births registered. Infant mortality has fallen from an average of 102 per year per 1000 live births in 1920-21 to 10.4 in 1980. This improvement is graphed in Figure 11.10. Both medical advances and economic growth and development have contributed to this improvement. The latter, for instance, has permitted better nutrition for mothers and infants, and this tends to lower infant mortality.

FIGURE 11.10   **Infant Mortality Rate in Canada 1920-21 to 1980**

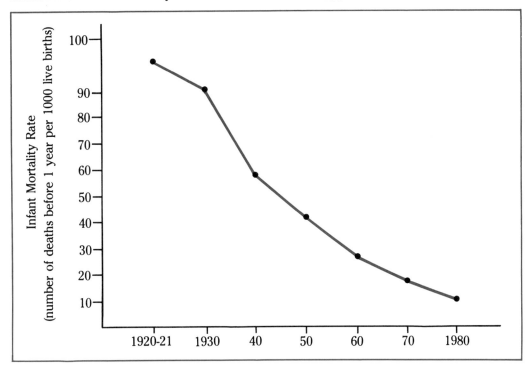

SOURCES: J. Overbeek, *Population and Canadian Society* (Scarborough: Butterworth and Co. (Canada) Ltd., 1980), Table 19; *Canada Year Book* 1980-81, Table 4.40; *Vital Statistics*, Statistics Canada, Catalogue 84-204, Table 23.

Many other characteristics of Canada's population can be studied. These include its religious affiliations, its racial or ethnic composition, the occupations of its people, and their location in urban and rural areas. Information about these is obtained in the censuses conduced by the Canadian government. The broad results are summarized in the *Canada Year Book* published by Statistics Canada. This can be used to obtain further data about characteristics of the Canadian population. It is interesting, however, to consider the regional location of Canada's population.

Regional Distribution of Canada's Population

Most of the Canadian population resides in a narrow band, approximately 350 km wide, along the border with the U.S.A. Table 11.7 summarizes the 1982 population size, and the percentage distribution of population for the 10 provinces and 2 territories in the Dominion of Canada.

The largest shares of the population are in Ontario and Quebec, and this has been the case historically. These two provinces accounted for slightly more than 60 percent of the total population in 1982. The Atlantic Provinces have 9.1 percent of the total. The share of these provinces (excluding Newfoundland) has decreased since Confederation, partly as a result of the opening up of the Canadian West. The Prairie Provinces (Manitoba, Saskatchewan, and Alberta) account for 17.6 percent of the total. A major boost in the population of these provinces occurred, according to Professor David Foot, with the immigration during the first decade of this century. British Columbia accounts for 11.3 percent of Canada's population. The Territories have 0.3 percent, which is less than that of Prince Edward Island. Considering the geographic location of the Territories, this small share is not surprising.

Regional populations may change as a result of natural increase, net international migration or net *interprovincial* migration. According to Professor Foot's study of Canadian Population, during the decade of the 1960s Ontario, Alberta, and British Columbia experienced net gains in population size as a result of interprovincial migration. All other provinces were net losers of individuals. These positions changed during the 1970s. The Atlantic Provinces as a group had become a net gainer whereas Ontario became a net loser. Quebec's net loss intensified as a result of a large outflow of anglophones whereas Alberta's net gain improved. Saskatchewan became a net gainer in the last half of the 1970s.

In 1980, 80 percent of the Canadian population was classified as urban. By way of comparison, in 1871 the urban population accounted for less than 20 percent of the total. In 1921, the population was roughly equally divided between urban and rural. From 1871 to 1971, Canada's population has shifted from rural to urban settings. The evidence for the decade of the 1970s, however, indicates that this trend reversed. The 1981 census shows that the rural

TABLE 11.7   **Distribution of Canada's Population 1982 (thousands)**

Province or Territory	Population Size	Percentage of Canadian Total Population
Newfoundland	571	2.3
Prince Edward Island	123	0.5
Nova Scotia	853	3.5
New Brunswick	701	2.8
Quebec	6470	26.3
Ontario	8700	35.4
Manitoba	1036	4.2
Saskatchewan	981	4.0
Alberta	2315	9.4
British Columbia	2783	11.3
Yukon Territory and Northwest Territories	70	0.3

SOURCE: *Economic Review*, Department of Finance, April 1983, Table 2.

TABLE 11.8   **Degree of Urbanization of Canadian Provinces in 1981 (%)**

Province	Urban	Nonfarm Rural	Farm Rural
Newfoundland	60	40	0
Prince Edward Island	35	54	10
Nova Scotia	54	44	2
New Brunswick	50	47	3
Quebec	77	19	4
Ontario	81	15	4
Manitoba	70	20	10
Saskatchewan	56	22	22
Alberta	77	14	9
British Columbia	78	18.5	3.5
Yukon	64	36	0
Northwest Territories	48	52	0

SOURCE: Statistics Canada, *1981 Census of Canada*, Catalogue No. 92-905, Table 4. (Calculations by the authors.)

sector grew by 8.9 percent whereas the urban area grew only 5 percent between 1976 and 1981. Canada is more urbanized that the U.S.A.

The degree of urbanization varies between provinces with Ontario,

(81.2%), Quebec (79.1%), British Columbia (76.9%), and Alberta (75%) being the most urbanized provinces in 1976. The most rural province in 1976 was Prince Edward Island with 62.9 percent. The degree of urbanization of the Canadian provinces is shown in Table 11.8. The percentage of Canadians living in urban areas of various sizes in 1976 is given in Table 11.9. Almost 10 percent of Canada's population live in 3 centres with over 500,000 people each. Table 11.10 shows the population size in 1976 of major Canadian metropolitan areas. The metropolitan areas for Toronto, Montreal, and Vancouver are much larger than their incorporated city size. The above 9 metropolitan areas accounted for 44 percent of Canadians in 1981.

TABLE 11.9   Population of Incorporated Cities, Towns, and Villages 1976

	Incorporated Centres	% of Total Population
Over 500,000	3	9.9
Between		
400,000-500,000	3	5.9
300,000-400,000	2	2.7
200,000-300,000	3	3.2
100,000-200,000	12	6.9
50,000-100,000	34	10.0
25,000- 50,000	52	7.8
15,000- 25,000	50	4.3
10,000- 15,000	69	3.7
5,000- 10,000	149	4.6
3,000- 5,000	179	3.0
1,000- 3,000	490	3.6
Under 1,000	1,033	1.8

SOURCE: Canada Year Book, 1980-81, Table 4.7.

TABLE 11.10   1981 Population of Selected Major Canadian Metropolitan Areas

Toronto	2,998,947
Montreal	2,828,349
Vancouver	1,268,183
Ottawa-Hull	717,978
Edmonton	657,057
Calgary	592,743
Winnipeg	584,842
Quebec	576,075
Hamilton	542,095

SOURCE: Census Tract Programme: A Review 1941-1981, Working Paper, Statistics Canada, Geography Division, Catalogue 92-x-507, Table 3.

KEY CONCEPTS
(FOR REVIEW)

Age Distribution of the Population

Birth Rate

Census

Death Rate

Degree of Urbanization

Drift from (to) rural areas

Fertility Rate

Infant Mortality Rate

Life Expectancy

Net Immigration

Net Reproduction Rate

Optimal Level of Population

Optimal Rate of Production Growth

Rate of Natural Increase of Population

QUESTIONS FOR REVIEW AND DISCUSSION

1. What is the most common concept of an optimal level of population? Illustrate such an optimum by a diagram.
2. Why might the level of population needed to maximize income per head of a population change?
3. Criticize the view that the optimal level of population is the one that maximizes income per head.
4. Do you believe that population can grow at too fast a rate?
5. Explain and outline the broad trends in the level of Canada's population since 1851.
6. What have been the two main components of population growth in Canada?
7. What is:

    a. the rate of natural increase of population?
    b. the birth rate?
    c. the death rate?

    How have these rates varied in Canada since the 1920s?
8. What is the net reproduction rate and why is it important to take it into account when considering replacement of a population?
9. Why has the net reproduction rate and the total fertility rate in Canada fallen since the 1960s?
10. Is the Canadian population as a whole starting to age? Why?
11. Why has life expectancy risen and the infant mortality rate fallen in Canada during this century?
12. To what extent is Canada urbanized? Is the degree of urbanization increasing?
13. What do you believe will happen to Canada's population growth in the future?

FURTHER READING

Foot, D.K., *Canada's Population Outlook.* Toronto: James Lorimer and Company Limited, Publishers, 1982.

Overbeek, J., *Population and Canadian Society.* Scarborough: Butterworth & Co. (Canada) Ltd., 1980.

Economic Growth and Development **12**

What Is Economic Growth and Is it Desirable?

Measuring Economic Growth

Economic growth occurs when the available amount of products and services in a country expands. Economic growth may increase the welfare of a country's population. An increase in the quantity of material goods or marketed commodities, however, can be accompanied by a decrease in welfare if there is a large reduction or deterioriation in nonmarket elements that are valued by individuals. If economic growth is accompanied by a deterioration in the environment or by an increase in anxiety, violence, and lawlessness, welfare may decline.

Economists have as a rule measured the economic growth of a nation by the expansion or increase in its GNP, which is an index of total production. Total production consists of different products such as coal, apples, hospital services, and bottles. GNP is the sum of production of these products and services when they are *valued in money terms*. Marketed commodities are as a rule valued at market prices and nonmarketed commodities such as those supplied by the government, e.g., defence, are valued at cost. Money values are used to make the production of different commodities addable and so give a single indication of total production, GNP. Although this is a useful method, under inflationary conditions the method can give a misleading impression of economic growth — the money value of national production may increase without an increase in the real output of goods and services occurring. This problem will be discussed later in the chapter. "Corrections" must be made to the estimates of GNP at current prices if the figures are to provide a reasonable indication of real economic growth.

Growth and Shifts in the Production Possibility Curve

As discussed in Chapter 1, economists have associated economic growth with an outward shift in the economy's production possibility frontier. This implies that the *potential* output of goods and services in the economy has increased. For instance, if we consider an economy that can produce only two commodities, wheat and cars, factors making for economic growth may, in the example shown in Figure 12.1, shift the production possibility frontier out from ABC to DEF. Annual production of both wheat and cars *may* expand. For example, the economy may shift from producing the combination of products corresponding to point B to producing the combination at point E.

Potential and Actual GNP

An economy's production possibility frontier corresponds to the *ceiling*, or current *potential*, for the production of goods and services, given the resources available in the economy. This potential may not be realized because resources are used inefficiently or labour is involuntarily unemployed. In Figure 12.1, these factors may cause production to be at point K rather than say at a point such as B. In most economies the actual level of GNP is less than the potential, or ceiling, level of GNP. The relationship between these might be like that indicated in Figure 12.2. In this case, the potential level of GNP is slowly rising with time. The actual level of GNP also increases with time, but fluctuates. The level of GNP may fluctuate, for example, because the general level of employment in the economy fluctuates.

As reported in Chapter 1, the Economic Council has estimated that the gap between potential GNP and actual GNP ranged between $7 billion and $10 billion during the 1974-79 period. In discussing economic growth, it is useful to keep in mind the distinction between growth in potential GNP and growth in actual GNP. It is possible that a country could experience growth in potential GNP, but, owing to a recession, experience less growth or even a decline in actual GNP.

Sources of Economic Growth

Growth in the potential and in the actual level of GNP may occur:

1. because of technological progress,
2. because of an increase in the amount and quality of education,
3. because total population rises thereby expanding the total available work-force, and
4. because the availability of other factors of production such as capital increase.

Other elements such as a growth in market size leading to economies of scale in manufacture and in transport, improvement in management and entrepreneurship, and greater willingness of members of the population to join the workforce can add to the growth of GNP. For instance, in Canada, participation of women in the workforce has increased since World War II, and this has been a factor contributing to the growth of GNP in Canada.

From 1961 to 1981, nominal GNP grew from $39,646 million to $328,501 million, an increase of 729 percent! Real GNP only increased by 144 percent, however. Most of the increase in nominal GNP was owing to rising prices. The Canadian inflationary experience of the 1970s was discussed in Chapter 10.

FIGURE 12.1   **Economic growth viewed as a shift outward in the economy's production possibility frontier**

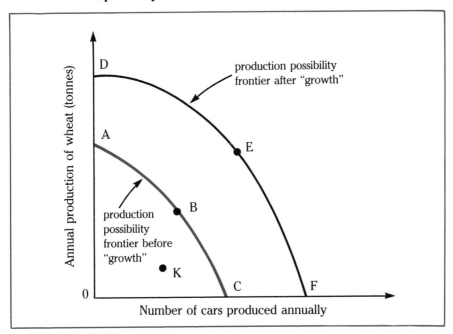

FIGURE 12.2   **In this example, both the potential level of GNP and the actual level of GNP grow with time, but some of the potential level of GNP remains unrealized.**

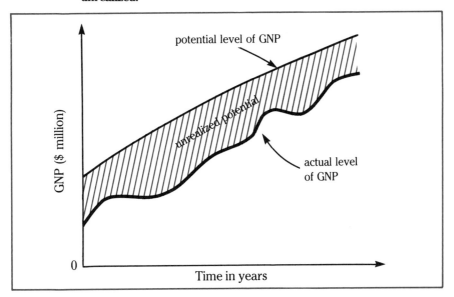

TABLE 12.1   **Nominal GNP, Real GNP, and Real Per Capita GNP, 1961-81**

Year	Current Prices ($ million)	Constant 1971 Prices ($ million)	Real GNP Per Capita*
1961	39,646	54,741	3001
1962	42,927	58,475	3147
1963	45,978	61,487	3248
1964	50,280	65,610	3401
1965	55,364	69,981	3563
1966	61,828	74,844	3739
1967	66,409	77,344	3796
1968	72,586	81,864	3956
1969	79,815	86,225	4106
1970	85,685	88,390	4150
1971	94,450	94,450	4379
1972	105,234	100,248	4598
1973	123,560	107,812	4891
1974	147,528	111,678	4994
1975	165,343	113,005	4979
1976	191,031	119,249	5186
1977	208,868	121,762	5235
1978	230,353	126,281	5379
1979	261,961	130,115	5494
1980	289,859	130,160	5438
1981	328,501	134,070	5543

*Based upon population at June
SOURCE: Economic Review, Department of Finance, 1982, tables 1, 3, & 4.

GNP per Capita

As pointed out in Chapter 4, the level of GNP is an inadequate indicator of the welfare of the residents of a country. In assessing welfare, one factor to be taken into account is the income per head of population. A country may have a large GNP but a low income per head of its population, as is the case in India for instance. Income per head of population in a country can be obtained from the following expression:

$$\text{Income per head} = \frac{\text{gross national income}}{\text{population size}}$$

$$= \frac{\text{GNP}}{\text{population size}}$$

$$= \text{GNP per capita.}$$

TABLE 12.2   Growth Rates for Real Per Capita GNP, real GNP, and Population

	Percentage Change In Real Per Capita GNP	Percentage Change In Real GNP	Percentage Change In Population
1961-1962	4.9	6.8	1.9
1962-1963	3.2	5.2	1.9
1963-1964	4.7	6.7	1.9
1964-1965	4.8	6.7	1.8
1965-1966	4.9	6.9	1.9
1966-1967	1.5	3.3	1.8
1967-1968	4.2	5.8	1.6
1968-1969	3.8	5.3	1.4
1969-1970	1.1	2.5	1.4
1970-1971	5.5	6.9	1.3
1971-1972	5.0	6.1	1.1
1972-1973	6.4	7.5	1.1
1973-1974	2.1	3.6	1.5
1974-1975	-0.3	1.2	1.5
1975-1976	4.2	5.5	1.3
1976-1977	0.9	2.1	1.2
1977-1978	2.8	3.7	1.0
1978-1979	2.1	3.0	0.8
1979-1980	-1.0	0.0	1.0
1980-1981	1.9	3.0	1.1

SOURCE: *Economic Review,* Department of Finance, 1982, tables 1 & 4.

Real GNP per capita or income per head for Canada from 1961 to 1981 is listed in Table 12.1. Real GNP per capita increased from $3001 in 1961 to $5543 in 1981. This is an increase of 85 percent. Income per head in Canada did not increase as much as total income. This is because the Canadian population had increased.

If gross national income, or GNP, rises faster than population, income per head rises. If population expands at a faster rate than GNP, income per head falls, as happened in Canada between 1974 and 1975 and between 1979 and 1980. The rates of growth in per capita GNP, real GNP, and population are shown in Table 12.2.

GNP and the Standard of Living and Economic Growth

The level of GNP in a country is an inadequate measure of the standard of living or well-being of its inhabitants. Not only must the aggregate level of GNP be related to the number of inhabitants of the country, but other considerations need to be taken into account. The amount of leisure available to the population or the length of their working week is one such consideration. The long-term tendency for real income per head to increase in Canada has been accompanied by a gradual decline in the length of the working week. The benefits of increased productivity, for instance, owing to technological improvements, can be taken out either in terms of more goods and services or more leisure.

Economic Growth Can Have an Adverse Effect on the Environment

Increased production is commonly accompanied by increased pollution. For instance, factories may release fumes into the air and discharge wastes into waterways. As most individuals value a "clean" environment, and as producers rarely pay the complete costs to the community of the disposal of their wastes, the value of production is less than indicated by GNP.

GNP estimates frequently include items that are costs of production. These may be more appropriately subtracted from estimated GNP rather than added to them. The costs associated with extra cleaning of houses and cars caused by industrial pollution is added to GNP because it reflects output of goods and services. It would be more appropriate to deduct these as a "cost". Again, the costs of travelling to and from work are added to GNP — the further one travels by a particular mode of transport and the greater its cost, the higher is GNP even though this travelling may reduce welfare. Costs of this nature tend to be high in developed countries. The level of GNP in these countries can give a misleading impression of the welfare of their inhabitants.

Economic growth is not in itself desirable. It is only desirable if it promotes the ends ultimately wanted by individuals. Mere growth in GNP does not always promote ends that are wanted by individuals. But the elements that make economic growth possible in a country open up a number of options for it. Technological improvements, for example, can be used to increase output or leisure or to improve the environment, and it is important to foster the desired mixture of these objectives.

Recent Economic Growth in Canada

In the 20-year period 1961 to 1981, the Canadian GNP (at 1971 prices) increased by 144 percent, and real GNP per capita rose by 85 percent. The increase in per capita GNP is smaller than the increase in total GNP because the level of Canada's population increased in the same period by 33 percent.

The annual growth performance of the Canadian economy is shown in Table 12.2 and graphed in Figure 12.4. As can be seen, the decade of the 1960s was a period of strong growth in real GNP. The annual growth average was 6.1 percent. According to Brox and Cluff, the economy was operating close to potential during this time period. The only year during the 1961-69 period in

FIGURE 12.3 **Changes in Canadian real GNP, level of population, and per capita GNP in the 21-year-period 1961 to 1981**

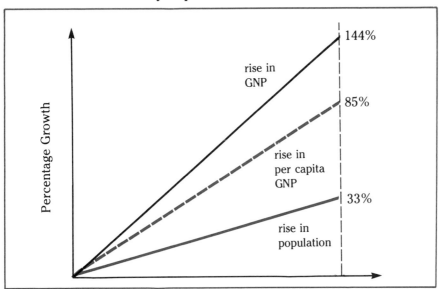

which GNP growth was less than 5 percent was in 1966-67 when the rate dropped to 3.3 percent. During this year, per capita GNP grew only 1.5 percent. The decade ended on the pessimistic side with growth in GNP falling to 2.5 percent in 1969-70.

Growth in the early 1970s was strong and comparable to that of the 1960s. Starting in 1973-74, however, the growth rates are much lower. Only in 1975-76 does the growth rate of GNP rise above 4 percent. In 1974-75, the growth in GNP of 1.2 percent is offset by population growth, and per capita GNP actually declines slightly. This slowdown in Canada was matched in other countries as a world-wide recession occurred following the rapid increases in the world price of oil in 1973-74. A similar problem occurred again in 1979-80 when once again the world price of oil increased substantially. In 1979-80, the growth in GNP was halted and per capita GNP declined by 1 percent. In the latter part of the decade, actual GNP fell substantially below potential GNP.

This poor performance in the latter years of the decade is apparent in the growth or lack of growth in productivity. Table 12.3 lists the growth rates in productivity for Canada 1962-80, and these are graphed in Figure 12.5. These show the sudden drop in productivity performance in the Canadian economy starting in 1974 with a slight recovery in 1976.

There may be many reasons for the decline in productivity. The Economic Council of Canada believes that it can explain only about half of the slowdown. One possibility is that during the recession, firms may have resisted laying off workers. When demand drops, firms reduce output while maintaining workers, and productivity falls. It is suggested that the growth in the service sector may

TABLE 12.3   **Growth in Canadian Productivity 1962-80**

Year	Output per Person Employed	Output per Man Hour
	(percentage change)	
1962	3.1	2.7
1963	2.5	2.9
1964	3.5	3.7
1965	2.3	2.7
1966	1.8	2.9
1967	2.2	2.8
1968	5.3	6.3
1969	2.5	3.6
1970	1.8	2.7
1971	4.1	4.8
1972	3.1	3.5
1973	3.0	3.1
1974	0.0	0.7
1975	-1.0	-0.2
1976	3.7	4.1
1977	0.6	2.0
1978	0.9	0.4
1979	-0.4	0.9
1980	-1.6	-1.5

SOURCE: *Economic Review,* Department of Finance, April 1982, Table 37.

account for some of the decline. Perhaps resources devoted to nonproductive activities such as pollution control have reduced productivity as currently measured.

Some General Issues about the Sources of Economic Growth

There is considerable debate among economists about the relative importance of different factors that contribute to economic growth. One school of thought places great emphasis upon the level of savings and investment (level of capital formation) in a society as a force making for economic growth. It has been suggested by Rostow, for example, that a nation must save and invest more than 10 percent of its GNP if it is to begin on the path of sustained or continuing growth. Investment is seen as probably the most important determinant of economic growth.

But this point of view is not accepted by all economists. Some see

FIGURE 12.4 **Canadian Growth Rate for Real GNP 1961-80**

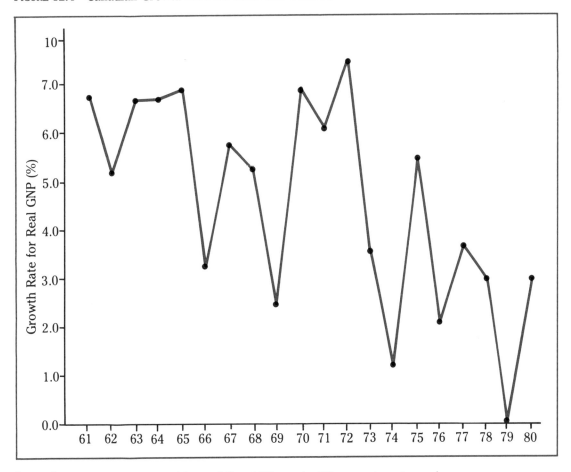

inventiveness, entrepreneurship, and the ability and willingness to put new inventions to commercial use as the most important ingredients of growth. Phyllis Deane, the noted economic historian, for example, points out that countries such as Great Britain, France, and Germany began on a path of development and sustained growth when they were saving as little as 5 percent or less of their GNP. Their growth was a result of business enterprise, and their ability to develop and to commercially apply new inventions. Savings and investment in these countries rose once they began to develop. Their high levels of investment were the result rather than the cause of their economic development.

Edward F. Denison has studied the sources of growth in developed economies in this century. His results indicate that improvements in the *quality* of capital and labour rather than increases in their mere *quantity* have become the major sources of economic growth in developed economies. Their quality of capital is improved by embodying new and more productive techniques in new machinery and other produced means of production. The quality of labour

FIGURE 12.5   Productivity Growth in Canada 1962-80

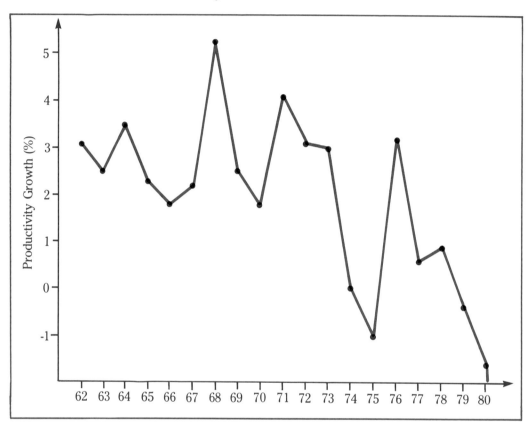

is raised by greater and improved education, and by improvements in the
health and fitness of the population.

The pattern of economic development of a country may be typically of the
type illustrated in Figure 12.7. Initially, the population may be at a subsistence
level, and the economy may remain in this underdeveloped state unless it obtains some impetus to growth (such as could come from discoveries of new
resources in the country, or inventions). It may then grow slowly at first, and
then at an increasing rate as incomes, savings, and capital accumulate. During
this phase, apart from developing its own technology, the country may draw
upon technology and ideas from abroad. This expansionary phase is likely to be
followed by a maturity or near-maturity phase in which economic growth of
the country slows down as it becomes more difficult for it to tap new markets
for goods, and as foreign technology is fully known and used.

This growth pattern, however, is a hypothetical one, and actual economies
may diverge from it. Furthermore, the typical pattern of economic develop-

FIGURE 12.6 **Students at the University of Calgary using computer terminals. Education and improved technology are important sources of economic growth in developed countries.**
Courtesy University of Calgary, Audio/Visual Services.

FIGURE 12.7 **Possible typical pattern of growth of real per capita income as a country develops**

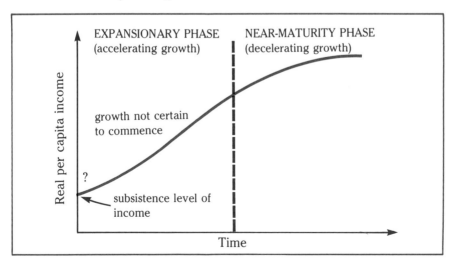

FIGURE 12.8 **Harvesting wheat in the Punjab, Pakistan by the traditional labour-
intensive method**

ment may have changed. Developing countries today are faced with different
obstacles and advantages from those of countries that commenced economic
growth during the last century. Developing countries today are surrounded by
developed countries with *much* superior technology (that they are continually
upgrading), and this may make it difficult (particularly as many of the
developed countries or blocs engage in protectionism) for developing countries
to make superior technical progress in any field, and to export products in such
a field. Some economists believe that differences in technical and scientific
knowledge play a large role in determining the pattern of world trade and the
gain from trade. On the other hand, recent advances have been made that
could make it easier for a developing country. For example, better and cheaper
birth-control techniques have been developed. Nevertheless, the obstacles facing developling countries wishing to embark on development and growth are
substantial.

Economic Features of Developing Countries

As mentioned in Chapter 2, about two-thirds of the world's population lives in
the developing countries of the world. There are countries in which the majority of people are poor and constantly struggling for economic survival. Many of

these countries are finding it difficult (or impossible in their current circumstances) to begin and then to maintain the process of economic development and growth that raises incomes and living standards. As a result of this, they are not developing, or are developing so slowly, that inequalities in the distribution of incomes or material wealth in the world are increasing. Growth and rising per capita incomes have been maintained in comparatively developed countries such as the U.S.A., U.S.S.R., Sweden, West Germany, and Canada. Per capita incomes have not risen significantly in developing countries such as India, Bangladesh, Pakistan, Indonesia, and Tanzania. Incomes in developed countries are rising relative to those in developing countries, and the difference between the two is increasing.

Developing countries tend to be characterized by the following features:

1. *Subsistence living and limited use of markets.* Most individuals in developing countries use their output for their own family — they provide the means of their own subsistence — and exchange little of their production. Most production in these countries is not exchanged or marketed. When marketing does occur, it is frequently by means of barter, which means that goods are exchanged for other goods rather than money. The barter system is cumbersome compared to the monetary system of exchange.

2. *A high proportion of the workforce in developing countries is engaged in agriculture and in other primary industries.* Whereas more than 50 percent of the workforce is likely to be engaged in primary industries in developing countries, less than 10 percent (often much less) is employed in this sector in economically advanced countries. The manufacturing sector and the tertiary sector in developing countries are also comparatively small.

3. *Technical change in developing countries is normally slow* and producers often cling to traditional methods. In some circumstances, however, traditional methods may be more appropriate than Western capital-intensive methods. Local methods may use a high proportion of labour and a low proportion of capital, and thereby accord more closely with relative resource scarcities than Western techniques of production. It may be more economical in a developing country not to use bulldozers to build a dam but to employ men carrying soil or fill in baskets.

4. *Savings are small and the rate of capital accumulation is slow.* Because most incomes are low — near-survival-levels savings in developing countries tend to be low. Individuals need to consume most of their production to survive. Furthermore, those on high incomes are reputed to spend most of their income on conspicuous consumption rather than to invest it in productive works. These factors combined mean that the rate at which capital is accumulated is slow. The resource capital is scarce and

the stock of this resource grows slowly in developing countries. This retards increases in production.

Table 12.4 sets out the gross capital formation in selected countries as a percentage of their Gross Domestic Product (GDP*), and allows for capital formation financed both from domestic savings and from foreign investment and aid. Without the inflow of foreign aid, capital formation would be lower in Tanzania, India, and Sudan, for example. The table indicates that, in relation to GDP, capital accumulation tends to be smaller in developing countries than in the economically more advanced ones. The annual absolute level of capital formation in economically advanced countries is much greater than that in the developing countries.

5. ***Business motivation or entrepreneurship of a productive nature may be lacking.*** In some societies, business is looked upon as a socially inferior means of employment. For instance, some tribal groups in Africa consider that to carry on commerce for gain is not socially acceptable. This helps to explain why immigrants such as Indians in many of these countries have largely fostered and have staffed the commercial sector. In some areas, those with funds to invest may have a preference for money-lending rather than for direct investment in, and *formulation* of, productive projects. Capitalistic entrepreneurship may be lacking.

6. ***Unemployment, labour-intensive methods, underemployment.*** Unemployment in the urban areas is often very high. In many instances, family members working on rural holdings are not efficiently employed because they lack adequate tools to work with — they are underemployed or employed in an inefficient way. The methods of production used employ a proportionately large amount of labour — they are labour-intensive. For instance, grain is likely to be separated from its hulls by winnowing it in baskets by hand.

7. ***Life expectancy is low, nutrition and health poor.*** As indicated by the statistics in Table 2.1, individuals in developing countries can expect to live for much shorter periods than those in more developed countries. This is the case because: a. nutrition is low in these countries, b. medical services are scarce (see Table 2.1, which indicates the number of inhabitants per doctor for various countries), and c. social provision for the supply of water and disposal of garbage and sewerage are inadequate or absent. This promotes the spread of diseases such as typhoid.

8. ***High growth rates of the population and a distorted age distribution of the population add to poverty.*** Although death rates are higher

---

*GDP, Gross Domestic Product, is a concept of national income sometimes used in place of GNP. GNP measures income received by Canadians whereas GDP measures Canadian production regardless of who is paid for the production.

TABLE 12.4   **Gross Domestic Investment as a Percentage of GDP in Selected Countries in 1980**

Country	Percentage
Developed countries	
Japan	32
Australia	24
Canada	22
Germany	25
United Kingdom	16
U.S.A.	18
Developing countries	
Tanzania	22
India	23
Sudan	12
Burundi	14
Ethiopia	10
Peru	16
Zimbabwe	18

SOURCE: World Bank, *World Development Report, 1982* (New York, Oxford University Press), Table 5.

in developing countries than in technically more advanced countries, birth rates are also much higher (see Table 12.5). Despite high rates of infant mortality and high death rates, populations in developing countries are increasing at a rate above the world average. The average rate of population increase in low-income and middle-income groups is three times as high as the average rate of increase in industrial-market economies. The higher rate of increase in the developing countries may reflect the less frequent use of birth-control techniques, and the effectiveness of modern medical techniques in reducing the spread or effect of disease. For example, the effectiveness of vaccination and "cheap" measures to eliminate or reduce carriers of disease (such as mosquitoes carrying malaria).

Because a high proportion of individuals die before they reach an economically productive age or die during the productive period of their lives, a high proportion of the population in developing countries is not of a productive age, i.e., a high proportion is economically dependent. There are proportionately fewer productive hands available in developing countries and proportionately more individuals are dependent than in the economically more advanced countries. This is indicated by Table 12.6, which shows that the proportion of the population under fifteen or

TABLE 12.5   **Annual Rate of Population Increase, Birth Rate, and Death Rate for
Selected Countries**

		Average Annual Population Growth 1970-80 (%)	Birth Rate 1980 (Per 1000)	Death Rate 1980 (Per 1000)
I	Low-Income Countries	2.1*		
	Bangladesh	2.6	45	18
	Viet Nam	2.8	36	9
	Pakistan	3.1	44	16
	Uganda	2.6	45	14
II	Middle-Income Countries	2.4**		
	Egypt	2.1	37	12
	Phillipines	2.7	34	7
	El Salvador	2.9	41	9
	Brazil	2.2	30	9
III	Industrial-Market Economies	0.8†		
	United Kingdom	0.1	14	12
	Australia	1.4	17	8
	Canada	1.1	17	7
	United States	1.0	16	9
	Germany	0.1	11	12
	Japan	1.1	14	6

*   Average for 33 countries in Group I
**   Average for 63 countries in Group II
†   Average for 19 countries in Group III

SOURCE: World Bank, *World Development Report, 1982* (New York, Oxford University Press),
Tables 17, 18.

over sixty-five years is higher in the low and middle-income groups of
countries.

9. *Urbanization problems, but a proportionately low urban population.* Economic change in many developing countries has been accompanied by a drift of population from rural areas to urban areas. Because of
shortages of capital, urban areas are not equipped to cope with the influx
of population from rural areas. Housing, sanitation, water supplies, and
roads are inadequate in many urban areas, and increases in their supply is
not keeping pace with the growth of urban population. Nevertheless, as
can be seen from Table 12.7, most of the population in developing countries live in nonurban areas, a position that contrasts with that in

TABLE 12.6 **Percentage of Population Under 15 or Over 65 Years of Age**

Low-Income Countries	41
Middle-Income Countries	45
Industrial Market Economies	34

SOURCE: World Bank, *World Development Report 1981*, (New York, Oxford University Press),
Table 19.

TABLE 12.7 **Degree of Urbanization: Percentage of Total Population Living in Urban Areas for Selected Countries in 1980**

Developing Countries		More-developed Countries	
Ethiopia	15	Canada	80
Rwanda	4	U.S.A.	73
Guatemala	39	Japan	78
Bangladesh	11	U.K.	91
Indonesia	20	Australia	89
India	22	Germany	85

SOURCE: World Bank, *World Development Report 1981*, (New York, Oxford University Press),
Table 20.

economically more advanced countries. The difference in urbanization reflects the fact that a much higher proportion of the population is engaged in primary industries in developing countries than in more-developed countries.

10. *Lack of social overhead capital.* Many of the public facilities that are taken for granted in economically advanced economies are unavailable in developing countries or are available in limited amounts. The supply of roads, ports, hospitals, schools, telephone services, water and sewerage facilities is limited. This is a reflection of overall poverty. The ability of the government to raise revenue for public works through taxation is limited as many incomes are close to subsistence level.

11. *Illiteracy is widespread* and the technical skills required in modern industry are in short supply.

12. *The distribution of income in developing countries is very uneven* compared to that in economically advanced countries. In many cases, too, the land is held by absentee landlords, and this can retard its economic development.

13. *Dualism.* Within many developing countries there are virtually "two economies" — an urban monetary economy consisting of individuals en-

TABLE 12.8   **The dependence of the value of exports of selected Developing Countries on one or a few products (1976, unless otherwise indicated)**

Developing Country	Main Exports	Percentage of Value of Exports Accounted for By Products in Column Two
Bangladesh	Jute goods and raw jute	79
Burma	Rice and teak	81
Burundi	Coffee	89
Chad (1974)	Cotton	65
The Gambia	Groundnut products	92
Ghana (1975)	Cacao	59
Mauritania (1975)	Iron ore	82
Mauritius (1974)	Sugar	86
Niger (1974)	Uranium	65
Rwanda	Coffee	80
Sri Lanka	Tea, rubber, coconut products	70
Sudan	Cotton, gum, groundnuts	76
Western Samoa	Copra, cacao	76
Zambia (1975)	Copper	91

gaged in Western-styled industry, and a rural traditional barter economy. Interaction between the two economies may be limited.

14. *Export dependence on one or two primary products*. Many developing countries rely on the export of one or two primary products to provide them with most of their earnings (see Table 12.8). Exports are important for development because they provide foreign exchange for the country concerned to import foreign capital, equipment, and skills that may be needed for development. But the value of such exports fluctuates considerably. The prices of primary products tend to be very unstable, and specialization in such a limited range of primary products (lack diversification) adds to risk as a rule. Furthermore, there has been a tendency for the price of primary products to fall in real terms so that it has become increasingly difficult for developing countries to maintain their export earnings.

Obstacles to Economic Growth and Development
Vicious Cycles of Poverty

Poverty itself is an obstacle to economic growth and development. Poverty limits the supply of savings and capital formation. Capital is one of the most important factors of production making for economic growth. Because individuals in developing countries have low incomes they can save little and can accumulate little capital. This means that their incomes rise only slowly because the amount of capital (tools, tractors, roads) used to assist labour in production rises only slowly. Their low incomes trap them in a low-income position from which it is difficult for them to emerge.

This has been called the vicious cycle of poverty, as far as the *supply* of capital is concerned, and is illustrated in Figure 12.9. This cycle is reinforced by the lack of demand for capital because the market for goods is small owing to low incomes. In turn, this implies that returns on capital investment may be low. If returns are low, it may not pay to borrow capital in order to invest in production and to sell the production. Thus, little capital is created, and productivity and incomes remain low. This, too, is a component of the vicious cycle of poverty, as far as the *demand* for capital is concerned, and is illustrated in Figure 12.10. Both of these cycles reinforce one another and help keep incomes low.

FIGURE 12.9 Cycle of poverty and capital creation as a result of lack of supply of capital

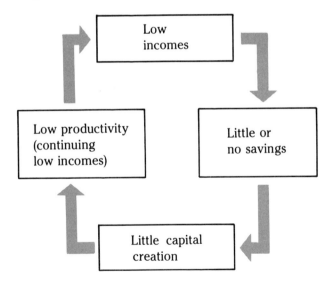

An *additional* reason why market demand is small is that markets are used only to a limited extent. Because transport costs can be high owing to poor roads and communication facilities, internal trade is limited in most developing countries. Improvements in the communication systems of developing countries would assist the wider use of markets and their development, but these improvements require the use of capital and skills that are scarce.

FIGURE 12.10 **Cycle of poverty and capital creation as a result of lack of demand
for capital**

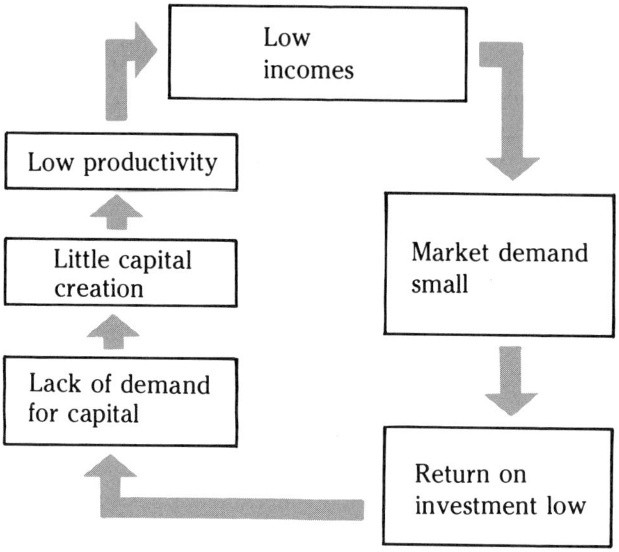

```
                    ┌──────────────┐
                    │  Low         │
                    │  incomes     │
                    └──────────────┘

┌──────────────────┐
│ Low productivity │
└──────────────────┘
                              ┌──────────────────┐
┌──────────────────┐          │ Market demand    │
│ Little capital   │          │ small            │
│ creation         │          └──────────────────┘
└──────────────────┘

┌──────────────────┐          ┌──────────────────┐
│ Lack of demand   │          │ Return on        │
│ for capital      │          │ investment low   │
└──────────────────┘          └──────────────────┘
```

Traditional Attitudes

Traditional attitudes in developing countries are sometimes not conducive to
economic growth. As mentioned earlier, in some societies businessmen are
looked down upon, and this does not encourage entrepreneurship. In some
underdeveloped countries, one's economic position is determined by birth. In
India, there are still strong social pressures for sons to follow the occupations of
their fathers and to remain within the occupation of their caste. This means that
the economic positions in society are not filled according to abilities, and thus
output is not maximized.

The size of families may also be influenced by religious beliefs. Hindus as a
rule wish to have a son to light their funeral pyre and may have extra children
to ensure this. Roman Catholics may have large families because of their
values. Religious beliefs can make it difficult to restrain population growth in
developing countries, as can ignorance of birth-control techniques as well as
the cost of birth-control measures. It is necessary to educate the population in
developing countries in birth-control techniques and make control methods
available at low cost. Otherwise, the danger increases that the population of a
developing country may increase as rapidly as the increase in production. Increased population may absorb any increase in output, and income per head
may remain stationary at a subsistence level. Population growth may trap a
developing country in a situation where incomes per head remain low, and savings and capital accumulation are low.

Policies to Promote Economic Development

Scarcity of resources limits the policies open to governments of developing countries to promote the development of their countries. Because incomes in these countries are low, their governments are limited in their access to resources to carry out policies. The revenue and loans that can be obtained within the country by the government are limited because incomes and savings are low. Furthermore, the government's capacity for borrowing abroad and repaying such loans with interest is limited because the value of exports by developing countries, and therefore their earnings of foreign exchange, are low. They must earn sufficient foreign exchange to repay foreign loans and interest unless foreign credit is available on a continuing basis. It is necessary to keep the resource restraint in mind. It is useless advising a country to spend heavily on the provision of *social overhead capital* if it does not have the means to do this. Given the limited resources available to the government of a developing country, it is important for it to make wise choices in allocating these funds between various projects that can assist development.

It is very difficult to generalize about the relative benefits of government expenditure on different public goods such as education, roads, railways, scientific research, and health care. But there are some types of government expenditure that may do little to promote development such as military expenditure and expenditure on "collective" consumption goods such as expensive sports stadiums and state banquets.

Public effort is needed in a number of areas. Some economists believe that public expenditure on birth-control education gives a substantial return to the community. If population increase is limited, income per head may rise. In turn, higher incomes provide a greater source for savings, government revenue, and capital formation.

Other ways in which the government of a developing country may be able to assist development of the developing country are by:

1. *Improving the operation of markets.* When private monopolies exist and restrict trade, it may be possible to break these up and create more competition. Where individuals are producing for a market (say coffee beans for a foreign market), it may be possible for the government to provide information about developments in prices likely in the future. Where custom or tradition prevent factor mobility, or result in discrimination against particular groups in society, the government can take positive action by legal means to reduce such discrimination, and can ensure that it does not occur in the public service. In India, for example, the government has taken positive action to increase the social and work mobility of the "untouchables".

2. *Fostering the spread and development of new techiques of production and ideas.* It may be desirable for the government to operate an extension service for agriculture and to undertake research to develop new

techniques of production relevant to the country, or to modify techniques developed elsewhere to make these more suitable to its environment. Small changes in agricultural practices (such as crop rotation, use of pesticides) may cost little and yield high returns. Improved varieties of plants such as rice and of animals (upgrading of local poultry) may bring high returns at little cost. The so-called "green revolution" in Asia that resulted in greater rice yields was a result of the experimental development of new types of rice. Effort of this type may also be needed to assist small manufacturers and to modify Western techniques to the more labour-intensive conditions existing in developing countries.

3. *Government enterprise.* As in developed countries, there is a need for the government to provide various social overheads such as roads and other facilities for communication. It may also be desirable for the government to engage in business enterprises such as steel production where these involve considerable capital cost. But there are dangers in this: there is no guarantee that a government business is likely to be more efficient than a privately owned one. Indeed, as its survival may not depend on its efficiency and profitability, there is not as strong an incentive for a public enterprise to be efficient as there is for a privately owned one to be efficient.

4. *Market and other interference designed to promote the development of one or more substantial manufacturing industries.* Rostow considers that one of the essential preconditions for the economic development of a country is the growth of one or more substantial manufacturing industries. It may be an optimal strategy to concentrate on the development of a narrow range of industries (including a narrow range of manufacturing industries) in a limited region, and, as development of these proceeds, fan out the development to a wider region and a range of industries. The government can aid the development of selected manufacturing industries:

   a. by providing taxation concessions to these industries,
   b. by protecting them from competing foreign imports by tariffs or other means,
   c. by subsidizing their production or exports, and
   d. by supplying adequate rail, road, and other public facilities in areas where the industries operate or are expected to operate.

But not all economists are convinced that an "unbalanced" approach to promoting economic development is best. Some economists argue that a balanced approach is best — that is, an approach that aids a wide range of industries. Traditional industries such as agriculture should not be ignored in the development process. Indeed, some economists argue that developments in agriculture can provide a lead (a surplus of income) to aid economic development elsewhere in the economy. Opinions are thus divergent about the best path for the government of a developing country.

5. *Land reform.* It is sometimes claimed that concentration of land ownership in the hands of a limited number of landlords, many of whom are absentee landlords, makes for the inefficient use of land. It has been suggested that governments should take action to ensure a more even ownership of land, and that more farmers should actually own their own land. But once again, opinion is divided about the likely impact of such reforms on agricultural productivity.

6. *Planning and co-ordination of economic activity.* As the funds available to the government in a developing country are extremely scarce, it is important that they be used to best advantage. This requires the government to forecast changes in the economy and to plan its own expenditures in accordance with these. Whether or not government involvement in planning and implementing economic change should extend to all parts of the economy depends to some extent on one's political philosophy. Some believe that complete government control of a developing economy can result in greater efficiency in resource use and to the sweeping away of cultural and social barriers to economic development. Others see complete control as inefficient and bureaucratic. Supporters of this view believe that administrative skills are in limited supply in developing countries, and that government officials are likely to be poorly equipped to direct an economy fully.

    Even if the government does not fully direct resource use in an economy, however, it may adopt *indicative planning* as a means of influencing economic development. Indicative plans consist of predications or forecasts about developments in the economy and its structure. They provide perspectives for plans by individuals in the economy, and need to be widely publicized and discussed. Individuals may be provided with incentives, such as taxation concessions, to assure that their actions are in accordance with developments desired by the government.

    Direct planning is associated with direct control of the economy by the government. It was used by Soviet Union in its starkest form during its early development under War-time Communism. It involves the government in directing all or most economic activity, and works poorly when planners and administrators are incompetent. The Soviet Union used this method to build up its capital and heavy industries, relying on a surplus forceably taken from the agricultural sector to support workers building up heavy industries. Consumption was also restrained.

7. *Mobilizing savings for capital accumulation.* Facilities for investing one's savings in developing countries are limited. It may be possible for

their government to encourage greater savings through extensions of the banking system, and by guaranteeing the solvency of various financial institutions.

8. *Appropriate taxation policies for growth.* Although the governments of developing countries can only raise a limited amount of revenue by taxation, their taxation policies can affect development. Taxes not only provide revenue for the government, but also have an impact on economic activity. Whereas personal income tax is an important source of government revenue in developed countries, in poorer countries, it is not an important source of revenue. There, such a tax is difficult to administer as a high proportion of the population is illiterate and does not keep business records. Furthermore, a considerable amount of production is not marketed but is directly consumed by its producers.

Many developing countries have a capitation tax, that is, fixed payment to be made to the government per individual or per dwelling. This is relatively simple to administer, but some individuals may not have the means to pay it. In such cases, it is important for the government to allow them to contribute a number of days of unpaid labour toward public works.

Taxes on the value of land and other assets also provide sources of revenue for governments in developing countries. Such taxes can encourage a more productive use of these resources. To help provide for the tax, landlords are less likely to leave land idle or to use it unproductively. Other taxes may also have a desirable economic impact. Taxes on consumption such as sales taxes and import taxes or tariffs on consumption goods can help to reduce consumption and use of foreign reserves for consumption purposes. But sometimes other taxes such as those on imports and exports are used to raise revenue in developing countries because they are administratively convenient.

As discussed earlier, taxation concessions may be used to encourage the growth of particular industries (such as particular types of manufacturing) that are considered to be important in fostering development. The government may also give "tax holidays" to foreign firms willing to invest and begin selected business operations in a developing country. As a result of a tax holiday, a firm is exempted from paying taxes or selected taxes for a number of years.

9. *Encouraging foreign investment.* The government of a developing country may find it worthwhile to encourage direct foreign investment. Such investment (business operations) may bring new skills into the country, as well as additional capital, and it may result in the replacement of imports by local production, a development that helps to save scarce reserves of foreign currency. Inflows of foreign private investment may increase employment and help to raise living standards.

But we cannot be certain that foreign private investment in a developing country will always have desirable effects. Some control may be necessary. For instance, foreign enterprise may drive out local enterprises in some fields in which local enterprises are not as technologically sophisticated as the foreign ones but that could, within a reasonable time, become so. Entry of foreign firms in such a case may be premature. Again, foreign investment is sometimes criticized on the grounds that it results in the import of inappropriate technology, and contributes to dualism in developing countries. Foreign firms may use the technology developed in countries with plenty of capital, and this may not be the optimal technology to use in countries where capital is in short supply. Industry developed by foreign firms may have weak linkages with the rest of the economy, and the persons employed in it may form a separate enclave. Consequently, there may be little "spin-off" of ideas to other parts of the economy.

10. *Improve "Basic Needs".* In the 1970s, it was recognized that more attention needs to be given to "basic needs" of the population in developing countries. The benefits of economic growth were not "trickling down" to the majority of poor people in these countries. Health-care systems were of the curative type rather than of the preventative type. The fact that these health centres were frequently located in urban areas meant that the majority of the very poor were unable to receive attention. Improvement in health and nutrition of the population is an important aid to economic growth. Studies have also shown that the social returns from education, particularly from primary education, are very high. A more educated populace is more likely to be aware of better hygiene and nutrition, and of birth- control measures. Education may be the most important basic need. It also seems particularly important that females receive this education as they manage the households in many developing countries.

Foreign Assistance and Trade and Aid

On the whole, economically advanced countries are well endowed with capital, savings, entrepreneurship, and technical skills, and are knowledgeable about new techniques whereas developing countries are short of these factors. The economically advanced countries are in a position to assist the developing ones. This assistance may take the form of investment by private individuals, loans and grants by governments, as well as technical help and trade concessions. Let us consider these different forms of assistance.

Private Foreign Investment in Developing Countries

Private investment is undertaken by individuals for their own profit or gain, but usually also benefits others. Private investment may consist of either *direct investment* or *portfolio investment.* Direct investment involves participation in business or economic operations of the country concerned by individuals or companies. As a result of such investment, foreign persons or companies may be involved, for instance, in mining operations, in textile production, in tea production, in the growing of palms for vegetable oil, and in chemical and oil production. As a result of this direct involvement, some managers or entrepreneurs from more developed countries may be employed in developing countries, and may introduce *new* techniques. Local people employed in foreign-owned firms may obtain experience in management and entrepreneurship, and gain knowledge and skills that can be used eventually outside the foreign-owned firm.

FIGURE 12.11 **Mining ore at P.T. International Nickel, Indonesia, a subsidiary of INCO, Canada. Foreign investment may aid development.**
COURTESY INCO, Limited

The extent to which direct investment benefits the host country (the country in which investment is occurring) depends upon the nature of the investment. Investment in which the assets of a local company are merely taken over by a foreign firm, or investment in existing property or land, may provide few benefits to a developing country. Operations by a foreign company can stifle entrepreneurs in a developing country if overseas firms enter an industry in which local enterprise is in a state of embryonic development. Time may be required for the development of a viable local industry. The entry of foreign-owned firms possessing advanced methods may prevent local firms from surviving and developing to a technologically sophisticated stage. Another criticism sometimes made of direct investment by foreign firms is that it leads to the use of inappropriate techniques of production in developing countries. Frequently, such firms use the machinery and techniques appropriate to countries in which capital is plentiful and labour is relatively scarce. Because available resources in developing countries are quite different (labour is relatively plentiful), this may not be the best approach in a developing country. Furthermore, the operations of foreign firms in some industries, e.g., mineral extraction, employ few people in the host country and may be only weakly linked to the rest of the economy.

To the extent that foreign investment leads to an inflow of foreign exchange to a developing country, it provides foreign funds to finance the import of capital equipment, or to produce capital equipment at home importing consumer goods instead. One of the few advantages of portfolio investment (purchase of share and securities in existing companies) by foreigners is that it provides foreign exchange for the country in which the investment is taking place. In addition, however, it can provide sources of new capital when foreign investors subscribe to new shares in established companies. It may also make the shares of local companies more marketable and thereby encourage local investment.

Many developing countries consider it desirable to regulate foreign private investment, and there are circumstances in which this is called for. Inept government regulation or excessive controls, however, may deter foreign investment that would benefit the host country. In cases where there is a risk that government may not provide security for foreign investments, or even nationalize such investment, investment will be deterred or channelled into areas offering quick returns, and possibly excessive profits, as foreign investors attempt to compensate themselves for risk.

Aid to Developing Countries from Foreign Governments

Another important form of assistance to developing countries is through loans and grants from foreign governments or international agencies acting on behalf of a group of governments. These include various agencies of the United Nations and the International Bank for Reconstruction and Development.

Loans have to be repaid, and they may be given to developing countries on commercial terms or on noncommercial terms. Loans made at market rates of interest (taking into account the repayment period) are described as *hard loans*. Loans for which conditions or terms are easier than in the market (and therefore involve concessions and, in essence, a hidden gift) are described as *soft loans*. The rate of interest may be lower than normal, the period of repayment may be lengthier than usual, or the country receiving the loan may be allowed to repay in its own currency rather than being required to repay in a foreign currency.

In accepting a hard loan, a developing country needs to be careful to ensure that the return on projects for which it is used exceeds the determined rate of interest, and that foreign currency will be available to repay the loan when it falls due. Loans of this type are made available by the International Bank for Reconstruction and Development, usually after it has assessed the expected returns for any project for which the loan is sought.

Soft loans (loans at less than commercial rates) are sometimes "tied". Frequently, the recipient country is required to buy goods or equipment of various kinds from the lending country. This may reduce the value of the loan. On the other hand, loans of this type are sometimes made by international agencies without "strings attached".

Grants are gifts, and do not have to be repaid. Sometimes they may be earmarked for a special purpose, for example, for famine relief or for hospitals. This may reduce their value from the recipient country's point of view, but they may be essential for the purpose of obtaining political support for the grant in the donating country. It may also be necessary to guard against their use for military purposes or their expenditure on prestige projects of little value.

Aid may be given on a *bilateral* or a *multilateral basis*. *Bilateral aid* involves *two* parties — the recipient country and the donor country. Such aid is likely in many cases to be motivated by political considerations. *Multilateral aid* involves *many* parties. As a rule, a number of countries donate funds to a common pool that is used to assist in a number of developing countries. The advantage of this method is that it allows the relative needs of the possible recipients to be assessed, and it prevents one country from imposing "undue influence" on another through an aid program. It tends to be favoured by developing countries. In 1978-79, Canada spent $560 million on bilateral aid and $491 million on multilateral aid. Canada's bilateral aid is roughly evenly divided between grants and (soft) loans. Table 12.9 sets out the recipient regions for 1978-79.

Trade Concessions as a Means of Assistance to Developing Countries

Developed countries can also assist developing ones by making it easier for the goods of developing countries to be imported into developed countries. Tariffs

TABLE 12.9   **Canada's Bilateral Aid by Various Regions 1978-79**

Region	$ million
Asia	227
Francophone Africa	130
Commonwealth Africa	107
Latin America	47
Caribbean	35

SOURCE: Canada Year Book 1980-81, Statistics Canada, pp. 754-55.

(taxes on imports) and limitations on quantity of imports can reduce the international trade prospects of developing countries and lower both the volume of their exports and the prices that they receive for exports. Many developing countries prefer improved trading opportunities to foreign aid because it gives them an opportunity to finance their own development. But developed countries have been slow in reducing barriers to the import of goods from developing countries because of political pressure in developed countries from industries that feel they are threatened by imports of goods produced by "cheap labour" in developing countries. From the point of view of raising real incomes in developed and developing countries, it may be optimal for some existing industries to be reduced in size or eliminated in advanced countries, and these industries expanded in developing countries, thereby increasing the specialization of countries in products in which they have a comparative economic advantage.

Increasing trade opportunities for developing countries widen their market and enable them to earn foreign exchange. A widening of their market may foster economies of scale and bring their entrepreneurs into greater contact with new ideas that may stimulate economic change.

The United Nations' "Second Development Decade"

Members of the United Nations have been making a worldwide effort to foster development in developing countries. The 1960s were set as the first development decade, and the 1970s were declared as the second development decade. Presumably this co-operative effort of U.N. members aimed at assisting development will continue in the 1980s.

The United Nations recommended that advanced countries should give at least 0.7 percent of their GNP to developing countries in the form of Official Development Assistance(ODA). As shown in Table 12.10, the countries in the OECD group fall considerably short of this target. The U.S.A. is one of the lowest contributors in terms of percentage of GNP. Canada, in 1980, spent 0.42 percent of its GNP on ODA, which is one of the higher contributions; but is still

only 60 percent of the targeted level. In terms of percentage of GNP, the OECD
countries are substantially behind the contributions from countries in the
Organization of Petroleum Exporting Countries (OPEC).

TABLE 12.10   **Official Development Assistance (ODA) from selected OECD & OPEC
Members (1980 estimates)**

		% of donor country GNP
OECD		
	Italy	0.15
	New Zealand	0.27
	United Kingdom	0.34
	Japan	0.32
	Australia	0.47
	Canada	0.42
	United States	0.27
	Germany	0.43
OPEC		
	Nigeria	0.05
	Algeria	0.21
	Iraq	2.19
	Saudi Arabia	2.60
	Kuwait	3.87
	United Arab Emirates	3.96
	Qatar	4.50

SOURCE: World Bank, *World Development Report, 1981* (New York, Oxford University Press),
Table 16.

The developed countries, besides contributing more in aid, can assist
developing countries obtain technology appropriate to their needs, and make
trading easier for them. For instance, fluctuations in the prices obtained for the
exports of developing countries is a major problem for them. Advanced countries could show more willingness to enter into long-term contracts for purchase of the production of developing countries at stable agreed prices.
Alternatively, countries may co-operate through pooling arrangements (buffer
stocks) for commodities to stabilize the prices of these. Stocks of commodities
are built up in times of low world demand for them and released when world
demand is high. The result is that prices do not fall (when demand is lower) to
as low a level as otherwise, and do not rise (when demand is high) to such a
high level. Such schemes can reduce price fluctuations, and are seriously being
considered for implementation by the United Nations. But they are not costless,

and there are some possible problems. For instance, stocks will build up excessively if a long-term fall in demand for, or rise in supply of, a product is misjudged as a temporary one.

As mentioned earlier, much scope still exists for the more-developed countries to make trade concessions to developing countries.

KEY CONCEPTS
(FOR REVIEW)

Balanced Growth

Basic Needs

Bilateral Aid

Capital Formation

Constant Prices

Cycle of Poverty

Degree of Urbanization

Developing Countries

Dual Economies

Economic Growth

Export Dependence

Inappropriate Technology for
  Developing Countries

Income per Head

Life Expectancy

Multilateral Aid

Official Development Assistance

Potential GNP

Production Possibility Frontier

Real Economic Growth

Tariff Preferences for
  Developing Countries

Tied Loans

United Nations' "Second
  Development Decade"

QUESTIONS FOR REVIEW AND DISCUSSION

1. How have economists usually measured economic growth?

2. Show how economic growth can be viewed as a shift outward in the economy's production possibility frontier.

3. Why might an economy's actual GNP not reach its potential level? Is GNP in Canada below its potential level? If so, why?

4. What factors may cause an increase in GNP?

5. Why is it important to take account of income per head when assessing the welfare of a population? How is income per head measured? Why is it important to distinguish between real income per head and money income per head?

6. Why is the level of GNP in a country an inadequate measure of the standard of living, or well-being, of its inhabitants?

7. In the last couple of decades, there has been a great difference between changes in Canadian money GNP and changes in real GNP. Why?

8. Why has the rise in real *per capita* GNP in Canada in the last few years been less than the rise in real GNP?

9. To what extent do you believe that improvements in the quality of resources rather than the quantity of resources are responsible for economic growth? List some of the ways in which the quality of resources can be improved.

10. What are the main characteristics of developing countries?

11. How can a distorted age distribution of the population of a country add to poverty? How is the age distribution distorted in developing countries?

12. In what way does the relative size of the primary sector and the degree of urbanization in developing countries differ from those in developed countries?

13. Explain what is meant by dualism in the economies of developing countries.

14. "Traditional attitudes present in some developing countries may hinder their economic development." Explain, and give some examples.

15. Outline and discuss the policies that the government of a developing country may adopt in order to promote economic growth.

16. How can the development of new techniques of production help the development of developing countries? Why might the techniques from developed countries need to be modified for adoption in developing countries?

17. Is foreign private investment likely to assist the economic development of a developing country?

18. Discuss the various ways in which official development aid can be made available to developing countries. In doing so, distinguish between grants, hard loans, and soft loans. What are tied loans and grants?

19. Distinguish between multilateral and bilateral aid. What advantages does multilateral aid have for recipient countries?

20. How has Canada's official aid been divided between bilateral and multi-lateral aid? Which regions receive the major part of Canadian aid? How does Canada's net official development assistance as a percentage of GNP/GDP compare with that of other developed countries?

21. "The best way for developed countries to assist developing ones is to make it easier for developing countries to export goods to developed ones." Discuss. Has Canada provided any import concessions for developing countries?

22. What is the United Nations' "Second Development Decade"? What initiatives does the United Nations believe should be undertaken to help foster development of developing countries?

FURTHER READING

Blomqvist, A., Wonnacott, P., & Wonnacott, R., *Economics*, 1st Canadian ed. Scarborough: McGraw-Hill Ryerson Limited, 1984, chapters 18 & 33.

Brox, J., & Cluff, M., "Potential Output and the Real GNP Gap." *Canadian Statistical Review* (January 1979), pp. vi-xii.

Finance and Development, a quarterly publication of the International Monetary Fund and the World Bank.

Lipsey, R.G., Purvis, D.D., Sparks, G.R., & Steiner, P.O., *Economics*, 4th ed. New York: Harper & Row, Publishers, 1982, chapters 43 & 44.

Rostow, W.W., *The Stages of Economic Growth: A Non-Communist Manifesto.* New York: Cambridge University Press, 1960.

Samuelson, P.A., & Scott, A.D., *Economics.* Scarborough: McGraw-Hill Ryerson Limited, 1980, chapters 37 & 38.

13 Income Distribution and Poverty

Determinants of Income

Poverty is not confined to developing countries. It also occurs in the developed countries, and individuals in these countries can become trapped in a poverty cycle. Furthermore, in economically advanced countries, differences in income levels can be considerable. What factors determine the levels of income received by individuals in our society?

Many factors play a role. One theory suggests that an individual's income is determined by the resources he or she possesses, and the prices that the services of these resources sell for in the market place. The prices of resources in the market place are, according to this theory, determined by the forces of supply and demand. Other theories suggest that the custom or social factors, rather than market forces, play a large role in determining incomes, especially in large organizations such as government departments and big companies.

Consider the supply-and-demand approach. The demand for the use of a resource is usually a derived demand. It is derived from the demand for products that can be produced using the resources. To a large extent, for instance, the demand for carpenters, bricklayers, and plumbers depends on the demand for buildings. As the demand for buildings rises, we would expect the wages of carpenters, bricklayers, and plumbers to rise. The demand for a resource is also affected by its productivity. An increase in the productivity of a resource may, but need not, lead to an increase in the demand for the resource.

The relationship between the (marginal) productivity of a resource and the demand for it is complex. But resources of the same type that have the greater productivity usually earn a higher income. As an example, better quality (more productive) land for agricultural purposes normally earns a higher rent than land of lower quality. This is ensured by competition for the use of resources. If the rent of better quality land is equal to that of lower quality, firms, in an attempt to increase their profit, will try to rent the better quality land. Thus, the competition for such land will force up its price, in this case, the rent.

The quantity demanded of a resource in an industry (other conditions unchanged) normally increases as the price of it falls. The demand curve for a resource is as a rule downward-sloping like the one shown by D_1D_1 in Figure 13.1. Usually (other conditions unchanged) the higher is the price offered for the use of a resource in an indusry, the greater is the quantity supplied of the resource to the industry. The supply curve of a resource to an industry usually slopes upward, as, for example, the supply curve marked SS in Figure 13.1 does.

In Figure 13.1, D_1D_1 is the hypothetical weekly demand curve for drivers of transport trucks and SS is their hypothetical supply curve. These indicate respectively the number of truck drivers demanded per week and the number of individuals willing to work as truck drivers at alternative wage rates. The equilibrium wage rate and number of truck drivers to be employed correspond to the point at which D_1D_1 and SS intersect. Given the conditions of supply and demand shown respectively by curves SS and D_1D_1, the equilibrium wage rate for a truck driver is $200 per week and 1000 are employed.

The normal effect of a rise in demand for truck drivers (a shift upward in the demand curve) is, other things unchanged, to increase the wage rate of truck drivers and the number of people employed as such. In Figure 13.1, for instance, a shift upward in the demand curve for truck drivers from D_1D_1 to D_2D_2 raises their equilibrium wage rate from $200 per week to $250 per week, and results in an increase in the number employed in market equilibrium from 1000 to 1200. The demand for truck drivers may rise because of an increased demand to transport goods by road as a result of a rise in railway charges. Or again, demand for transport may temporarily increase owing to seasonal factors such as the pre-Christmas rush.

Shifts in the supply curve of individuals willing to work as truck drivers affects the equilibrium market conditions. Normally, when the supply curve shifts upward (indicating that a higher price must be paid to secure the use of any unit of the resource), the equilibrium price of the resource under consideration rises. Given the normally sloped curves shown in Figure 13.1, a reduction

FIGURE 13.1   **Supply and demand as determinants of wages**

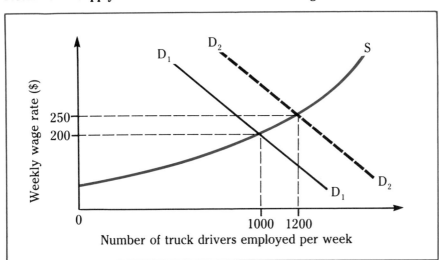

in the supply of truck drivers increases the equilibrium wage rate paid to them, and results in a decrease in the number employed. As well, the supply curve may shift upward because wage rates in alternative occupations, such as bus driving, go up.

The above discussion indicates how the forces of supply and demand help to determine the wage rate of truck drivers, and how the price paid for a resource tends to be higher the greater the demand for the resource is relative to its supply. According to this theory, the prices paid for other resources are determined in a similar way. The hiring charges for capital equipment such as air compressors tends to be determined in the same way. Figure 13.1 can be modfied to fit this case by indicating the number of air compressors along the X-axis and the weekly hiring charge of a compressor on the Y-axis.

Again, the rate of interest paid on loans may be seen as resulting from the interaction between the demand for and supply of loanable funds. Figure 13.1 can be modified to illustrate this case by indicating the quantity of loanable funds on the X-axis and the rate of interest on the Y-axis. The rent of land of a particular type depends on the demand for it and on its supply. It should be noted that the forces of demand and supply do not always operate freely in our society. Government regulations and market domination by large firms and trade unions can hamper the operation of these forces.

Personal incomes (the incomes received by individuals) depend upon the amount of *resources owned* by individuals, the going *market prices* of these resources, and the *willingness* of individuals *to market* their resources. Inheritance of property, inherent and acquired personal abilities and disabilities, and the accumulation of skills, knowledge, and property help to determine the resources available to an individual.

Although most of us can, within bounds, control our ownership or possession of resources, our individual fortunes depend to some extent upon chance. For example, some of us are born with severe personal disabilities or acquire these through accidents or ageing. On the other hand, we can add to our resources by undertaking training to improve our skills or by saving and accumulating capital.

Our incomes depend not only on the amount and quality of resources that we own but also on the prices that are paid for the use of these. As discussed above, these prices are determined to a considerable extent by the forces of supply and demand.

A further factor to take into account is the willingness of an individual to supply or market a resource he or she holds. For instance, a landholder may prefer not to rent his or her property for agriculture or for commercial gain and to use it merely for hunting. Another individual may prefer to take more leisure than others. He or she does not seek a second job and tries to avoid overtime. Incomes in these cases are lower than they might otherwise be. Incidentally,

3.4 percent of the Canadian labour force (more than 3 persons in every 100 in the labour force) held more than one job in January 1983.

The Distribution of Income in Canada

The way in which national output or income is shared between individuals or groups in society is referred to as the *distribution of income.* Sometimes the share of national income received by different types of factors of production is considered. For example, the proportion of national income accounted for by wages and salaries has been roughly 56-58 percent in Canada.[1]

The distribution of personal income in Canada may be illustrated by the use of a Lorenz curve as shown in Figure 13.2. A Lorenz curve indicates the percentage of total income received by recipients as a function of the percentage of recipients obtaining an income equal to or less than any specified amount. For instance, in 1977, the individuals in the lower 50 percent of the income distribution received less than 25 percent of total income. The top half received over 75 percent of the total income. The 20 percent of individuals on the lowest incomes received only 3.8 percent of the income. It can also be deduced from Figure 13.2 that the 10 percent of individuals with the highest incomes received roughly 27 percent of the total income in Canada in 1977.

The degree of inequality of income is indicated by the extent of curvature of the Lorenz curve away from the diagonal in Figure 13.2. When income is absolutely equal, the Lorenz curve coincides with the diagonal. In this case for example, the 10 percent of the population earning the lowest income earns 10 percent of the total income, and the 50 percent of the population earning the lowest incomes earn 50 percent of the total income and so on.

A statistical measure of the degree of inequality is given by the *Gini index.* The Gini index is the ratio of the area between the diagonal and the Lorenz curve to the entire area below the diagonal. If income is absolutely equally distributed, then the Lorenz curve coincides with the diagonal, and hence the area between the curves is zero. Thus, the Gini coefficient for a completely equal distribution of income is zero. The opposite extreme is the case where one person receives all of the income; the Lorenz curve then coincides with the edges of the box, and the area between the diagonal and the Lorenz curve is the same as the area below the diagonal. For a completely unequal distribution of income, the Gini index has a value of 1. In general, the Gini index has a value

---

[1]This is the proportion of GNP accounted for by wages and salaries. As a proportion of *net national income at factor cost* (GNP-[capital consumption allowance]-[indirect taxes less subsidies]) wages and salaries account for about 74-76 percent.

between 0 and 1. The smaller the value the more equal is the distribution of income. For 1977, the Gini index for Canada was 0.388.

The distribution of income is more equal in economically advanced countries than it is in many developing countries. Figure 13.3 shows that the distribution of income in Canada is more equal than that in Malaysia, but is less equal than the distribution of income in the Netherlands. Comparisons across countries may be misleading, however, because of different definitions of income, for example.

In Canada, the distribution of wealth (assets-debts) is less equally distributed across households than is income as shown in Figure 13.4. According to J. Podoluk, however, if the distribution of wealth is examined by income group, then wealth is more equally distributed than is income. The Gini index, in 1970, for wealth distributed by wealth group is 0.724, whereas the Gini index for the distribution of wealth by income group is 0.298. This result occurs owing to the fact that many low-income individuals are retired but have accumulated substantial wealth over their lifetimes.

FIGURE 13.2   Lorenz Curve for Canada (1977)

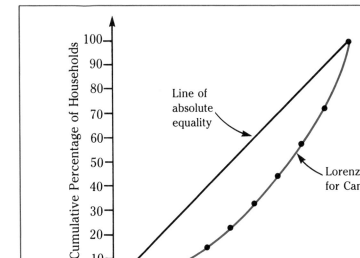

SOURCE: World Bank, *World Development Report, 1982* (New York: Oxford University Press), Table 25.

FIGURE 13.3 **Lorenz Curves for Canada, the Netherlands, and Malaysia**

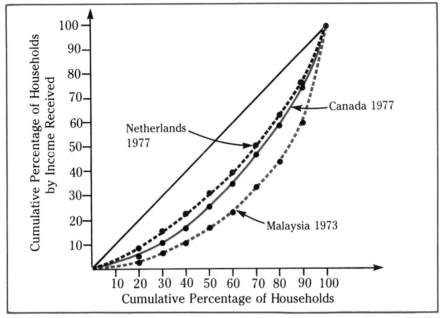

SOURCE: World Bank, *World Development Report, 1982* (New York, Oxford University Press), Table 25.

FIGURE 13.4 **Lorenz Curves for Income and Wealth in Canada**

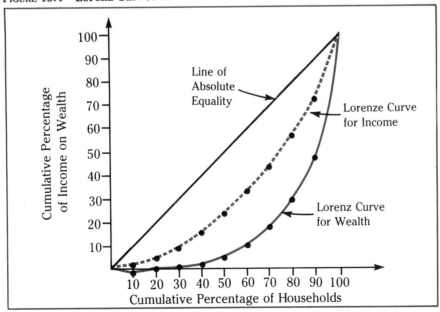

SOURCE: Data cited in I.J. Irvine, "The Distribution of Income and Wealth in Canada in a Lifecycle Framework," *Canadian Journal of Economics*, 1980, 455-74.

Factors Influencing Incomes in Canada

Most income recipients in Canada are principally wage-and-salary earners. In 1978, 76.8 percent of income recipients obtained their income from wages and salaries, and 9.1 percent obtained their income principally from government transfer payments. Only 5.5 percent earned their income through self-employment, and 5.9 percent received their income from investments. Over three-quarters of those earning over $35,000 in1978 received their income as wages and salaries. (These figures are shown in Table 13.1.)

TABLE **13.1** **Principal Source of Income of All Canadian Family Units 1978**

Principal Source of Income	Percentage of Recipients
Wages and Salaries	76.8
Net Income from Self-Employment	5.5
Investment Income	5.9
Transfer Payments	9.1
Other Money Income	2.6
Total	100.0

SOURCE: L. Osberg, *Economic Inequality in Canada*, (Scarborough: Butterworth & Co. (Canada) Ltd., 1981), Table 5.3.

Let us now consider some of the factors that are believed to influence the incomes that different people receive in Canada.

Age and Income

Incomes normally vary with the age of the individuals. In Canada (1977), income for families with a male head rises until age 45-54, and declines thereafter. For families with a female head, income rises until age 55-64, declines only slightly for 64-69, but declines more for 70 and over. For all families grouped together, income rises until age 45-54, and then declines thereafter. These trends are shown in Table 13.2 and Figure 13.5.

Education and Income

Another factor influencing income differences in Canada is the amount of education received by income recipients. Table 13.3 sets out the relationship between educational attainment of the family head and the mean (average) family income of families in Canada in 1977. The mean income of those workers with minimum educational achievement (left school by grade 8 or less) is 57 percent of the mean level of workers with a degree from a university. Income rises with the degree of educational achievement. But not all the difference in income between those with higher and lower levels of education can

TABLE 13.2   Age-Income Profile for Canadian Families 1977

| | Average Annual Family Income ($) | | |
Age Group	Male Head	Female Head	All Families
Under 25	16,593	7,319	15,455
25-34	20,182	8,448	19,178
35-44	23,465	12,349	22,412
45-54	25,563	14,274	24,478
55-64	21,180	15,272	20,686
65-69	13,836	15,172	13,973
70+	10,870	13,534	11,217

SOURCE: *Canada Yearbook, 1980-81*, Statistics Canada, Table 7.33.

FIGURE 13.5   Income-Age Profile 1977

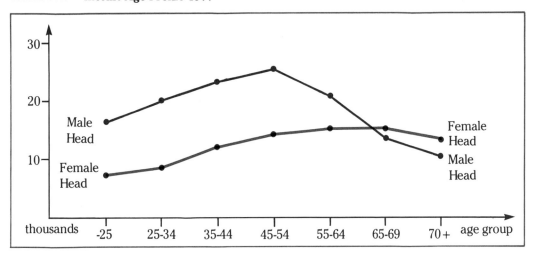

be attributed to education. On the whole, those undertaking more education may be more intelligent or from a wealthier background — factors that in themselves will tend to raise the individual's income. Nevertheless, education remains an important determinant of personal income in our society.

Sex-Marital Status and Income Differentials

The figures in Table 13.2 show that families with a male-head under age 64 receive higher family incomes than families with a female head. The average for all male-headed families was $20,947 in 1977 whereas the average for all female-headed families was $12,089. The female figure is roughly 60 percent of the male. Some of this differential may be attributed to more income earners in

TABLE 13.3   **Average Income of Families, Husbands under 65 Years, by Education of Husband and Wife in 1980**

		Average Family Income ($ in 1980)
I	Husband with University Degree	
	i) Wife with University degree	44,996
	ii) Wife with Secondary School	42,775
	iii) Wife with less than Secondary School	39,865
II	Husband with Secondary School	
	i) Wife with University degree	36,718
	ii) Wife with Secondary School	30,076
	iii) Wife with less than Secondary School	27,470
III	Husband with less than Secondary School	
	i) Wife with University degree	37,649
	ii) Wife with Secondary School	27,629
	iii) Wife with less than Secondary School	23,929

SOURCE: A. Rashid, "1981 Census of Population (Part 6): Changes in Work and Education Patterns and Family Income: 1970-1980," *Canadian Statistical Review*, December 1983, pp. xx-xxviii.

the male-headed family as it is family income. On the other hand, this figure has been quoted on other occasions as an unadjusted male-female differential. Not all of this differential can be attributed to discrimination against females, however. Females may be involved to a greater extent in part-time work or they may have lower levels of educational attainment. In order to determine how much of the differential is owing to discrimination we must adjust for other job-related characteristics. Adjusting for these other characteristics using the 1971 Canada Census, Professor Morley Gunderson determined that about 60 percent of the gap (of 40 percent) between Canadian male and female earnings could be attributed to discrimination. For the Ontario subset of individuals, Professor Roberta Robb found similar results; however, professors Shapiro and Stelcner found that in the Quebec sub-group, the degree of discrimination was somewhat lower at 53 percent.

Influences of Unions and Professional Licensing Groups

As discussed in Chapter 5, labour unions and professional licensing associations attempt to achieve higher wages and salaries for their members by restricting membership, etc., Studies for Canada suggest that other things being equal, the union/nonunion wage differential is roughly 15-16 percent.

Professors Muzondo and Pazderka, using the 1971 Census of Canada, determined that professions that restricted fee competition earned roughly 10 percent more than those that did not restrict fee competition. Their more interesting result, however, was that those professions that restrict advertizing earn roughly 33 percent more than those without such restrictions.

Public Sector and Private Sector Salaries

Using the 1971 Census of Canada, Professor Gunderson has determined that males in the public service earn roughly 6 percent more than comparable males in the private sector. For females in the public sector, the benefit of being in the public sector was a wage differential of almost 9 percent. Most of the benefits, in terms of higher wages, in the public sector accrued to those in the low-level occupations.

Poverty in Canada

Poverty, as we noted earlier, is not confined to less-developed countries; it occurs to some extent in developed countries. According to the Statistics Canada definition of what constitutes poverty in Canada, slightly less than 20 percent of Canadian family units in 1975 were living in poverty. Whether or not a family unit is regarded as being in poverty depends upon whether its income equalled or fell below a predetermined level — *the poverty line.*

Statistics Canada in the 1970s defined as poor those families that spent more than 62 percent of their income on the basic needs of food, shelter, and clothing.[2] For a family of 4 this results in an income level of $8446 in 1978. Below this line the family is in poverty. The Statistics Canada definition is not the only definition of what constitutes poverty, and different definitions may result in quite different estimates of the number of people that live in poverty. The Special Senate Committee on Poverty argued that for a family of 4, poverty sets in when less than 30 percent of income is available for discretionary purposes. The threshold income level in this case was $11,876 in 1978. Another definition, proposed by the Canadian Council on Social Development (CCSD), suggests that the poverty line for a family of 4 is determined at 50 percent of the average income for Canadian families. In 1978, this meant that those families (of 4) earning less than $10,605 were living in poverty.

Factors Associated with Poverty

Using a 1974 Statistics Canada Survey, the National Council of Welfare found that 60 percent of Canada's poor were to be classified as "working poor", that is, they earned more than half of their income from employment income. Thus,

---

[2]For the early 1980s, the percentage used by Statistics Canada has been revised from 62 to 58.5. "Canada's Forgotten Poor," (*Maclean's*, January 30, 1984).

the problem of poverty will not be remedied simply by recourse to employment creation.[3] The bulk of those in poverty are already working.

Sixty-one percent of the working poor live in Ontario and Quebec, which is not surprising as we saw in Chapter 11 that the bulk of Canada's population lives in these two provinces. Relative to population size, however, Quebec has a larger share of working poor than does Ontario. In 1973, the Atlantic Provinces and the Prairie Provinces also had a larger share of poverty relative to their share of Canada's population. British Columbia, on the other hand, was in the same position as Ontario with a smaller share of working poor than would be dictated by their share of population.

Half of the working poor lived in cities of 100,000 or more, yet 25 percent of them lived in areas with 1000 or less or in rural communities. The numbers for the nonworking poor are roughly similar. Twenty-six percent of unattached individuals were either working poor or nonworking poor. This figure is high compared to the 13 percent for families with children and 7 percent for other families. Nonetheless, of the working poor, 67 percent were families with children. In the nonworking-poor group, 53 percent were families with children. Twenty-four percent of families that were poor (working or non-working) with children, had 4 or more children.

Twenty-six percent of families with a head under 25 years of age were poor. Of the working poor, this group accounted for 30 percent of the total. Forty-four percent of the working poor were aged 25-44. Thirty-five percent of the nonworking poor were aged 55-64. Thirty-five percent of the working poor families had a head with less than grade-8 education.

The incidence of poverty among females was higher than among males. Thirty-three percent of unattached females were poor compared to 20 percent of unattached males. For female one-parent families, 49 percent were classified as poor whereas only 10 percent of male-headed families with children fell below the poverty line.

Of the working poor, 46 percent worked for 50 weeks or more per year. For the nonworking poor, 73 percent worked zero weeks per year. Some individuals are unable to work because they are too disabled. There may be as many as 2 million disabled Canadians. About 400,000 disabled are unable to work. Roughly one-third of these are permanently disabled, whereas the rest are temporarily absent from the labour force.

Assisting Those in Poverty

The National Council of Welfare concluded that the diversity of individuals classified as working poor meant that no single government policy could be

---

[3]In times of recession, of course, more people will fall below the poverty line owing to increased unemployment. Employment creation will alleviate some poverty in these circumstances.

designed to solve all the problems. They did conclude that low-income workers need an income-supplementation program that will guarantee a certain level of income.

The purpose of the *guaranteed income scheme* is to ensure every individual a minimum level of income by the government, paying each an allowance equal to this minimum when he or she receives no income from other sources. As income rises this supplement to income is reduced until it peters out at some level of "earned" income. Beyond this level of "earned" income, the individual pays income tax. An example of this is illustrated in Figure 13.6. In this case the minimum income level per year is set at $3000. Those with no "earned" income obtain a supplement or grant from the government equal to $3000 per annum. Once income is earned, the grant in this case is reduced by 50¢ for each dollar earned so that at an income of $7000 no grant or supplement is paid. In the case shown, income earners with more than $7000 income per year pay tax. At present, there is no general *negative income tax* or income-supplement scheme of this nature operating in Canada (although an experimental scheme was implemented in Manitoba during the last half of the 1970s). Although no tax is paid on low incomes in Canada, one is not entitled to

FIGURE 13.6 **Example of an income guarantee scheme based on government supplementation of low incomes and tax on high incomes**

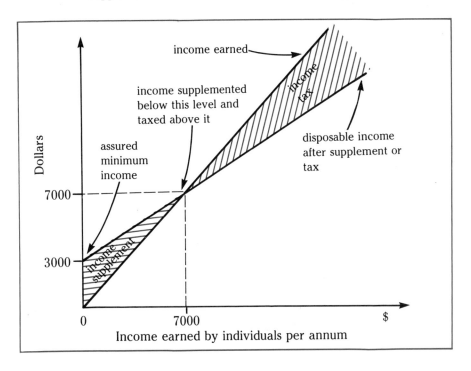

an income supplement by the mere fact of earning a low income. Some supplement may, however, in certain circumstances be obtained through social welfare payments — for instance through old age or invalid pensions and unemployment benefits. Old age pensioners may receive a Guaranteed Income Supplement (GIS). The maximum GIS monthly payment is reduced by 50¢ for every 1 dollar income earned.

It needs to be stressed that measures of poverty in more-developed countries are relative. Indeed, some workers in this field have proposed that poverty be determined in relation to income inequality. The Canadian Council on Social Development has suggested that for a family (of 4) having an income of half or less than half of the average income in the country might be regarded as being in poverty. By this measure, about 25 percent of families or households in Ontario in the mid-1970s could be regarded as being in poverty.

KEY CONCEPTS
(FOR REVIEW)

Derived Demand for a Resource
Discrimination and Female Incomes
Distribution of Income
Gini Index
Guaranteed Income Scheme
Life Cycles and Income
Lorenz Curves of Income
    Distribution
Marginal Productivity

Minimum Wages
Poverty Cycles
Poverty Lines
Public Sector/Private Sector Wage
    Differentials
Standard Hours of Work
Supply and Demand as
    Determinants of Income
Union/Nonunion Wage
    Differential

QUESTIONS FOR REVIEW AND DISCUSSION

1. Explain the type of poverty cycle that poor individuals or families in Canada could become trapped in.
2. Speaking generally, what factors determine the level of income received by individuals in our society?
3. "The demand for the use of a resource is usually a derived demand." Explain.
4. Show in principle (using a diagram to illustrate your answer) how the wages of grape-pickers might be determined by conditions of demand and supply. What effect would an increase in the demand for grape-pickers (shift to the right in the demand curve) have on their wage rate?
5. Draw figures to illustrate how the prices for the use of the following resources mentioned in Chapter 13 might be determined by conditions of demand and supply:

a. air compressors, and

b. loanable funds.

Price in the first case is the rental rate, and in the second case, the rate of interest.

6. "Personal incomes depend upon resources owned, willingness to market these, and their market prices." Explain and discuss.

7. What does the distribution of income refer to? Is the distribution of income in Canada even? How uneven is it?

8. What are the main sources of income in Canada? Do interest, rents, and dividends provide a large proportion of income?

9. In what way do incomes tend to vary with age? Explain the pattern that occurs. Why is the mean income of females in Canada so much lower than that of males?

10. Income in Canada tends to rise with degree of educational attainment. To what extent do you think that educational attainment is the reason for this higher income?

11. What is a poverty line? Are such lines arbitrary? What are the definitions of the poverty line used in Canada?

12. Among what groups does poverty seem to be most prevalent in Canada? Why does poverty occur in these groups?

13. Outline some of the ways in which those in poverty can be assisted by economic measures. In doing so, pay particular attention to the guaranteed-income scheme, or negative income tax, as a means for helping those in poverty.

14. What percentage of the Canadian population is in poverty?

15. What is meant by Canada's "Working Poor"? Will employment creation solve the poverty issue for Canada? Explain.

16. What are the characteristics of Canada's "Working Poor"?

17. Does Canada have a negative income tax?

FURTHER READING

Gunderson, M., "Decomposition of the Male/Female Earnings Differential: Canada 1970." *Canadian Journal of Economics* (1979), pp. 479-85.

Gunderson, M., "Earnings Differentials between the Public and Private Sectors." *Canadian Journal of Economics* (1979), pp. 228-42.

Lipsey, R.G., Purvis, D.D., Sparks, G.R., & Steiner, P.O., *Economics*, 4th ed. New York: Harper & Row, Publishers, 1982, chapters 20-23.

Muzondo, T.R., & Pazderka, B., "Occupational Licensing and Professional Incomes in Canada." *Canadian Journal of Economics* (1980), pp. 659-67.

National Council of Welfare, *The Working Poor* (1977).

Osberg, L., *Economic Inequality in Canada.* Scarborough: Butterworth & Co. (Canada) Ltd., 1981.

Podoluk, J., "Measurement of the Distribution of Wealth in Canada." *Review of Income and Wealth* (June 1984).

Reuber, G., "The Impact of Government Policies on the Distribution of Income in Canada: A Review." *Canadian Public Policy* (1978), pp. 509-29.

Robb, R.E., "Earnings Differentials between Males and Females in Ontario, 1971." *Canadian Journal of Economics* (1978), pp. 350-59.

Samuelson, P.A., & Scott, A.D., *Economics.* Scarborough: McGraw-Hill Ryerson Limited, 1980, chapters 5, 27, 28, & 29.

Shapiro, D.M., & Stelcner, M., "Male-Female Earnings Differentials and the Role of Language in Canada, Ontario, and Quebec, 1970." *Canadian Journal of Economics* (1981), pp. 341-48.

The Role of the Government in the Economy

14

The Need for a Government Sector and for Government Intervention in the Economy

In both socialist and nonsocialist countries today, governments intervene or are involved to a great extent in the operation of economies. In complex economies, such as our own, *free markets do not satisfactorily solve all economic problems*. This explains to a large extent the prevalence of government interference in the workings of market economies.

The present consensus in our society is that markets do not ensure a fair or *equitable distribution of income*, and the government should intervene to improve the distribution of income. Governments in most countries, for example, attempt to aid the poorer members of society by paying pensions to the handicapped and the aged from taxes collected from those earning higher incomes. Furthermore, in a market economy, *equality of opportunity* is not fully assured. The desirability of equality of opportunity is widely accepted in Western economies, but access to educational opportunities, for example, may be extremely unequal in the absence of government intervention. The children of less-well-off parents could be expected to obtain less or inferior schooling in the absence of the supply of free or subsidized school facilities by governments.

The *market system may fail to produce some desired goods or services* or may produce less than the optimal amounts of these. This is because some goods and services are difficult to market: once they are supplied, it is hard to make their use by consumers dependent on the payment of a price. For example, once a radio station begins transmitting it is difficult to make listeners pay according to the amount of time that they spend listening to the station. Furthermore, it is not optimal to exclude any listener from listening to the station by charging a price for listening. This is because no additional cost is incurred by the radio station if an additional person tunes in to the station. In cases like this, a private owner or supplier of a commodity (in this case a radio station) may not supply the commodity or may supply it in smaller quantity than if he could appropriate a greater amount of its value. Thus, it may be optimal for the government to supply the commodity or subsidize its supply. Governments provide other services of this nature, such as defence, and law and order. If national defence were left to private individuals, it would be underprovided and would not be efficiently organized: some individuals might not contribute anything toward national defence even though they would gain from the national-defence effort of others. Some services are supplied by the government *to promote national cohesiveness*, and because society does not accept market or economic power *as a fair arbiter* of these services. Justice would appear to be of this nature. In our society, we accept the principle that justice and the rule of law should be available equally to all. This principle is likely to be most nearly satisfied when justice is meted out by government through the courts. The judicial system is therefore supplied by the government.

The occurrence of natural monopolies and the need (in the interest of economic efficiency) to avoid duplication of supplied facilities frequently explains why a good or service is supplied by the government. In Canada, water and sewerage, roads, electricity, and postal delivery are supplied by governmental bodies because the duplicated supply of these facilities in any region would add to costs. Just imagine the extra cost of supplying electricity if two companies distributed it in each street, duplicating electricity poles and electricity mains. Although supply by one company is most economic, this gives the company a monopoly (a natural monopoly because competition is uneconomic) that it may use to charge high prices. In theory, this can be overcome by the government's supplying the services and charging moderate prices, or by the government's regulating the private supply of the service. In Canada, for instance, telephone services are supplied largely by a private company, Bell Canada, but the maximum prices it can charge are regulated by the government. There is no guarantee, however, that the prices of a government monopoly or a regulated monopoly will be moderate.

A government may also produce goods and services *to provide competition* where a private company has no competition or limited competition in supplying commodities in an important market. In theory, the government-owned railway, the Canadian National Railway (CNR), provides competition for the privately owned railway, Canadian Pacific Railway (CPR). Similarly, Air Canada, the government-owned airline, provides competition for the private airline CP Air and other private airlines.

The government not only intervenes in the production of goods but also in their exchange. In Canada, the government has declared various trade practices to be illegal. It is illegal, for example, for a company to engage in the practice of resale price maintenance. That is, to oblige retailers to resell a product at a minimum price. It is illegal in Canada for employers to pay less than the minimum wage, except in those sectors that are specifically exempted such as domestic service in private homes.

Governments have passed laws to give greater protection to consumers. In Canada, new motor vehicles must satisfy minimum vehicle safety and en-

FIGURE 14.1   **The Parliament Buildings in Ottawa. Total spending by Canadian
governments amounts to roughly 40 percent of GNP.**
COURTESY Archives of Ontario

vironmental protection standards. In order to protect children in Canada, there
are regulations governing car seats, cribs, toys, and rattles.

Even in economies where markets play a major role in allocating
resources, governments intervene to modify the distribution of income, to produce or control the supply of various goods and services, and to regulate the
exchange of many goods and services.

Furthermore, governments can control overall economic activity. Governments, through their policies, can greatly influence the level of employment in
an economy and the rate of inflation. A market economy does not ensure full
employment, and economic activity in a market economy may fluctuate to a
greater extent than is desirable. By pursuing suitable policies, governments can
raise employment in an economy in times when business activity is depressed,
and can restrain excessive demand when business activity is booming, thereby
evening out the rhythm of economic activity.

The Government Sector in Canada

It is difficult to quantify the importance of the government sector in any
economy. The extent of spending by the government, or the proportion of the
workforce employed by the government, can only provide a rough guide to its
economic importance.

If we use total spending by the government sector as a proportion of GNP
as a guide to the relative importance of the government sector in the economy,
we find that for each year in the last half of the 1970s, total spending by government was slightly in excess of 40 percent of GNP. Total expenditures by level of
government in 1982 are given in Table 14.1.

TABLE 14.1   **Total Expenditures by Level of Government, 1982**

Level of Government	Total Expenditure ($ Millions)
Federal	85,957
Provincial	72,020
Local	32,839
Total Government*	165,557

*excludes intergovernmental transfers

SOURCE: *Economic Review*, Department of Finance, April 1983, tables 49, 51, 56, & 58.

The provincial governments' spending is almost as large in terms of total
spending as is that of the federal government.

Although total spending by Canadian governments is a significant propor-

TABLE 14.2   **Total Government Spending as a Percentage of GNP or GDP for
Selected Countries 1980**

	%
Australia	33.9
Austria (1977)	46.6
Canada	41.7
Denmark (1976)	43.7
France	45.9
Germany	45.2
Italy	44.0
Japan	31.7
Netherlands	62.5
Norway	49.1
Sweden	61.7
United Kingdom	44.6
United States	35.1
Average	45.2

SOURCE: *Economic Review*, Department of Finance, April 1983, Table 47.

tion of GNP, it is not large in comparison to the proportions for some other countries listed in Table 14.2.

Total spending by the Netherlands government sector amounts to 62.5 percent of GNP, 61.7 percent by Sweden, and 49.1 percent by Norway. The average for the group is 45.2 percent. By this measure, the economically advanced "market" economies of the world have substantial government sectors.

Although total government spending in Canada exceeds 40 percent of GNP, not all of this spending goes to providing government goods and services. Some of this spending is merely a transfer of income from government to private individuals or to other levels of government. It is important to include these transfers as they reflect government involvement in the economy through its income redistribution function; however, the inclusion of these transfers overestimates the degree of government activity in terms of real resources allocated to the public sector. If we exclude transfers, then government spending in 1982 was 24.7 percent of GNP. The major component of government spending is current expenditure on goods and services. Gross fixed capital formation by governments amounted to only 3.0 percent of GNP in 1982.

We may also try to measure the size of the government sector by the proportion of employees employed by the government. Table 14.3 shows the employment in the government sector by level of government for September 1982.

TABLE 14.3   **Government Employment, September 1982**

Level	
Federal	590,798
Provincial	426,625
Local	298,395
Total	1,316,395

SOURCES: *Federal Government Employment*, Statistics Canada; *Provincial Government Employment*,
      Statistics Canada; *Local Government Employment*, Statistics Canada.

The total employment of roughly 1.3 million people represents 12.5 percent of those employed in the labour force in September 1982.

Features of Government in Canada Resulting from Confederation

The nature of government activities in Canada is influenced by the fact that,
from a political point of view, Canada is a federation of ten provinces and two
territories.

According to the *Constitution Act*, 1867, the federal government would be
responsible for issues of general or common interest to the country, and the
provinces would be responsible for issues of local or specific interest. For
example, the federal government would be responsible for national defence,
but the provinces would be responsible for schools and hospitals. The *Act* also
specified the means of raising government revenues. The federal government
was granted the right to raise tax revenue through any means of taxation
whereas the provincial governments were restricted to the use of direct taxes
only.

It was easy for the demands placed upon the provincial governments to
outgrow their financial resources because of their more restricted taxation
powers. As a result, the federal government and the provincial governments
have entered into various tax-sharing agreements and shared-cost programs.
For example, the federal government has been involved in the provincial
domains of health and education since 1919 and 1912 respectively. In recent
years, the shared-cost programs in these areas have been governed by the pro-
visions of the *Established Programs Financing Act* of 1977.

In 1982, provincial governments received roughly 22 percent of their total
revenue as a transfer from other levels of government whereas local governments were more dependent upon other levels of government, receiving 46
percent of their revenue from such transfers.

FIGURE 14.2 **Education is one of the largest components of expenditure for provincial and local levels of government.**
Courtesy University of Guelph Illustration Services

Expenditure or Outlays by Governments in Canada

Table 14.4 sets out the general categories of outlays by all government bodies in Canada, in 1982. From the table, the largest government spender on goods and services is the local government sector. Expenditure on goods and services by provincial authorities also exceeds that made by federal authorities. Local and provincial governments are also responsible for the major portion of gross capital formation by the government sector, with each of the local and provincial levels spending close to three times as much as the federal level in 1982. The largest outlay by the federal government is for "transfers to persons". Transfers to other levels of government form the largest outlay for provincial governments whereas expenditures on goods and services is the largest outlay for local governments.

Table 14.5 provides a more detailed picture of general expenditure by Canadian governments. The largest category of expenditure for the federal government is social services, which accounts for slightly less than one-third of its gross general expenditure. The second largest federal expenditure is the interest charge on the public debt. Resource conservation and development, and protection of persons and property are the next major outlays.

TABLE 14.4   General Categories of Expenditures by Level of Government 1982
              ($ Millions)

	All Gov't.**	Federal Gov't.	Provincial Gov't.	Local Gov't.
Goods and Services	75,748	18,636	21,155	25,278
National Defence*	6,969	6,969	-	-
Transfers to Persons	42,630	24,644	13,629	478
Interest on the Public Debt	25,238	16,440	6,245	2,451
Subsidies	7,600	5,649	1,951	-
Capital Assistance	2,588	2,288	300	-
Transfers to Other Levels of Government	-	15,768	24,659	141
Gross Capital Formations	10,694	1,493	4,081	4,535
Transfers to Nonresidents	1,059	1,039	-	-
Total Expenditures	165,557	85,957	72,020	28,193

* Included in Goods and Services
**Includes Hospitals

SOURCE: *Economic Review,* Department of Finance, April 1983, tables 49, 51, 56, & 58.

The major expenditures for the provincial government sector are for
health, education, and social services (in that order). These three groups account for roughly 60 percent of provincial spending. The largest component of
local government spending is education, which accounts for over 40 percent of
local government general expenditures.

Table 14.6 indicates the economic classification of the total gross general
expenditures by the federal government presented in Table 14.5.

Slightly less than 70 percent of general expenditures by the federal government are in the form of transfers to persons, business, governments or noncommercial institutions. Almost 60 percent of the transfer payments are made to
persons or noncommercial institutions. Twenty-seven percent of transfers went
to provincial governments.

Financing Government Expenditure

Table 14.7 indicates the major sources of government general revenue. A
major proportion of gross general revenue is collected through taxation by
federal and provincial governments. The main source of governmental taxation receipts is the income tax. The personal income tax accounts for two-thirds
of federal income tax and 80% of provincial income tax. Consumption taxes
are the second largest source of federal revenues and third largest source of
provincial revenues. The major consumption tax for both federal and provin-

TABLE 14.5   Components of Gross General Expenditure for Levels of Government 1981 ($ Million)

		Federal* Gov't.	Provincial** Gov't.†	Local Gov't.‡
1.	General Services	3,482	4,667	1,631
2.	Protection of Persons and Property	6,372	2,311	2,423
3.	Transportation and Communications	4,255	4,715	3,981
4.	Health	4,391	16,938	1,320
5.	Social Services	21,514	10,273	931
6.	Education	2,513	15,251	12,882
7.	Resource Conservation and Industrial Development	7,246	3,720	276
8.	Environment	343	964	2,634
9.	Recreation and Culture	538	928	1,911
10.	Labour, employment, and immigration	777	154	-
11.	Housing	1,002	615	56
12.	Foreign Affairs and International Assistance	1,076	-	-
13.	Regional Planning and Development	162	760	337
14.	Research Establishments	1,073	55	-
15.	General Purpose Transfers to other Levels of Government	4,387	-	-
16.	Transfers to own Enterprises	1,427	809	350
17.	Debt Charges	7,320	5,492	2,174
18.	General Purpose Transfers to Local Government	-	1,519	-
19.	Other	2	119	80
	Total Gross General Expenditure	67,880	69,286	30,985

*   Fiscal year ending March 31, 1981
** Includes Yukon and Northwest Territories
†   Fiscal year ending March 31, 1982
‡   Estimates for 1981

SOURCES: *Federal Government Finance*, 1980, Statistics Canada; (June 1982) catalogue 68-211; *Provincial Government Finance*, 1981, Statistics Canada (November 1982), catalogue 68-205; *Local Government Finance*, Estimates 1981, Statistics Canada (September 1982), catalogue 68-203.

FIGURE 14.3   **Economic Classification of Federal General Expenditures in Canada**

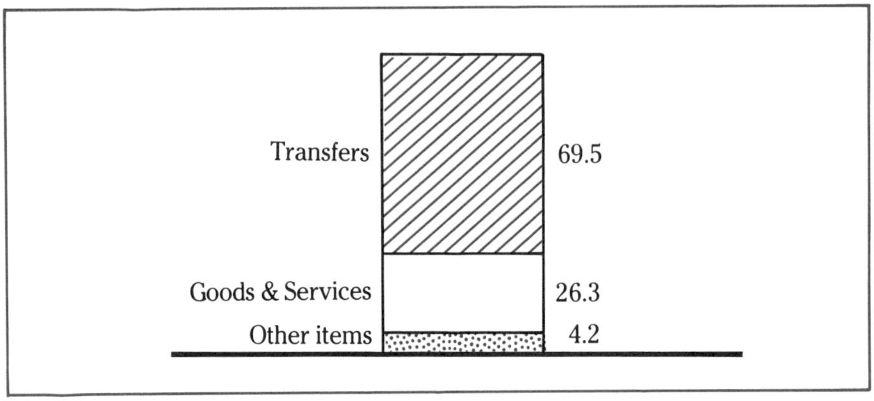

Transfers	69.5
Goods & Services	26.3
Other items	4.2

FIGURE 14.4   **Allocation of Federal Transfer Payments in Canada**

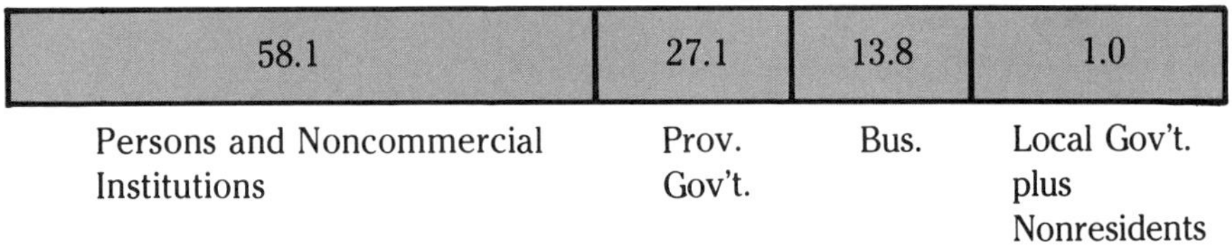

58.1	27.1	13.8	1.0
Persons and Noncommercial Institutions	Prov. Gov't.	Bus.	Local Gov't. plus Nonresidents

cial levels is the general sales tax. Customs duties are also a significant consumption tax at the federal level, and the motor fuel tax is an important provincial consumption tax.

At the federal level, health and insurance levies, return on investments, and sales of goods and services are important revenue sources. These are comparable to the major consumption taxes in terms of the size of their contribution.

The second largest component of provincial revenue is the group of various transfers from other government. This group is almost as large as the provincial income tax. The major portion of transfers come in the form of specific-purpose transfers. Natural resource revenues, health and insurance levies, and return on investments are also major sources of revenue for provincial governments.

For local governments, the most important source of revenue is specific-purpose transfer payments. Virtually all of these transfers were from provincial governments. Taxes formed the second major revenue source.

The Government Budget Constraint

Comparing tables 14.7 and 14.8 with Table 14.5 reveals that gross general revenue may not be equal to gross general expenditure. For the year presented, the provincial governments (collectively) generated a small *budget*

TABLE 14.6   **Economic Classification of Federal Gross General Expenditures, Fiscal Year ending March 31, 1981 ($ million)**

1.	Goods and Services	(17,867)
	a. Salaries and Wages	7,303
	b. Other	10,564
2.	Transfer Payments to	(47,141)
	a. Provincial Governments and Territories	12,797
	b. Local Governments	310
	c. Persons and noncommecial institutions	27,370
	d. Business	6,504
	e. Nonresidents	140
3.	Other Items	2,872
	Gross General Expenditure	67,880

SOURCE: Federal Government Finance, 1980. Statistics Canada, (June 1982), catalogue 68-211.

surplus, that is, their revenue exceeded their expenditure. This is a form of government, or public, saving.

The federal government, on the other hand, generated a *budget deficit* because their expenditures exceeded their general revenues. How does the federal government finance the excess of expenditure over revenue? One option is for the government to spend from past savings by drawing on their bank balances held with the banking system. This method of financing the deficit is unlikely to have additional repercussions on the economy.

If the government does not want to reduce its bank balance, then it must borrow to finance the deficit. Borrowing to finance the deficit is likely to have further repercussions on the economy. The nature of the repercussions depends upon the source of the borrowed funds. The government may choose to borrow from the Bank of Canada. In this case, the government sells bonds to the Bank of Canada in return for money. These proceeds will result in an increase in the money supply; this method is commonly referred to as *money financing* of the deficit. Following the discussion of Chapter 8, this will tend to reduce interest rates in the economy. This may stimulate private investment and raise national income. On the other hand, if national income is close to potential then money financing may be inflationary.

The government may also borrow from the private sector. In this case, the government raises the money by selling bonds to private individuals. This increase in the supply of bonds in the bond market will tend to depress bond prices and thus raise interest rates. There is no change in the money supply

TABLE 14.7   **Components of Gross General Revenue for Federal and Provincial Government ($ Millions)**

		Federal Gov't.*	Provincial** Gov't.†
1.	Income Tax	(30,293)	(19,906)
	a. Personal Income tax	21,296	16,152
	b. Corporation Income Tax	8,130	3,754
	c. Tax on payments to nonresidents	867	-
2.	Consumption Tax	(10,850)	(10,977)
	a. General sales	5,429	7,217
	b. Motor fuel	453	2,336
	c. Alcoholic beverages	699	7
	d. Tobacco	811	919
	e. Racetrack Betting	8	128
	f. Air transportation	166	-
	g. Custom duties	3,188	-
	h. Amusements and admissions to places of entertainment	-	4
	i. Other	96	366
3.	Property Tax	-	146
4.	Miscellaneous Taxes	2,722	1,158
5.	Health and Insurance Levies	5,941	5,938
6.	Natural Resource Revenues	47	7,148
7.	Privileges, Licences, and Permits	69	1,724
8.	Sales of Goods and Services	3,292	1,412
9.	Return on Investments	4,305	7,042
10.	Other Revenues from Own Sources	842	832
11.	General Purpose Transfers from Other Levels of Government	-	4,728
12.	Specific Purpose Transfers from other Levels of Government and their Enterprises	-	9,476

	Federal Gov't. *	Provincial** Gov't. †
13. Transfers from Local Government	-	108
Gross General Revenue	58,362	70,593

*   Fiscal year ending March 31, 1981
**   Includes Yukon and Northwest Territories
†   Fiscal year ending March 31, 1982

SOURCES: *Federal Government Finance*, 1980, Statistics Canada (June 1982) catalogue 68-211; *Provincial Government Finance*, 1981, Statistics Canada (November 1982) catalogue 68-205.

TABLE 14.8   **Components of Local Government Revenue (1981 Estimates) ($ millions)**

1.	Taxes	10,856
2.	Privileges, licences, permits	199
3.	Sales of goods and services	2,546
4.	Other revenue from own sources	528
5.	General Purpose Transfers	1,865
6.	Specific Purpose Transfers	12,263

SOURCE: *Local Government Finance*, Estimates 1981, Statistics Canada (September 1982) catalogue 68-203.

once the government spends the money that was previously held by individuals. The increased interest rates may retard private investment expenditures. This method of financing the deficit is commonly referred to as *bond financing*. Bond financing a deficit may lead to a *crowding out* of private investment — that is, a reduction in private investment expenditures.

The Full-Employment Budget versus the Actual Budget

If the government is running a budget deficit, does this mean that the government is conducting an expansionary fiscal policy? On the surface it may appear so as the goverment is injecting more into the economy with its expenditure than it is withdrawing in the form of tax revenues. This does not mean, however, that the fiscal policy is *designed* to be expansionary. As income taxes form an important source of revenues, the government's *actual* budget may be in a deficit position because recessionary pressures have reduced incomes and hence income tax revenue. In order to determine if the fiscal policy is expansionary, one must examine the *full-employment budget*, that is, the budget value that would occur if the economy were operating at full employment. It is quite possible that the full-employment budget position may be a surplus, but the actual budget position may be a deficit, as shown in Figure 14.5.

FIGURE 14.5   **The budget position as a function of national income**

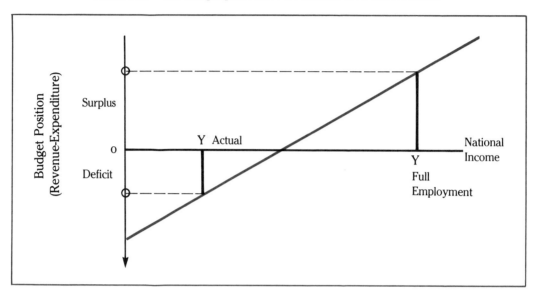

The reader may easily verify that if the actual budget is in a surplus position, then the fiscal policy is indeed contractionary as the *full-employment budget position* is a surplus, also.

Some Problems Encountered in Government Economic Policy

Objectives of Canadian Economic Policy

In its *First Annual Review* (1964), the Economic Council of Canada specified five basic economic and social goals for the economy each of which taken individually seem like reasonable objectives. These goals were:

1. Full Employment,
2. A High Rate of Economic Growth,
3. Reasonable Stability of Prices,
4. A Viable Balance of Payments, and
5. An Equitable Distribution of Rising Incomes.

To this list, one may wish to add:

6. Economic efficiency in the operations of the economy,
7. Reasonable stability of the exchange rate, and
8. Desired environmental quality.

General Difficulties of Policy Making

Governments encounter many difficulties in putting economic policies into effect. First, there is the difficulty of obtaining consensus or agreement about desirable objectives. It is not always possible to obtain agreement, except in very general terms, about economic aims. Secondly, once aims are formulated it may turn out that they cannot be achieved simultaneously. For instance, the aim of increased employment and the objective of reduced inflation may be impossible to achieve simultaneously during a given time period. Some trade-off between inflation and employment may be necessary in the short run. The nature of this trade-off was discussed in Chapter 10. In that chapter, we showed that the long-run relationship between inflation and unemployment may be vertical at the natural rate of unemployment. This means that in the long run, the government may be able to control the rate of inflation but not the rate of unemployment.

Not all economists believe that the long-run Phillips curve is vertical. Some believe that the long-run curve is steeper than the short-run curve, but that it is still negatively sloped indicating the existence of a long-run trade-off between inflation and unemployment. In this case, the options open to society are like the ones shown in Figure 14.4 by the curve ABC. In this case, a zero rate of inflation occurs only when 12 percent of the work force is unemployed. A zero rate of unemployment can be achieved only when the rate of inflation is raised to 30 percent. In circumstances such as this, it is necessary to decide how much

FIGURE 14.6   **It is frequently impossible for a government to attain all the goals that it seeks. In this case, it is impossible for it to achieve a zero rate of inflation and a zero rate of unemployment simultaneously.**

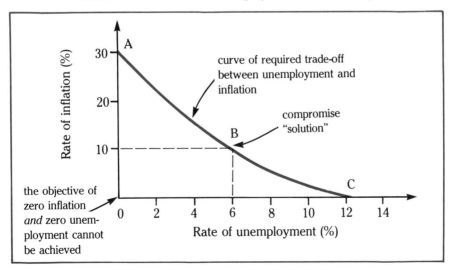

of one desired end to trade off to attain more of the other. After considering preferences, it may, for instance, be decided to aim for 6 percent unemployment in the knowledge that this will be accompanied by a rate of inflation of 10 percent.

Consider another example. The balance of payments may be adversely affected by policies designed to raise employment if exchange rates are fixed. If the government increases the money supply to lower interest rates and stimulate domestic investment, it may also cause people to lend their money in other countries in order to earn a higher return. This may worsen a deficit situation in the balance of payments. If the exchange rates are not fixed, then the expansionary monetary policy will result in a depreciation of the Canadian dollar. Although newly employed members of society benefit, purchasers of imported goods are made worse off.

It needs to be remembered that the public sector is large and complex, and is involved in much interaction between individuals and pressure groups representing diverse interests. The concept of the public sector as a monolithic, well-co-ordinated, and centrally directed body does not appear to be the appropriate one. Rather it is a body that is not perfectly co-ordinated, and one in which there is internal conflict (for instance, between and within government departments), and in which many decisions are decentralized.

A further difficulty facing government is that of accurately predicting future economic developments. Most economic policies take time to implement and to have an impact. Policies that only take account of recent experience and ignore independent, possible developments during the period of their economic impact may prove to be very damaging. For instance, as a result of a boom in the demand for Canadian exports, the government might plan to reduce its spending to dampen down the possible inflationary impact of the increase in demand for Canadian goods. But, if it does this, and the demand for Canadian exports subsequently slumps, this policy will add to the possible recession in the Canadian economy — a recession that may follow the slump in demand for Canadian exports.

Canada's Economic Future

It is extremely hard to predict future events. Social and economic circumstances throughout the world can change rapidly. But it seems clear that the economic climate faced by Canada is changing and will change in this century.

Unemployment and Inflation

When the Economic Council of Canada presented its first annual review, it believed that a reasonable objective for unemployment was 3 percent, and that a reasonable objective for inflation was between 1.4 percent and 2.0 percent.

Canada, in the 1980s, faces a very different picture than it did in the 1960s.

Indeed the unemployment rate has not been within 2 percent of the 3 percent target since 1970. Since 1975, the unemployment rate has been above 7 percent. The recession in Canada pushed the 1982 unemployment rate to 11.0 percent with the December 1982 rate standing at 12.8 percent. Current predictions suggest that the Canadian unemployment rate will remain above 10 percent until 1987.

There are concerns that technological and structural change will result in increased unemployment. Technological change usually does eliminate some jobs, but it also usually creates new jobs in the process. For example, in the 1970s, many jobs were lost as a result of technological change, but new jobs created a net increase of 2.8 million jobs. Nonetheless, it is likely that some additional unemployment will be generated as a result of the disruption that will take place in the short run as the individuals displaced will not normally have the required skills for the newly created jobs.

The inflation rate has not fared much better. The rate of inflation measured by the CPI has been above 4 percent since 1972. For most of the 1970s, the rate was above 7.5 percent. For the early 1980s, the rate was in the double-digit range. The recession was taking its toll in early 1983, and there were signs of inflation abating significantly. It remains to be seen what the impact of economic recovery will have on inflation rates.[1]

Economic Growth

In 1964, the Economic Council believed that a growth target of 5.5 percent growth in real output was reasonable. This target was attained for several of the years between 1964 and 1973. From 1973-1982, however, the growth rate fell short of that target, achieving it in only one year, 1975. This is partially explained by significant decline in productivity growth, and for some years a decline in productivity itself. As much of the poor productivity performance is not yet explained, it is difficult to assess the future trend. Much depends upon the recovery from the recession.

But whatever economic challenges await us in the future, we need to remember that material wealth is not the sole aim of life, even though it can enable us to achieve a great deal. In making social choices, we must consider all the values of our society because the price of material wealth can be too high in terms of its adverse impact on the environment, individual freedom, justice, individual opportunities for creativity, family life, and compassion and concern for one another. Material wealth, in our view, is best regarded as a means to other ends, rather than as an end in itself. Economics and economiz-

---

[1]It is likely that the inflation rate for 1985 will be slightly less than 4 percent — the lowest since 1972.

ing must be seen as a part of society, and as a part of a wider human context. It is clear that our economic system has shaped our modern society and its institutions to a considerable extent, and will continue to modify and shape these. We must be on our guard, however, to ensure that it does not shape our society and its institutions in a way contrary to our fundamental values and aspirations.

FIGURE 14.7 **Robots increase the daily output of automobiles, and rather than displacing human workers, they create higher skilled jobs. "Even a robot needs a human helping hand to get started."**
Courtesy Ford Motor Company of Canada

KEY CONCEPTS
(FOR REVIEW)

Bond Financing a Budget Deficit
Budget (Surplus or Deficit)
Conflict between Policy Aims
Consumer Protection
Consumption Taxes
Crowding Out of Private
  Investment
Customs Duties
Economic Growth
Equitable Distribution of Income
Full Employment
Full-Employment Budget Position
Government Financing Constraint

Income Tax
Market Failure
Money Financing a Budget Deficit
Natural Monopolies
Public Expenditure on Goods and
  Services
Public Goods
Regulation of Competition
Regulation of Overall Level of
  Economic Activity
Sales Tax
Taxation
Trade-off Between Objectives
Transfer Payments

QUESTIONS FOR REVIEW AND DISCUSSION

1. Why is there need for a government sector and for government intervention in the economy?
2. How does the relative size of the public sector in Canada compare with that in other countries? What is the relative size of the public sector in Canada and how is employment shared between tiers of Canadian government?
3. What are the main tiers of Canadian government? What financial relationships exist between them?
4. The main public outlays in Canada are made for what purposes? How important are transfer payments?
5. What shares do the tiers of Canadian government have in some of the largest types of public outlays?
6. What are the main sources of finance for the Canadian public sector? What is the relative size of these sources as a proportion of total public finance?
7. What are the main sources of taxation receipts in Canada?
8. To what extent do provincial and local governments depend for their financing on grants from other levels of government?
9. What is the government's budget? What is the full-employment budget? Does a deficit in the actual budget mean that fiscal policy is expansionary?
10. "In policy-making it is sometimes difficult to formulate aims, and once they are formulated, it is sometimes impossible to meet them simultaneously." Discuss.

11. Give some examples in which economic aims cannot be simultaneously satisfied.
12. What are or have been the main objectives pursued by governments in the Canadian economy?
13. What is the government's financing constraint? How will bond financing and money financing of a budget deficit differ in their impact on economic activity? Which do you think is preferable as a means of financing a prolonged period of deficit spending? Why?

FURTHER READING

Auld, D.A.L., *Issues in Government Expenditure Growth.* The Canadian Economic Policy Committee and the C.D. Howe Research Institute, 1976.

Auld, D.A.L., & Miller, F.C., *Principles of Public Finance: A Canadian Text.* Toronto: Methuen Publications, 1982.

Breton, A., *The Regulation of Private Economic Activity.* C.D. Howe Research Institute, 1976.

Economic Council of Canada, *Reforming Regulations*, 1981.

Lipsey, R.G., Purvis, D.D., Sparks, G.R., & Steiner, P.O., *Economics.* New York: Harper & Row, Publishers, 1982, chapters 18, 24, 25, & 34.

Osberg, L., *Economic Inequality in Canada.* Scarborough: Butterworth & Co. (Canada) Ltd., 1981, Chapter 12.

Reuber, G., "The Impact of Government Policies on the Distribution of Income in Canada: A Review." *Canadian Public Policy* (1978), pp. 505-29.

Samuelson, P.A., & Scott, A.D., *Economics.* Scarborough: McGraw-Hill Ryerson Limited, 1980, chapters 8 & 9.

Index

91164